PRAISE FOR

PERSONAL INTELLIGENCE

"Innovative . . . Mayer's new theory of personal intelligence is a welcome starting point for analyzing 'how people think about themselves and one another.'"   —*Publishers Weekly*

"I find Mayer's optimism heartening and his theory convincing:
Strengthening personal intelligence could certainly improve communication and understanding in professional and personal relationships . . . I realized personal intelligence—though I've never called
it that before—is key to reading about both fictional characters and
real people."   —Deb Baker, *Concord* (New Hampshire) *Monitor*

"Mayer makes his case for personal intelligence by synthesizing decades of scholarship, supporting it with examples of high achievers from Ludwig van Beethoven to the late *Washington Post* owner
Katharine Graham, and suggesting how people can improve their
own personal intelligence."   —Janice Harayda, *UNH Magazine*

"John D. Mayer has done so much to get us to think about human
personality in new ways, from his theoretical models to his empirical research on emotional intelligence (on which I have been thrilled
to collaborate). With *Personal Intelligence*, Mayer once again challenges us—arguing that there is a set of skills that may determine
what sets successful people apart from those who seem oblivious to
the needs and desires of those around them. He is a clear thinker
and a beautiful writer, and his arguments compel us to broaden our
understanding of what constitutes an intelligent individual."
                          —Peter Salovey, president and Chris Argyris
                          Professor of Psychology, Yale University

"This lively book vividly illustrates the importance of personality
and the judgments we make of one another. John D. Mayer sur-

veys a wide range of classic and up-to-the-minute modern research, along with engaging personal histories, to make a compelling case in support of his innovative theory of personal intelligence."
—David C. Funder, Distinguished Professor of Psychology, University of California, Riverside, and author of *The Personality Puzzle*

"John D. Mayer takes us on a comprehensive journey through his theory of personal intelligence. Along the way, he shows just how vital personal intelligence is to understanding ourselves as well as navigating our social world. Making sense of others is an essential skill, and *Personal Intelligence* shows us how we use it, when we use it, and why it matters."
—Elaine Fox, director of the Oxford Centre for Emotions and Affective Neuroscience and author of *Rainy Brain, Sunny Brain*

JOHN D. MAYER

PERSONAL INTELLIGENCE

John D. Mayer is a professor of psychology at the University of New Hampshire and a key innovator in intelligence research. He has written more than 125 scientific articles, books, and psychological tests, including the internationally known Mayer-Salovey-Caruso Emotional Intelligence Test (MSCEIT™). His writing has appeared in *Scientific American, Psychology Today*, and *The New York Times*, and his work has been covered in *Time* and *The Washington Post*. He lives in New Hampshire. Visit his website at http://personalintelligence.info/.

PERSONAL INTELLIGENCE

PERSONAL INTELLIGENCE

THE POWER OF PERSONALITY
AND HOW IT SHAPES OUR LIVES

JOHN D. MAYER

SCIENTIFIC AMERICAN / FARRAR, STRAUS AND GIROUX
NEW YORK

Scientific American / Farrar, Straus and Giroux
18 West 18th Street, New York 10011

Copyright © 2014 by John D. Mayer
All rights reserved
Printed in the United States of America
Published in 2014 by Scientific American / Farrar, Straus and Giroux
First paperback edition, 2015

The Library of Congress has cataloged the hardcover edition as follows:
Mayer, John D., 1953–
     Personal intelligence : the power of personality and how it shapes our lives /
John D. Mayer.
        pages   cm
     Includes index.
     ISBN 978-0-374-23085-2 (hardback) — ISBN 978-0-374-70899-3 (ebook)
     1. Personality.   2. Emotional intelligence.   I. Title.

BF698 .M3437 2014
155.2—dc23

                                                                              2013033926

Paperback ISBN: 978-0-374-53501-8

Designed by Jonathan D. Lippincott

Scientific American / Farrar, Straus and Giroux books may be purchased for
educational, business, or promotional use. For information on bulk purchases,
please contact the Macmillan Corporate and Premium Sales Department at
1-800-221-7945, extension 5442, or write to specialmarkets@macmillan.com.

www.fsgbooks.com • books.scientificamerican.com
www.twitter.com/fsgbooks • www.facebook.com/fsgbooks

Scientific American is a trademark of Scientific American, Inc.
Used with permission.

P1

To those of us who are confused and who seek direction; to the friends, neighbors, and teachers who guide us with sensitivity; and to all of us who are captivated by the mystery of who we are

The winds and the waves are always on the side of the ablest navigators.   —Edward Gibbon

CONTENTS

PERSONAL INTELLIGENCE

INTRODUCTION: DOES PERSONALITY MATTER? . . . AND OTHER PRELIMINARIES

We try to make sense of the people around us and anticipate how they will act. At the gym we notice the high-strung guy and the urgency with which he encourages other weight lifters—imagining he must look down at our own slighter efforts. We seek out a colleague from Information Technology because she seems intrigued by our questions about a new kind of software. We expect that our uncle who's always late will be late again for his upcoming visit. We're always curious to know what people will do next—and what is best for us to do.

Evolutionary theorists now believe that our ability to understand people began to develop half a million years ago as human beings adapted to life in ever-larger social groups. Those who could better figure out the people around them possessed an advantage relative to others. They knew their own preferences better—and as a consequence could make choices that motivated themselves; they understood other people's needs well enough to know how to cooperate with them, and they could identify the troublesome members of the group and keep an eye on them. Our ancestors who were successful readers of personality were more likely to survive and reproduce, passing down the genetic bases for this problem-solving potential to their descendants. Today, we each possess some skills in understanding ourselves and others. If our perceptions are weak or fall into disuse, we're likely to be regularly blindsided by the unpredictability of people around us. If our perceptions are strong, we'll develop a readiness to cope with how people will act.

Our collective interest in personalities is reflected throughout recorded history. For example, between roughly 2500 BCE and 200 BCE, political advisers, philosophers, and religious leaders wrote about the different kinds of people around them—sociable types, misers, and country bumpkins—as well as about the need for self-knowledge, in the hope of solving problems in human conduct and relationships. This interest in personality spread into the world of medicine as well. Physicians described the normal variations of personality, and attempted to treat the diseases of character to which we might fall prey, such as "hysteria" and melancholy. Dramatists and novelists have filled their pages with passionate lovers, by-the-book administrators, resourceful children, eccentric entomologists, and the many other personalities who drive the world we live in. These philosophers, physicians, and writers thought about people in very different ways, which may have masked a quality they shared in common: a heightened capacity to understand people's characters.

This discussion of people and human nature developed for two millennia until the science of psychology emerged. In 1887, Wilhelm Wundt established the first psychological laboratory; Wundt and his students asked research participants about their perceptions of weight, pattern, and color, and often timed the participants' answers, to see how people converted sensory phenomena into psychological experience. Apart from his empirical focus, Wundt foresaw the need for the study of all a person's mental systems, from perception to memory to motives and emotions—the study of a "psychical personality."

Wundt's vision of a personality psychology became a reality in the early 1900s as Sigmund Freud, Carl Jung, Gordon Allport, and others crafted grand theories of how people operated psychologically. These psychologists and psychiatrists represented a modern generation of specialists who were particularly talented at understanding personality. They drew mostly on their own observations, coupled with their knowledge of philosophy and literature from past centuries, and translated their insights into an emerging scientific language of the new field. Freud, for example, drew together work in evolutionary biology, linguistics, philosophy, theatrical drama, and the case studies he made of his patients. He viewed a person's mind as a brew of animal instincts, logical reasoning, and conscience. As he saw it, from this heady mixture of elements, people sought to satisfy their often animal-like personal desires by means of civilized social behavior. Carl Jung drew on Western, Hindu, and Buddhist traditions to describe what he viewed as universal types of personalities—heroes, villains, and clowns, among others—whom we identify with and might even try to imitate, sometimes so extremely that we become caricatures of our true selves. Gordon Allport was interested in describing the mental traits—the psychological consistencies—that people exhibit; it was also Allport who recommended that the term "personality psychology" be applied to the field.

Freud, Jung, and other early theorists, including Alfred Adler, Harry Stack Sullivan, and Henry Murray, argued their perspectives on personality in compelling language, but they worked in a data-poor environment. Despite the contributions of Wundt and others, the procedures for carrying out research in psychology remained in an embryonic stage over the early decades of the twentieth century. Psychological measurement was in its infancy; psychologists were developing the first research designs for use with human participants, and applied statistical methods were crude at best. As a consequence, although these grand theorists had many brilliant insights, they lacked dependable empirical findings, and that made it hard to know which among their ideas about people were correct and which were misguided.

In 1959, Professors Calvin Hall and Gardner Lindzey reviewed those theorists' work and suggested, ever so tactfully, that psychologists might want to end their project of describing personality by drawing on philosophy, literature, and case studies. Instead, members of the field should use their rapidly developing scientific methods to collect some data to see what personality is *really* like and what people *really* do. A new generation of psychologists did just that, and infused the field with rich empirical findings concerning personality traits, mental defenses, self-control, and the perception of other people.

Their conclusions upended at least a few long-held beliefs about personality. For example, although a person might repress her traumatic memories, as Freud suggested—blocking them out of memory for decades at a time—many other people found such traumas impossible to forget, and indeed might think of them frequently. As such information accumulated, researchers found they needed more powerful (and extensive) explanations for what was taking place, including new ideas of how repression, normal forgetting, and posttraumatic stress occur.

Today, many psychologists are developing new accounts of how personality works based on the rapid accumulation of findings of the field. I am one of them. In this book, I describe my theory of a new human intelligence—a mental capacity that I believe we use to guide our lives—to reason about ourselves and other people. I call this ability to draw out information about personality and to reason about it "personal intelligence."

We use our personal intelligence to recognize information from sources that include a person's appearance, possessions, and behavior, and use that to label our ideas of her and to match our impressions to similar people we've known. From such clues, we deduce how to behave with the person and how she will treat us in return. And we use clues about ourselves to better understand our own needs and to map out our future plans.

I will use this theory of personal intelligence to organize many studies from around the world that reveal how people think about themselves and one another. Researchers are actively studying aspects of this reasoning process today, examining how we gauge whether someone is conscientious, disagreeable, or creative, how well we set our personal goals, and more. Their laboratories are conducting some of the most exciting studies in the history of personality psychology.

That said, I won't be able to avoid several areas of controversy when I write about personality and personal intelligence. For one, many of our leaders assert that everyone is equal, and yet my account presupposes that people are different in consequential ways. In addition, we are taught from the time we are toddlers not to judge others, but I will point out that we are engaged in assessing one another all the time. It's also the case that many psychologists believe our behavior is a product of the situations we encounter and has little to do with our individual choices. For personal intelligence to matter, however, people must behave with enough consistency so that we can reasonably forecast what they do. If social situations are totally responsible for determining our behavior, as some have suggested, there is little point to discussing any intelligence about personality. From my standpoint, these disagreements over whether we are the same or different, whether to judge one another, and whether personality is consistent form a key backdrop to the concept of personal intelligence, so they are worth taking a serious look at as we get under way.

Ideas of "human sameness" have been explored for centuries, and philosophers of the seventeenth century emphasized our equality as a means to promote social justice. For example, Thomas Hobbes argued that all men are equal, and in the eighteenth century, Jean-Jacques Rousseau began his *Confessions* by saying that he was no better than others. But Hobbes, perhaps realizing his argument was more idealistic than accurate, acknowledged that we might truly be unequal; his primary goal was to promote peace and justice. And Rousseau added, with evident satisfaction: "I am, perhaps, like no one in existence."

Appeals to our sameness remain a familiar trope today. During his acceptance of the Nobel Peace Prize, the fourteenth Dalai Lama emphasized that "no matter what part of the world we come from, we are all basically the same human beings," and continued, "We all seek happiness and try to avoid suffering. We have the same basic human needs and concerns."

These sentiments rightly encourage us to cut through the categories that set us apart to recognize our shared humanity. Although I appreciate the values behind the narrative, there's something to be said for pointing out our differences. As a brief aside to illustrate this idea, the Dalai Lama's remarks reflected beliefs from Hindu and Buddhist traditions that describe how a person's true self (or atman) draws on a universal force, yet religious teachers from those same traditions distinguish among students with different personalities. They may use Jnana yoga for a student who is reflective, studious, and intellectual, because it focuses initially on scholarship, but use Bhakti yoga for a student who is more devotional, emotional, and loving, because it emphasizes adoration of the spiritual.

If any empirical evidence was needed to prove that each of us is different, then Alexander Thomas, Stella Chess, and Herbert Birch provided it in a study they began in the 1950s. The three physicians followed 141 infants in their New York City medical practices, sorting the two-to-three-month-olds into three groups: those who were adaptable, positive, and cheerful—the "easy" infants; those who were distressed, slow to adapt, and negative in mood—labeled "difficult"; and those who were "slow to warm up" and had a low activity level and mildly negative emotion. The researchers then followed those individuals for fourteen years, and the members of the individual groups *still* differed from one another as they reached adolescence. Eighty percent of the easy infants were regarded as well-adjusted adolescents, and just 20 percent were seen as needing some form of psychological intervention such as family therapy or psychiatric medication; among the adolescents who had been difficult infants, nearly 70 percent were evaluated as needing psychological interventions, with the rest regarded as well-adjusted. This is one study among many—the point here being that although we share a basic humanity, there are also plenty of differences among us even when we are just a few months old. The deeper understanding here, as I see it, is for us to acknowledge our equal claims to humanity, but whether we are promoting social justice, working in an office, or teaching in a classroom, it makes sense to appreciate our individual differences as well.

Even if we grant that people do differ from one another, isn't it impolite to point out these differences? After all, if someone notices our shortcomings and points them out to us (or, even worse, points them out to a mutual friend who shares their feedback with us), we can easily feel hurt. But at the same time, the doctrine that differences are unmentionable has made us so uncomfortable talking about character among our close friends and colleagues in particular that we've done a disservice to our society as a whole—because the differences exist and we can make life easier for ourselves and others by acknowledging them. When I speak about understanding personality, I do include judging people to a degree—and although that rightly raises a bright red flag for many of us, there are many benefits to accepting our differences and discussing them.

Throughout this book, I'll refer to the personally relevant feedback we receive—positive or negative—as conveying "hot information" about ourselves. The information is "hot" in the sense that it affects our motivations and our feelings, and can overwhelm our self-control: a person who comments on one of our qualities may draw from us a warm flush of embarrassment, or the heat of anger if we feel unjustly characterized, or the rush of appreciation for a compliment. Our reactions are complex at times: we may experience praise as a double-edged sword, because we perceive it as mere politeness, false flattery, or aimed at something we're not actually proud of. Protecting the sensitivities of others is one of the good reasons we're taught to refrain from remarking on the personalities of others. But if we can *listen* to such information without reacting defensively— for example, hear that someone finds us to be controlling—we may be able to develop a more intimate knowledge of who we are and use that to better develop ourselves, and to relate more positively to our friends and family.

Like everyone else, I've felt the pain of being judged—and the hot information it conveys—many times. When I was an undergraduate at the University of Michigan, I lived in the Residential College with a group of students, many of whom were taking courses in drama, or in creative writing and literature. Many of us in those majors competed with one another for literary awards and for having our plays performed at the university. I often came up short in those contests and was having doubts about my talents as a writer. The judgments of my instructors and fellow students, in the form of passing over my own works for awards or selecting other students' plays to produce, led me to question whether my skills were advancing as well as those of my classmates. I felt unappreciated as a result, and it didn't feel good.

Judgments have their consequences, and I began to step back from the competition: when I had the chance to live elsewhere in my junior year, I moved to a student cooperative on the university's North Campus, a sprawling open space at the time, which seemed like it would be a calmer setting. In this instance, my self-perceived inadequacy—based on judgments—drove me out of a community, but it also meant I joined a new one where I felt more comfortable. Critical feedback is rarely easy to take, and yet information that tells us about ourselves is crucially informative. The feedback helped me improve as a student, and in the long run I felt free to consider alternative occupations, ultimately changing fields and attending graduate school to study psychology.

We are, all of us, exposed to evaluations from other people, and I won't present an easy answer to the question of when to share our thoughts about another person—that's a different book—but I do believe there are actual, observable qualities each of us possesses that are knowable through scientific research and often simply from observing ourselves and others, and we can use what we perceive about people to guide our social interactions.*

My tale of being judged as a student has a plot twist related to the theory of personal intelligence. After moving to North Campus, I spent most of my evenings with students who were studying engineering and law. While I continued to craft stories for my theater and writing courses, they were honing their skills in legal reasoning, logic, and mathematical computation. I sensed they questioned the work of the artistic types I hung out with during the day. What were

---

*I acknowledge, when I claim that we can observe another person accurately, that, for example, a person may behave differently with me than with someone else. When I observe an individual, the person I see may be different from what that same person is like with others, and different from what they are like inside. Nonetheless, I regard each person as possessing her own unique constellation of inner qualities and interpersonal styles, and those qualities are in principle knowable to a degree (whether I know about the person well in practice or not).

those aspiring writers and dramatists learning, after all? What was the reasoning involved in telling stories?

So long as I was studying short stories, novels, and drama, I was determined to understand how good storytellers operated. As I read literary critics I began to understand how constructing a piece of fiction involved its own logic of character types and their inter-actions, of emotions, and of the unfolding of lives. R. S. Crane, a leader of the Chicago School of criticism, argued that the story lines of naturalistic novels serve as simulations of real-world events, al-lowing readers to reason about the characters and the consequences of making certain choices. Crane wrote that a novel's plot "imitates in words a sequence of human activities, with a power to affect our opinions and emotions in a certain way." He believed that the best plots allow readers to evaluate the quality and ethics of the charac-ters, according to their "actions and thoughts vis-à-vis the human situations in which they are engaged."

As I completed my Ph.D. in psychology, researchers in the al-lied field of cognitive science were becoming increasingly interested both in the emotions and in stories. By 1983, Wendy Lehnert, Michael Dyer, and colleagues at Yale University had developed an expert computer system named BORIS that could "read" stories and infer the emotions of the characters involved. For example, when the researchers gave BORIS a story about Richard, who was driving when he nearly hit an old man, and stopped shortly afterward for a drink, BORIS was able to deduce that Richard had been upset by the near-accident and decided that he needed to imbibe to calm his nerves (someone else drove Richard home, I guess).

By the mid-1980s, Peter Salovey, then an assistant professor at Yale University, and I were both studying how emotions influenced thought. We discussed the emerging research on the regularities of emotions, and the logic of reasoning with them, and slowly wove those ideas into a new theory that we published in a 1990 article entitled "Emotional Intelligence." Peter and I claimed that there was a logic about emotion that some people understood and used in their lives to promote their well-being, but that remained a mystery to many others.

In 1995, Daniel Goleman, then a journalist at *The New York Times*, featured our theory in his lively book also entitled *Emotional Intelligence*. His account created a great deal of interest in our work. Since 1990, Peter and I have worked productively on emotional intelligence, joined later by our colleague David R. Caruso. As a personality psychologist, however, I hoped, ultimately, to develop a theory that would more centrally capture how we understand individuals as a whole—to examine a person's *overall* character, as Crane had put it—and to describe the impact that witnessing character had on each of us. It might seem like a small step from an emotional intelligence to one that concerned personality, but there were several obstacles to making the intellectual journey.

First among the obstacles to creating a theory of personal intelligence was the widespread belief among academic psychologists at the time that personality didn't matter. If personality was irrelevant to an individual's life, then no theory of personal intelligence would be necessary. And, in the 1980s and 1990s, many psychologists subscribed to the idea that personality was an illusion—a will-o'-the-wisp that came and went without any consequences for an individual's life. These psychologists argued that healthy people are so adaptable and responsive to the environment that their behavior is due far more to the situation in which they find themselves than to any inner qualities. Psychologists fought out whether the person or the situation was more important in what became known as the "person-situation" debate of the latter part of the twentieth century— and it still casts a shadow on the field today.

The issues surrounding the person-situation debate can be illustrated with the real-life example of two college baseball players at Arizona State University who were hoping to play professionally: Jeff Larish and Dustin Pedroia. The day before the 2004 draft, scouts from major-league teams were invited to watch the college players at ASU. Larish was a highly ranked player expected to dominate the scouts' attention, but he had a wrist injury and his hitting suffered as a result. Pedroia ended up playing one of the best games of his life up to that time—he later remarked that he was especially relaxed because he believed all eyes were on Larish. When the Red Sox called the Arizona State coach, it was for Pedroia, and Larish had to wait another year before he got called up by the Detroit Tigers.

Psychologists taking a situational perspective would argue that the situation determined who played the best: the expectations of Larish were too high, especially coupled with his wrist injury; Pedroia could be relaxed and play well because no one expected him to be a focus of attention. Psychologists taking a "person" approach would say that Pedroia's performance was due to his personality, including his motivations and attitudes, his athletic skills, and his mental preparation.

The situationist perspective had found its first advocates years before, in the 1920s, among three forward-looking professors, Hugh Hartshorne and Mark May at Yale, and Edward Thorndike of Columbia. They founded a project called the Character Education Inquiry to explore whether schools could mold personality to make students more "persevering," "honest," and "good"—qualities that leaders in public education wanted to instill in their young charges.

The Inquiry project was massive in scope. Working from 1925 to 1930, the researchers developed their procedures and administered more than 170,000 tests to 10,500 public and private school students to better understand those young people's personality and behavior. For example, to assess honesty, the researchers set up multiple situations in which the schoolchildren could cheat. In one situation, the "duplicating technique," students took a quiz and then turned it in to their teachers. Unbeknownst to the students, the researchers recorded their original answers to the quiz overnight. The next day the teachers passed the quizzes back and asked their students to self-grade their responses—which allowed the children an opportunity to covertly change their original answers. The researchers then checked the students' self-graded results against their original responses to see who had changed their answers. Using approaches like this, the investigators recorded the honesty of a given pupil in each of several situations. To their surprise, they found far less consistency in honesty across situations than they had expected; their findings helped set off the person-situation controversy.

It's worth taking a close look at what they found. The relationship between any two variables—such as honesty measured in one situation and then in a second situation—is often measured with a statistic known as a correlation coefficient. A zero correlation indicates no relationship between two variables; a correlation of 1.0 indicates a perfect relation. For example, if students in class were given a course grade that was entirely based on their performance on a single test, then the test grades and course grades would be perfectly correlated. Returning to the Character Education Inquiry, if the relation between honesty in the quiz situation and honesty in a second situation (such as peeking when you should keep your eyes closed) were random, the correlation would be zero. If honest behavior in the quiz situation perfectly predicted honesty in the peeking situation, the correlation would be 1.0. Given the zero-to-one scale for a positive relationship, psychologists of the time had likely expected a high correlation between students' honest behaviors across situations—perhaps a .70 or .80 along that zero-to-one continuum.

The researchers at the Character Education Inquiry found, however, that the correlation for honesty across two situations was closer to about .30. And they concluded on that basis that students changed their behaviors so much from one classroom setting to another that the stability of personality appeared negligible. The project leaders expressed their conclusions in extreme terms: they could find "no evidence" for honesty, and no evidence for character more generally.

At first the findings had little impact on the field of personality. Perhaps psychologists found the idea implausible; or scholars may have been distracted by major events going on at the time—the stock market crashes from 1929 to the early 1930s, the Great Depression that followed, World War II. During the war years, many psychologists left academe to work for the military effort. In the postwar period, however, psychologists continued to teach the theories of Freud and Jung, and the new theories of Carl Rogers and Abraham Maslow, which made no contact with the research of the

Character Education Inquiry. The issue of whether personality was consistent was simply not dealt with.

But that all changed when Walter Mischel, then a professor at Stanford, published his book *Personality and Assessment* in 1968. Mischel drove home the situationist perspective by arguing that people adjust how they act in different situations, and their adaptability places severe limits on any predictions we can make from an individual's traits. For example, whether you're a noisy person or a man of few words, you will nonetheless become quiet in a library, and even the rowdiest party animal can be found standing obediently in line in a crowded supermarket. Although we might perceive others we know as consistent, Mischel argued, our perception is an *illusion*: we classify those around us by using "prototypes" of people much as we may stereotype different national or ethnic groups. Once we have pegged someone as a particular "type," we continue to see him through that lens: if we believe someone is "emotional and dramatic," we will fit whatever he does into an "emotional" template, forgetting the many times he has behaved in a perfectly calm fashion.

Many social psychologists and cultural anthropologists loved Mischel's position because it celebrated the power of social influences and discounted the role of personality in behavior. The situationist idea became so pervasive in the 1970s that still today, when I travel on a speaking engagement here or overseas, many human resource professionals and psychologists trained during that time are surprised that I bring up personality at all in my lectures. Hadn't they learned it was elusive?

But, of course, the situation regarding situations was more complex than those who sought to dismiss personality had supposed. In independent articles published in the seventies and eighties, prominent psychologists including Kenneth Bowers, Seymour Epstein, David Funder, and Daniel Ozer pointed out a rather embarrassing problem for the situationists. They concluded, after reviewing a number of studies, that situations, far from being all-powerful, appeared to predict people's behavior at about the same level as personality had. In other words, people weren't easy to predict no matter *how* you tried: we seem to modify our behaviors to meet both our inner needs and the requirements of the situations we find ourselves in. Psychologists began to wonder about still another possibility: if the correlation from personality traits to a person's acts was so low—and if predicting from situations was no better—was there something about the way we were interpreting the correlation that was problematic?

Robert Abelson, a Yale psychologist, had been arguing the situationist position with a colleague by pointing out that an athlete's performance was often due to "freaky and unpredictable events such as windblown fly balls, runners slipping in patches of mud, baseballs bouncing oddly off outfield walls . . ." His colleague argued for the power of personality, contending that regardless of circumstances it was an obvious fact that "good teams usually win, [and] that even under freaky circumstances . . . skilled players will better overcome difficulties than mediocre players . . ."

To clarify the situation, Abelson studied the batting averages of baseball players—the number of hits a player gets per time at bat. Major-league players averaged about .270 overall in 1986, with individual players averaging hits from the .200s to the .300s for the most part—a considerable range. For example, a player with a .320 batting average compared with a player with a .220 average had nearly a *50 percent greater likelihood* of getting a hit during a single time at bat. So Abelson was quite surprised to find that, when he correlated batting averages with the likelihood of a player's hitting the ball at a single at-bat, the correlation was just .11. Surely, batting averages described the skill of the batter, yet batting averages were a poor predictor of a single at-bat performance.

Abelson pointed out that the apparently low correlation between a person's skill level and his behavior in an individual situation masked the important consistencies a person expresses as his behaviors accumulate *over time*—and these consistencies matter when we try to estimate the behavior of a friend, a supervisor, or a spouse. For example, if you had two friends who had "batting averages" of being late of .220 and .320, and you met them a few dozen times over the course of a year, the friend with the .320 average would be late nearly 50 percent more often—a considerable inconvenience to you, *unless you recognized it* and accommodated to it. So, you could arrange to meet him in places that were comfortable to wait, and bring something to do until he arrived.

More generally, a person who behaved like a "random decider" would pick the more suitable of two possible individuals for a friendship or for a job 50 percent of the time (by chance alone); but someone who was just a bit perceptive might choose the person who is a better fit for the relationship, say, 53 percent of the time, and the less good one 47 percent of the time. And it seems entirely possible that still more perceptive individuals might choose the more suitable member of the pair 65 percent of the time versus 35 percent.* Even people who choose just a bit better than chance are likely to benefit from substantial advantages in their relationships because they will make those better choices time and again, situation after situation, over a lifetime.

Some people can pick up clues to personality that others miss. For example, as the Red Sox scouts considered recruiting Dustin Pedroia, they likely gathered whatever information about him they could. The clues they sought would have included his performance over time as reflected in his batting average and other statistics— and also some of his attitudes about playing baseball generally. According to family lore, Pedroia's parents gave him a bat and allowed him to swing at anything just after he learned to walk. By the time he was a young child, friends of his parents who watched him hit would admire his ability. Most parents find themselves reminding their children not to play with baseball bats or throw things in the house. But life for Pedroia was different. In his words, he would practice throwing and catching baseballs inside: "[I'd] fire the ball off the bricks [of the fireplace], catch it, then turn and fire it at my mom, who was sitting on the couch. She's such a good athlete, she was

---

*There aren't any well-worked-out estimates I could find that specifically addressed how accurate we are at selecting the better of two people for a given task or relationship. The basis for my suggestion that the rates could reach as high as 65 percent versus 35 percent is explained in the Notes section.

having no problem taking my throws and then throwing them right back to me." And when he knocked a clock off the wall and it broke a table, his mother said, "Don't worry about the clock or the table . . . just keep throwing the ball." A scout who took such personality-relevant information seriously might reason that Pedroia's natural interest in sports, his upbringing, his determined practice, and his training by talented coaches would all contribute to his success as a ballplayer. Pedroia's personality was shaped by all these qualities as he arrived to play ball on Scout Day at Arizona State.

One national team representative who watched Pedroia play that fateful day confessed that "the only tool I saw he had was the ability to hit for average. He couldn't throw. He didn't run. He wasn't an average fielder at that time . . ." Maybe the Red Sox scout was more observant than that, or maybe it was just luck that led him to choose so well: Pedroia would move up from a farm team to play in the major leagues by 2006. In 2007, he was named Rookie of the Year and would help the team win two World Series. Regarding whether the scouts could really know how good Pedroia would be, the same national scout remarked: "I can't think the Red Sox are this smart." But we can think of baseball scouts and all the rest of us as having a batting average when it comes to evaluating people—and ourselves.

I avoided the person-situation debate during my early career, focusing instead on intelligence and cognitive skills (and emotional states). Walter Mischel—who had pointed out people's inconsistencies—had acknowledged that intellect, knowledge, and mental capacities were relatively stable parts of personality. We are inconsistent in part, he argued, because we use our intelligence to *figure out what to do in a given context*. Still, as the debate progressed, a consensus developed that people expressed many other aspects of their personalities across situations in meaningfully consistent ways—their sociability, conscientiousness, optimism, and much more. That resolution opened the door for a possible intelligence regarding personality, but what reasoning would it involve?

Psychologists divide our thinking about personality much as philosophers have before them: they speak of "self-knowledge" when we reason about ourselves, of "reading people" when we observe others, or of becoming our "optimal selves" when we perform well in life; and then there is also "personality psychology" itself, a field that focuses on how our overall mental system works.

In the summer of 2007, I was wondering what it meant to be "smart" about personality. Over the preceding weeks, I had been grappling with three concepts that I saw as somehow related: one concerned self-knowledge, a second concerned how personality functioned, and a third concerned the traits of "high-functioning" people. One morning, I awoke to realize that to understand ourselves, to perceive others accurately, and to do well, we just might draw on a group of everyday rules of thumb about how personality operated—and people likely varied in their ability to use those rules. If such a mental capacity existed—that joined self-knowledge, reading people, and functioning well—then perhaps thinkers who studied those different areas all were drawing from the same evolved ability to reason; perhaps all of them were drawing on a personal intelligence.

I began to draft a theory of personal intelligence. The term itself had been used on an occasional basis over the past century—"Personal Intelligence" appeared as the title of a magazine column tracking the comings and goings of notable people, and as a reference to a person's own individual (traditional) IQ score. The Harvard psychologist Howard Gardner had proposed an intrapersonal intelligence, which he paired with an interpersonal one. At least a few researchers shortened Gardner's term from "intrapersonal" to "personal intelligence" when writing about it. And Imrich Ruisel, of the Institute of Experimental Psychological Sciences of Slovakia, expanding on Gardner, had used the term to refer to a "meta-intellect"—an introspective awareness of one's personality and intelligence together. But what I had in mind was different from these earlier ideas. The personal intelligence I envisioned—focused on personality as it was—had not yet been described or explored with a valid psychological measure that might test whether such a coherent group of skills actually existed. It seemed like a good time to affix the "personal intelligence" label firmly to this new conception.

On the empirical side, I found suggestions that an intelligence like this might exist. In a 1948 report, a J. Wedeck had hoped to understand whether there was an ability for understanding people separate from Charles Spearman's general intelligence. Wedeck administered a series of questions to 203 adolescents, including questions that were related to personal intelligence (as I see it today). Participants tried to guess the personality characteristics of 40 people based on their photographs—Hard-hearted? Ascetic? Self-conscious?—and, on another part of the survey, tried to estimate people's personalities from written descriptions of them. The findings were a bit murky, but Wedeck believed there was evidence for "psi (Ψ)"—an ability to think psychologically—that was potentially different from general intelligence. A more recent study by Neil Christiansen and his colleagues at Central Michigan University identified a "dispositional intelligence" that concerned how well people understood the meanings of personality traits; they found clear evidence of reliable individual differences in how people reasoned in the area. Together, the two studies suggested to me that an ability such as personal intelligence might exist.

I recounted my theory to two colleagues, David R. Caruso of Yale and A. T. (Abigail) Panter of the Thurstone Psychometric Laboratory of the University of North Carolina, and gauged their interest in exploring whether personal intelligence might exist. I was delighted when they both wanted to join me to test and to further refine the theory. I also discussed the idea with Peter Salovey, with whom I have worked closely on emotional intelligence. David, Abigail, and I began to translate areas of personality-relevant reasoning into test questions that potentially measured people's understanding of the area. We were able to generate questions in a number of different areas of reasoning about personality—of which I provide examples throughout this book. And, more crucially, using the test we developed, we were able to support our conception of the mental ability.

Early on in this book, I'll examine a century of intelligence studies and explain how researchers identify a new intelligence, describe some examples of intelligences that have intrigued psychologists, and show how reasoning about personality fits into what we now know about mental abilities. I'll frequently describe case examples to illustrate how reasoning about personality plays out in real-life contexts, so as to connect the science to our everyday experience.

The theory of personal intelligence I employ suggests that there are several areas of reasoning that are key to understanding personality. The middle chapters of the book address these areas. To begin with, each of us regularly identifies and gathers information about ourselves and others. I'll discuss the most helpful clues to personality that psychologists presently have identified. But gathering information is just the beginning of understanding someone; we also combine that information into a more complete representation of the individual: we understand that if a person is highly sociable, for example, she is also likely to be lively and to enjoy taking a few risks. To understand ourselves, we use many of the same principles we employ to understand other people, yet there are some differences when it comes to self-understanding, as I'll also point out. For example, we obtain feedback about ourselves, and when we do, we *feel* the judgments of ourselves; these evaluations contain the hot information I spoke of earlier that roils us, attracts our attention, and sometimes disturbs our equilibrium. People high in "PI" (as I sometimes call it) develop rules for understanding their own needs and styles, and when they make choices, they take their personal qualities into account.

In the later chapters of the book I'll examine how personal intelligence develops. Most of us already understand something about traits and evaluating other people by the time we're in elementary school, we learn to estimate what other people are thinking, and we continue to learn more as we grow. Certain adults employ practices of lifelong learning about personality, enhancing their lives by establishing coherent, self-directed plans. Finally, at the end, I'll examine how personal intelligence contributes to society and how society, in turn, can support our skills by providing education about personality. And I'll speak to the significance of personal intelligence at home, at work, and in our social relationships.

Some of us will examine personal intelligence as curious spectators: we have enough of it or don't feel the need to develop it further—each of us has our own profile of strengths. But even if we don't care to develop the skill ourselves, being able to recognize its operation among the people around us can help us better appreciate human capabilities, and respect those who are good at it. Some of us may hope to enhance our own thinking about personality through the numerous research findings and case examples I'll report on. To my mind, one of the best ways to understand ourselves and others is by absorbing the lessons of psychologists who have been studying the area over the past decades, as well as by thinking about examples that illustrate some of the principles of reasoning in the area. No matter who you are and what has brought you to this book, I hope you will join me for a look at how reasoning about people unfolds. My wish is that you will feel enriched by seeing how we all use personal intelligence to reason about ourselves and others, and that you will come to appreciate this set of abilities in a new way.

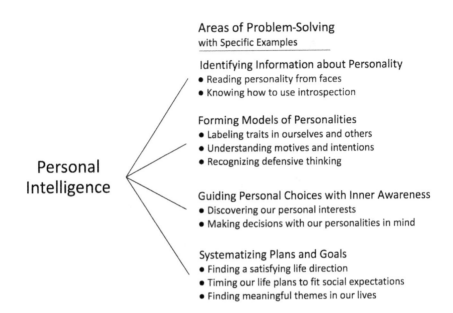

Areas of Problem-Solving
with Specific Examples

Identifying Information about Personality
- Reading personality from faces
- Knowing how to use introspection

Forming Models of Personalities
- Labeling traits in ourselves and others
- Understanding motives and intentions
- Recognizing defensive thinking

Personal Intelligence

Guiding Personal Choices with Inner Awareness
- Discovering our personal interests
- Making decisions with our personalities in mind

Systematizing Plans and Goals
- Finding a satisfying life direction
- Timing our life plans to fit social expectations
- Finding meaningful themes in our lives

An Overview of the Theory of Personal Intelligence. The overall intelligence is divided into four interrelated areas of problem-solving: identifying information, forming models, guiding personal choices, and systematizing plans. Each area, in turn, is made up of more specific problems to solve, some examples of which appear in the bulleted lists.

1

WHAT IS PERSONAL INTELLIGENCE?

During the course of our day, we might pass a group of men in athletic gear in the morning walking toward the neighborhood gym and bantering about baseball. Other people on the same sidewalk look like they don't want to talk to anyone until they've had their first cup of coffee. There are gregarious people we meet on our commute to work who will stop and talk to anyone who will listen, and less sociable folks who pass us by, eyes straight ahead. At work, we receive a hard-to-decipher e-mail from a colleague who has trouble expressing herself—we'll speak with her to find out what she needs. Buying lunch, we walk to the register, where the owner knows most of his patrons' names and orders by memory. In the afternoon, we negotiate a timeline with a client we are getting to know, wondering if she's married and has children. By the time we pack up our belongings and head home for dinner, we've responded to and juggled countless personalities, and there are still more to come, in slightly more removed fashion as we discuss the characters in the day's news: an actor who ranted about his costar and was fired from his show, or a baseball player who started a charity.

Later, as we fall asleep, we think of these people and we may think of ourselves, too—what we did well or might have done better, why people have acted in the ways they did and what they might do next. And it continues: if we were to wake up briefly a few hours later, and glimpse the light on in the home across the way, we might wonder, "What are they up to so late at night?" We can't help ourselves from being so inquisitive. We are naturally curious about what people do.

Our curiosity is no accident. We have evolved to try to understand one another so as to anticipate how others might behave. And to understand other people, we draw on our unique capacity to reason about personality, an ability that is a legacy of our evolutionary past and is augmented by our everyday learning. Our ability to reason this way serves as an inner guidance system that helps us navigate the people and situations we encounter and to attain our goals in life, be they to find a pleasing lunch mate or to choose a more inspiring direction to our life. And some people are especially talented when it comes to understanding personalities. The idea that people differ in the ability to understand one another isn't new, but the intelligence I will describe provides an explanation for why we think about other people and how we reason well about others, and draws together a diverse set of findings in personality psychology that haven't been examined together before—and, in some cases, were not even regarded as related. For example, scientific reports indicate that people vary in specific skills such as decoding faces, judging traits and motives, and demonstrating self-knowledge. I argue throughout this book that these skills—although they may seem diverse—mostly arise from a common ability. I call this ability "personal intelligence."

"Personal intelligence," as I mean it here, is shorthand for an intelligence about personality, and in order to unpack the idea I'll begin with a look at some present-day views of intelligence more generally. I'll use the term "mental ability" to refer to an individual's capacity to carry out a given psychological task, such as defining a word or putting together a puzzle. An intelligence represents a group of related abilities—a person's mental capacity to correctly solve a broad set of related problems of a particular type that our society recognizes as being of importance.* Scientists consider these abilities

---

*I also recognize a continuum that runs from intellectual potential, at one end, to learned competence, on the other. I'll mostly use "intelligence" and "capacity" to emphasize an individual's intellectual potential, and the terms "skills" and "competencies" to refer to a person's learned performance in an area.

to form an intelligence when the problems involved are valued, when only some individuals can reliably solve them, and when the ability leads to specific accomplishments. For example, the intelligence named "verbal comprehension" (or just "verbal") contributes to a wide range of skills, from understanding the definitions of individual words to recognizing the meaning of a written passage; verbal intelligence helps us communicate clearly with one another and, in so doing, helps us accomplish tasks from texting a friend to communicating with our team members at work. By contrast, our ability to remember nonsense words from a randomly sequenced list is a narrower enterprise—it may be one of the many abilities that contribute to verbal intelligence—but it is insufficiently meaningful to be considered an intelligence by itself.

To identify a specific type of intelligence, researchers carefully analyze what human beings do in a given setting and then try to identify the abilities that have characteristics in common. For verbal comprehension, the abilities include word knowledge (vocabulary), sentence comprehension, and certain forms of logical reasoning. To identify this, or any other intelligence, scientists engage in a process much like reverse engineering: they look at the problems people solve, and then try to figure out the abilities needed to find the correct solution.

Among the most successful investigations of how people solve problems was Alfred Binet's analysis, in 1905, of how certain students thrived in school. In 1904, the French government appointed a commission of educators and scientists to develop an objective means of distinguishing students who could learn in the nation's classrooms from those who were, in the language of the period, "mentally subnormal" and required special help.* Binet was appointed a member of the commission and was one of those who took on the task for the government.

Binet deduced from his observations of classrooms that successful

---

*Today, organizations such as the American Psychiatric Association (in their *Diagnostic and Statistical Manual of Mental Disorders*-5) refer to individuals who have general difficulties in learning and comprehending information as having intellectual disabilities. (See, for example, dsm-5-intellectual-disability-fact-sheet-1.pdf.)

students paid attention, followed instructions, imitated others, understood language, and remembered what they learned, among other abilities. To see if these were the key ingredients to school achievement, Binet, along with his colleague Theodore Simon, created a mental test with questions that evaluated a child's abilities to perform in those areas. The 1905 version of Binet and Simon's test, for example, contained one set of questions for which a test examiner asked a child to "do as I do." Then the examiner clapped his hands together, put them in the air, and raised his foot. If the child followed the instructions and imitated the acts, she passed that part of the test. For another part of the test, the examiner asked questions such as "Where is your head?" "Where is your nose?" and "Where is your eyebrow?" and prompted the child to point to them. The examiner assessed vocabulary specifically by asking for the definitions of words ("What is a dog?") and assessed memory by asking the child to repeat sentences of varied lengths.

Binet's test did indeed predict which students did well in school, indicating that he had successfully analyzed a core set of abilities necessary to achieve in that setting. Some critics pointed out, however, that Binet's instrument was dominated by items that required test-takers to understand words and language; and included only a few questions that inquired as to visual and spatial thinking, let alone questions about the children's social behavior. Binet and Simon nonetheless had brought about a remarkable advance, but one that had only begun to assess intelligence. With the benefit of hindsight, researchers would describe the area of ability that these early measures assessed as focused on verbal-comprehension intelligence.

As Binet was developing his tests, Charles Spearman, who in 1906 would become the University of London's first psychology professor, published a scientific article arguing that there might just be one *general* intelligence; Spearman had administered his own mental tests to students and he observed that the brightest children were able to answer most of the questions correctly, whereas the intellectually disabled children had difficulties with nearly all the test questions. If Spearman was correct that a given person's different problem-solving abilities were either all high, all low, or all in the middle, then Binet's test could be an adequate indicator of general intelligence even though it focused mostly on verbal reasoning, because a person's verbal IQ would reflect his other mental abilities as well. Spearman's observation was, generally speaking, correct, and still today, researchers regard verbal-comprehension intelligence, even by itself, as highly predictive of a pupil's grades in school, as well as predictive of success on the job.*

Although Spearman regarded intelligence as mostly general, other researchers of the time observed that many people were better in some areas of problem-solving than others. In 1920, another intelligence expert, E. L. Thorndike, concluded based on his studies: "The primary fact is that intelligence is not one thing but many." If there were multiple intelligences, then what lay beyond verbal IQ? Writing in *Harper's Monthly* on the virtues of studying people's problem-solving, Thorndike introduced his idea of social intelligence as ". . . the ability to understand and manage men and women, boys and girls—to act wisely in human relations." This intelligence, he continued, ". . . shows itself abundantly . . . on the playground, in barracks and factories and salesroom . . ."—and it had its start "in the nursery."

After briefly raising his idea, however, Thorndike returned to his central topic of the virtues of psychological testing, leaving social intelligence in its infancy. Other psychologists rushed in to nurture the castaway; they suggested that social intelligence included the "ability to get along with others," possessing "social technique," and comprehending the personalities of others. The overall picture of social intelligence was as if seen through a kaleidoscope—colorful in its design, but fragmented. And, even several decades later,

---

*When I say "highly predictive" in this book, I mean so relative to other psychological (and sociological and economic) variables. Researchers regularly identify clear relationships between variables such as intelligence, on the one hand, and positive life outcomes, on the other, and many of the relationships have practical significance. That said, any statement of the form "Intelligence X predicts outcome Y" represents a relationship that holds for people in general but may not hold for a specific individual. So although I might say that verbal intelligence is an important predictor of school grades, it is with the acknowledgment that other influences—personal motivation, family and community support, teacher qualities, sheer luck, and much we don't know about—also come to bear.

psychologists remained more comfortable with Binet's test, with its clear emphasis on verbal intelligence, and paid scant attention to alternative IQs.

David Wechsler finally coaxed psychologists to explore the precincts beyond verbal reasoning in 1939. Wechsler was a psychologist at Bellevue Hospital in New York City, and he faced a practical problem at the time. The city's police department, courts, and social agencies were sending his way recent immigrants to the United States who had engaged in a number of offenses, including vagrancy, public intoxication, disturbing the peace, and other petty crimes—and the authorities requested that Wechsler and his colleagues evaluate whether these new arrivals had any psychological difficulties, including intellectual disabilities.

These immigrants' native tongues ranged from Croatian to Yiddish. Any of these newcomers might have exhibited verbal intelligence in their homeland, but they were in a city that now offered them scant opportunity to employ their native language on the job or outside of their communities. Fortunately, intelligence researchers had already raised the point that people solved nonverbal problems all the time as well as verbal ones. Among these non-English-speakers would be found master carpenters who could plan, measure, and fit together wooden pieces into exquisite inlaid designs, garment workers who could stitch together intricate fashionable patterns, and mechanics who knew how to disassemble, repair, and reassemble motors and generators. Wechsler viewed such expert problem-solvers as able to perceive and understand the visual patterns of objects, and he proposed the existence of a perceptual-organizational intelligence to account for their reasoning.

To test his idea, Wechsler created a new measure of intelligence for which test-takers were asked to identify patterns in pictures, and to assemble puzzle pieces into designs. When Wechsler studied English-speakers and compared their verbal intelligence with that of their perceptual-organizational intelligence, the two were highly correlated: if a person was good verbally, she was also good at perceptual-organization tasks (and vice versa), generally speaking. And if a person was poor at one skill area, she was poor at the other.

Perceptual-organizational IQ, in other words, provided a reasonable alternative to verbal intelligence as an indicator of people's overall mental ability. Practically speaking, it meant we could test for perceptual-organizational intelligence rather than verbal intelligence among non-English-speaking test-takers. The perceptual-organizational IQ could then be used as an estimate for the person's overall intelligence.

To many psychologists, the strong relationship between verbal and perceptual-organizational intelligences provided more support for the existence of a general capacity to carry out abstract thought, and to them, one number—g, for general intelligence—approximated by an overall IQ score, was enough to gauge the overall sharpness of a person's intellect. If, on the other hand, intelligences were *multiple*—articulated in different areas of thinking—then a person's intellect would be more like a Swiss Army knife with multiple components, some of which may be particularly sharp and others that may be a bit rusty or even broken off. Then we would need more than one IQ score, one for each function.

Many people are baffled by the claim that a general intelligence could exist. They raise objections such as "I *know* I can critique a literary classic with great skill, but I'm not good at all when it comes to math," or "I am good at playing the piano but I'm really not much of a reader." Yet advocates of general intelligence argue that we all have similar natural abilities across diverse areas but, for reasons of personal motivation and experiences at home or in school, we become discouraged and end up being "no good" at a given subject despite our original potential.

Scientists who adhere to the g position ask us to think about people *all along* the intelligence spectrum. People with *severe* intellectual disability—typically with IQs of 20 to 35—have impaired language and need to rely on gestures and facial expressions to communicate, and are unable to take care of themselves generally. At these levels of intellectual function, they are hardly able to perform on a children's intelligence test at levels much above chance. At the opposite extreme, people with exceedingly high levels of intelligence— with IQs above 170 or so—are likely to perform above average at everything from analyzing prose to solving complex equations and to acquire new concepts at a lightning-fast clip. Psychologists who witness these extremes are likely to accept general intelligence as a reasonable index of how well a person will function in intellectually demanding environments. At the middle range of intelligence—which includes most of us—our differences in skill across areas of problem-solving are plainer. Our friend's claim that he can handily pick up a new language but is terrible at math seems reasonable to us. But intelligence researchers may remind us that, against the backdrop of the full range of intellect, our friend's abilities are solidly somewhat above average: his language skills, though excellent, fall short of those with the highest IQs, and his math skills, though relatively weak, far exceed the skills of people who are intellectually disabled.

Many clinical psychologists regularly conducted mental assessments of people with severe intellectual disabilities and people with tremendous potential; their professional experiences predisposed them to be natural allies of the general-intelligence position. Throughout the latter part of the twentieth century, general intelligence, and the verbal-comprehension and perceptual-organizational intelligences that were a part of it, seemed sufficient for most practical purposes, and indeed predicted important life outcomes. From this perspective, any new IQ was unnecessary—it would be just more of the same. Then Howard Gardner came along and picked up the argument for multiple intelligences once again.

Gardner, a professor of education at Harvard University, hoped to revise and broaden how people looked at human abilities. He caught the public's imagination in the early 1980s with a book entitled *Frames of Mind* that proposed seven intelligences. Gardner argued that intelligences were identified in part because societies had a need for problem-solvers in a given area. For example, spatial intelligence was crucial in some societies, including

the Puluwat people of the Caroline Islands in the South Seas. In the case of Puluwats, the highly developed skill is that of navigation, one found in a minority of individuals who are allowed to sail canoes. Within this well-trained population, there occurs a flowering of skills that has filled Western-trained navigators with awe . . . To navigate among the many islands in their vicinity, the Puluwats must recall the points or directions where certain stars rise and set around the horizon.

In addition to the cultural valuation of mental skills, Gardner appealed to evidence from intellectual prodigies in each area of ability he proposed, and from brain injuries that could eliminate a mental skill and therefore provided evidence for the ability's specificity. His list included verbal comprehension, but carved out a mathematical intelligence from it. And he proposed intra- and interpersonal intelligences, roughly denoting an intelligence about emotions and identity, and an intelligence about reading other people, influencing them, and understanding social laws, justice, and morality.

Gardner's clarion call was that children who might have difficulty performing at a subject such as math might be intelligent in spatial or musical terms (he had also proposed a musical intelligence). This appealed to many educators who found it inspiring to think about the undiscovered talents of their students. It resonated beyond the classroom as well, to those of us who harbored a hope that we might possess intellectual abilities that have gone unrecognized.

But Gardner rather inexplicably brushed off any empirical test of his theory that involved the construction of a new battery of mental tests. So far as he was concerned, evidence from intelligence tests was uninformative given the strength of the arguments he had marshaled; and he seemed to express more interest in what brain science might ultimately tell us about learning. This was a surprising position that left psychologists little leeway to assess his theory. And although he was open to the idea that his seven intelligences could be verified through brain research, it wasn't exactly clear how—or when—that would happen. Many psychologists were disappointed and troubled because Gardner's emphasis on the relative independence of one intelligence from another appeared to dismiss widely accepted findings that intelligences generally rose and fell together.

Even advocates of multiple intelligences, such as Robert J. Sternberg, then of Yale University, were troubled by the lack of research support necessary to drive home points. When psychologists did attempt to test Gardner's theory, their findings weren't obviously consistent with his ideas.

Other psychologists of the time also advanced alternative models. Robert Sternberg had identified three somewhat independent intelligences, including analytical intelligence (the sort measured by traditional IQ tests), creativity (which Sternberg regarded as his second form of intelligence), and, with his colleague Richard K. Wagner, a practical intelligence. People with practical intelligence pick up on the unspoken rules of social behavior and use them to improve their lives. To measure this, Wagner and Sternberg posed lifelike problems to test-takers. In one instance, they described a new manager at a company who wanted a promotion—and then asked people how the manager could best meet his goal. Test-takers were instructed to choose what the manager should do from a long list of possibilities that included getting rid of deadwood employees, appearing on a local PBS talk show, and matching an employee's strengths to the tasks at hand. Correct answers were identified by experts from the relevant field of management. Wagner and Sternberg found promising evidence that practical reasoning predicted successful performance in related work contexts, and research on the new ability continues today.

Although scientists at the time often bickered about general versus multiple intelligences, there was a growing middle ground as to how the abilities might fit together. John Carroll, an emeritus professor at the University of North Carolina, proposed one key version of the integration. Carroll depicted intelligence as a hierarchy of three "strata," or levels. General intelligence was at the top, and beneath it were eight or so broad intelligences, including verbal comprehension, perceptual intelligence, cognitive speediness, long-term memory, and several more, based on his reanalyses of previously collected data from various laboratories. At the lowest level were over sixty specific abilities, such as speed of reasoning, free-recall memory, spatial scanning, and maintaining rhythm. Today, many contemporary researchers regard multiple intelligences as embedded in a hierarchical structure like the one Carroll proposed; they use g (the top stratum) as a convenient benchmark for predicting a person's overall ability, but they also examine the broad intelligences at the middle level of the hierarchy (the second stratum) to understand the implications of a given ability profile.

And a person's profile of broad intelligences matters. For example, in a study of 400,000 high school students and their subsequent occupational choices, Jonathan Wei of Vanderbilt University and colleagues studied learners with comparable verbal and arithmetical abilities but spatial abilities that differed. Those students who were relatively low in spatial ability were more likely to enter careers in the performing arts, law, and education, compared with matched participants higher in spatial abilities, who gravitated to the visual arts, engineering, and the physical sciences.

This was the intellectual landscape in 1990—very roughly speaking—when my colleague Peter Salovey of Yale University and I published our article "Emotional Intelligence" and a second article providing evidence that the intelligence could be measured. We had reasoned that because the brain had evolved relatively distinct areas for emotion and emotional processing, an emotional intelligence might exist and might be partly distinct from other intelligences. This idea attracted many enthusiasts among the public, helped along by Daniel Goleman's journalistic account of our newly proposed theory in his 1995 book.

But many scientists were skeptical of the idea at first—wondering if emotional intelligence could be measured and whether it was a unitary ability. To address those questions, Peter and I, along with David Caruso, began developing a series of tests to assess people's reasoning in the area, culminating with the Mayer-Salovey-Caruso Emotional Intelligence Test (MSCEIT). Researchers could use that measure to study people's profiles of ability in the area. Scientists who have examined our work have succeeded in replicating and extending our key findings. And although they have not been shy about pointing out technical limitations of our early measures, the tests were good enough to convince many of our colleagues, first, that the intelligence existed, and later, that EI predicted important outcomes. Those with emotional intelligence were better liked by others, had better social relations, and attained greater well-being than others.

But there were limitations inherent in our concept. We had described an ability that was focused on the emotions, and yet there is much more to people than feelings. At least some journalists had, in their enthusiasm, equated our theory of emotional intelligence with a person's *overall character*, going well beyond anything we had written. But as important as emotions are, they have little to say about people's intentions, traits, motives, or life stories. So, just a few years after Salovey and I had published our work, I began to look for common rules and principles that people used to think about personality—starting with the rules used by personality psychologists themselves. I constructed, over a few years' time, an outline of psychologists' core beliefs about how we function. For example, almost all psychologists agree that personality represents the overall organization of a person's psychological life; they agree that our personalities emerge from our motives and emotions, thoughts and intelligences, social skills, and self-control—the larger mental systems that make us up. Those larger systems, in turn, emerge from lower-level mental processes, and the lower processes themselves emerge from the neural activities of the brain. Our personalities also are constantly responding to (and influencing) our physical location, the situations we face, and the groups to which we belong. As I worked on this new project, I would periodically wonder whether emotional intelligence represented just a *slice* of a broader form of reasoning about personality.

As time passed, evolutionary theorists began to explore the advantages that might have accrued to our ancestors who better understood one another's characters. About 600,000 years ago, our brains grew in size dramatically relative to those of other primates. Robin I. M. Dunbar, an anthropologist and evolutionary psychologist at Oxford University, pointed out that most primate groups are limited to about thirty members—small enough so that each member comes in contact with all the others. He suggested that *Homo sapiens* sought to live in larger groups, and this created a selective pressure that favored those with bigger brains. As these groups grew in size, ancient humans needed to keep track of one another, and to do so people began talking about what the members of the group were up to. Through gossip, Dunbar argues, people discovered what other members of the broader, extended group were like—who was trustworthy, who was hardworking, and who was skilled—and this enabled them to better control their social environment. Martie Haselton and David Funder added that we evolved an instinctual urge to judge other people, which is reflected today in the rapidity with which we make judgments about one another.

David Buss of the University of Texas at Austin further suggested that we evolved "difference detectors" when it came to evaluating other people. Our hunter-gatherer ancestors who possessed the skills to evaluate the industry and generosity of their fellow food-seekers would fare better than others, he has argued. For example, they'd be able to choose hunting partners who could be counted on to obtain and share food. Buss also argued that women would acquire skills to evaluate the loyalty and potential success of their male mates to ensure their own well-being and that of their offspring during childbearing and child-rearing. He asserted that individuals who could better make such predictions were apt to experience a meaningful adaptive advantage over time and to pass along such a facility to their descendants.

Although we cannot know with confidence what people were thinking or talking about half a million years ago, we do know that among the earliest documents of recorded history were judgments of personality. Writing 4,500 years ago, Ptahhotep, a political adviser in ancient Egypt, counseled leaders to hold a private conversation with an individual so as to evaluate his character before trusting him, and to listen carefully to what the person had to say. And by 2,500 years ago, written records across many ancient traditions—including from Buddhist writings, from the philosophies of ancient Greece and the Hellenic region, the Hebrew Bible, the Hindu Upanishads, and from Confucianism—attested to a global interest in types of personality.

Many of these writings described different types of people. For example, in ancient Greece, Theophrastus outlined different kinds of character, such as the flatterer, the country bumpkin, the avaricious, and the superstitious. Plato's emphasis was on understanding oneself. Superficially, personality types and self-knowledge might seem like different topics—until you stop to consider that personality lies at the heart of both. It seems to me that we cannot know either ourselves or other people well without knowing something about the human personality we all share in common.

The intertwined nature of our self-knowledge and our ability to comprehend others is illustrated in a classic study from 1949 by Bertram Forer, a clinical psychologist at the Veterans Administration in Los Angeles. Forer was teaching a class in introductory psychology when his students asked him to give them a personality test—a matter of considerable interest for young adults. So the next week, he administered a questionnaire that asked his students their attitudes about themselves, about authority figures, and about their levels of realism and of idealism. A week later, Forer gave the students their own personal results sealed in an envelope—and instructed them not to compare their own feedback with others, but to open the envelope and just read through what they saw. For example, one student's responses included "You have a great need for other people to like and admire you," "You have a tendency to be critical of yourself," and "While you have some personality weaknesses, you are generally able to compensate for them." That student's list of thirteen attributes concluded with "Security is one of your major goals in life."

Forer then asked each student to rate the feedback they received as to its accuracy in "revealing personality." All but one of the students rated the statements at a four or a five on a five-point scale (very good to near perfect). Following up, Forer requested a volunteer to read his description aloud, and the class burst into laughter as they realized they all had exactly the same description of themselves. Forer's trick of convincing the students that the test feedback he used for everyone was actually personalized information had worked.

Psychologists interpreted Forer's study as revealing that students were naïve and overly willing to accept feedback about themselves from an authority. They referred to Forer's finding as the "Barnum Effect"—after the circus proprietor P. T. Barnum, who said that a sucker is born every minute. One of Forer's central points was to warn his students against being unduly impressed by horoscopes, palm readings, and other occult practices. In fact, Forer selected his feedback statements for the students from a book of horoscopes.

I originally shared that interpretation of Forer's findings, but more recently I have drawn a different lesson. To me, Forer's results revealed the surprisingly close relationship between who we are as human beings and who we are as specific individuals—and the genuine challenge of distinguishing between the two. I imagine that the astrologers from whom Forer had drawn his descriptions had gradually amassed character descriptions that were widely applicable to the public. Those astrologers learned that most of us don't recognize how generally applicable the descriptions are. In Forer's class, the students who agreed with the statement "You have a tendency to be critical of yourself" likely didn't pause to consider how many other people felt the same way (nor did Forer ask them to).

In fact, if test-takers receive *two* sets of feedback—one based on the average of the sample, and the other specifically tailored to themselves—the participants do rate the feedback generated from their own test responses as more accurate than the average profile, although their ability to do so is sometimes modest.

Forer's legacy, to me, was his demonstration of how much we share in common with other people—often without knowing it. This speaks to a cornerstone of my theory: that reasoning about ourselves and about other people is in many respects the same. The understanding of the personality we share with most others provides a key foundation for the mental reasoning involved in personal intelligence.

Some of us are limited in our understanding of personality—we just don't reason well in this realm. We have all encountered people who are challenged in making good judgments about others—and there are many case reports of such phenomena. As just one example, Dr. Hazel Ipp, a Toronto psychoanalyst, worked with Gayle, a client who had a blind spot about her behavior that led her to seek professional assistance. According to Ipp, Gayle was tall, lean, attractive, and invariably well dressed. She had a real presence when she entered a room. Although Gayle could be charming and engaging, she could also disapprove of others "in cynical and cutting tones." When she was in her thirties, Gayle had impressed people in the Toronto arts community with her energy and her discerning eye as to quality creative expressions. Using such talents, she had built a thriving business amid the city's arts scene. Gayle attended glitzy parties and amused guests with clever observations. Her elegant manner extended to a lovely summer home she maintained, at which she frequently entertained. And she had many loyal clients—until recently.

At the time Gayle sought Ipp's help, she had just lost several faithful business clients. Gayle was lonely even though she was surrounded by people who shared her interests, and she had written off relationships with men. She lived in an apartment in the city she regarded as a "pigsty," she confessed to Dr. Ipp. Gayle was undermining herself, it turned out, by her harsh evaluations of other people. Rather than accepting that each of us is flawed and imperfect by nature, Gayle assessed the people around her in the same cutting tone she might have used for an inferior piece of art. She seemed to expect a level of coherence and perfection that only a work of art might attain. Perhaps her understanding of personality was weak to begin with; perhaps people with higher personal intelligence would be less prone to make such errors.

Those higher in personal intelligence, I believe, evaluate individuals more accurately and therefore make more allowances for others' foibles; they are better at acknowledging their own limitations too. Those who are talented at this reasoning power make better guesses about how people are likely to behave (including themselves). And they have a generally good idea about how their acquaintances, colleagues, and friends perceive them—they know their own reputations. At still deeper levels, these individuals recognize that their perceptions of the people around them might require revision at times.

There are no schools for reading people, no institutions where the highly perceptive among us hang out, and so I turned to biographies and autobiographies for examples of these problem-solving styles. One of the examples I found that nicely illustrates some of these ideas was Katherine (Kay) Graham's account of the period around 1963 when she took over as publisher of *The Washington Post*—a position she would fill for the next sixteen years. Graham had been married to Phil Graham, then the *Post*'s publisher, but in 1963, sadly, her husband committed suicide during his struggle with bipolar disorder. In the aftermath, Graham changed her life's direction. I perceived some personally intelligent reasoning in her self-descriptions at the time.

Graham made the newspaper's success her mission after her husband's death, exhibiting a sense of self-direction that drew on her self-knowledge. She declined offers from others to buy the *Post* from her, writing that "having stood by my father and husband as they built [the *Post*] up with such zeal and devotion, I would never sell; it was unthinkable." She mulled over the possibility of taking over the *Post* and running it herself, prudently soliciting opinions from friends and family about whether she could carry it off. And although she decided to go ahead, she clearly recognized her limitations—that she had never before managed *any* company. She openly acknowledged her inexperience to her colleagues at the newspaper—which, I suspect, helped her to form relationships with the key staff members and executives. Graham thought a great deal about how others perceived her: only some of the staff welcomed her presence, she remarked, whereas others viewed her as "an ignorant intruder" and most staffers likely didn't care much—a plausible picture of how others must have seen her at the time. And, of course, she sought out people whom she could trust and rely on for guidance.

Like any of us doing something for the first time, Graham was rough around the edges as she embarked on her new leadership role. That said, she also labored under the shadow of her husband's legacy. As she began to run the paper, she was troubled by the sense that her own leadership was a step down from her husband's. She puzzled over this idea until she realized that just by acknowledging her husband's exceptional leadership, she and her colleagues might be further exaggerating it in their recollections. Granting his very real talents, she concluded, "Not only had I mythologized him, but others shared the same idolatrous view . . ."

One key to personal intelligence is our ability to distinguish our own perception of another person from who the person really is. Graham realized she had made things harder on herself by comparing herself with her idealized view of her husband—and, although acknowledging his genuine strengths, kept the difference in mind. She then concluded that she could not become him and, to improve in the role of publisher, would need to develop her own leadership style.

Other people might be less impressed by Graham's account than I was, or read it differently than I have, but the passage increased my sense that there was a cohesive mental ability lurking in the problems she solved. Some people might wonder if this is really a kind of social intelligence, but if Graham used social intelligence, as I would define it, she would have been far more focused on issues of who wielded power, the rewards and punishments she might dole out, the exchange of favors with others, who owed what to whom, and factions in the office. Although Graham no doubt thought about these matters as well, her focus was on the personalities of those around her and on herself. Her problem-solving involved who she was and what she could do, accurately perceiving others, and fitting her own strengths and weaknesses into her interactions with others.

To test whether other people might also observe what I was seeing in Kay Graham's description of herself, my lab members and I conducted a study for which we examined biographical information from eight well-known business leaders in the United States. We assembled quotes and life data for each person and, based on this information, independent judges (who didn't know how we ranked the eight leaders) evaluated the individuals as to their appearance of personal intelligence. Oprah Winfrey was ranked highest among these leaders (who also included Warren Buffett, Bill Gates, Steve Jobs, Charles Schwab, Martha Stewart, Donald Trump, and Jack Welch). Winfrey, then the champion of daytime talk, had spoken openly about her self-knowledge. In one interview, for example, Winfrey remarked:

> I am a colored girl born in Mississippi in 1954 and all that that means: poverty, isolation, discrimination, deprivation, lack of information, low self-esteem. The expectation for me was to work in white people's kitchens. I am here because I have walked across the backs of people who made this way for me. That's in everything that I do. I'm black and I'm female and . . . I find strength and honor in that. My responsibility is not just to myself.

Winfrey also described how she used parts of her autobiography to motivate herself:

> I relate to the core of everyone's pain and promise because I've known pain and promise . . . Having that understanding and that connection has really given me wings to fly.

The average judge in the study ranked the leaders' personal intelligence similarly to how we had, and this increased our confidence in the idea. Of course, many public figures represent themselves in the media to promote their public personae and careers; and the more powerful the individual is, the more her public appearances may be controlled by publicists and other assistants. Obviously, we couldn't prove that any given individual really possessed such reasoning power from this study—but we had found some evidence that people could perceive a quality such as personal intelligence from samples of biographical information.

To obtain more pertinent evidence as to whether an intelligence like this really existed, David Caruso and A. T. Panter, who have joined me in studying this phenomenon, developed more than a dozen categories of questions about personality for test-takers to grapple with, and then wrote multiple-choice questions of each type. I'll explain the kinds of problem-solving the test measures throughout this book, but as a first example, to understand people, it often helps to know what character traits tend to go together in a given person. We measured such knowledge with questions like this one:

> Susan is depressed and self-conscious. Most likely, she also could be described as:
> a. calm and even-tempered
> b. self-controlled
> c. anxious and impulsive
> d. fairly thick-skinned

People who are depressed and self-conscious, studies show, are also prone to be worried and, at times, rash. The best answer is therefore "c. anxious and impulsive." Some people may object that the alternatives are a bit imprecise. After all, people use "anxious" to refer to states that range from mild concern to intense fear. Philosophers sometimes call these categories "fuzzy"—and they argue that we are able to reason with these imprecise ideas without much difficulty by using "nonclassical" logic. Our capacity to use approximations while thinking allows us to recognize that depressed people are more often anxious and impulsive (alternative "c") than they are thick-skinned (alternative "d"), for example. We wrote more than a hundred such items, each in multiple-choice form, and in each case designated which answer was correct. Our goal was to use this diverse set of problems to measure personal intelligence.

This tried-and-true method of testing ability is the gold standard for measuring an intelligence—really, the only standard. It's not possible to accurately measure intelligence by asking people how smart they are—attempts have been made, but we lack the necessary insight to estimate our own intelligence. And although brain scientists hope to unlock the workings of intelligences by imaging the brain, their neurological research depends on such test questions as well: to localize an intelligence, people have their brain activity recorded while they solve well-defined problems. To find out if personal intelligence exists, in other words, there was little choice but to develop a good measure of problem-solving.

After we wrote our questions, we hoped to show that the test problems formed a conceptually coherent group—all described within the theory of personal intelligence. We called this first group of items the Test of Personal Intelligence 1.0—or the TOPI 1.0, for short. To show that personal intelligence existed, our first steps were to show whether people varied in their ability to solve the problems: that some people would be able to solve most or all of the problems, that other people would lack the ability to solve them, and that most people would fall somewhere in between.

In a 2012 article, our team reported findings that found just that: people who could perceive personality in people's faces also knew how personality traits were interrelated—and were better at setting goals as well. We also found that personal intelligence was related to emotional intelligence—which makes sense given that understanding personality includes understanding the emotions that are part of the broader system. In addition, we could distinguish personal intelligence from general intelligence—indicating that we were measuring something new.

So what does this wide area of thinking involve? When we reason about personality, we can think of ourselves as beginning by observing the outside of a person. We notice that some people have very "strong" personalities—they have lots of charisma or are very controlling and demanding, or all of those wrapped into one. We may think of someone else who we have little reaction to as having "no personality." According to the psychologist David Funder, we perceive each other accurately when we spot cues a person gives as to his behavior and use that information correctly to make predictions about what he might do next. Funder finds that we are particularly good at spotting the traits of others that are outwardly visible, such as a person's sociability and dominance; we are much less accurate at discerning inner qualities, such as his tendency to daydream or his intelligence. I'll describe a number of such outwardly visible clues in the next chapter.

As important as these outward signs of personality are, they are just a beginning. A. A. Roback, who wrote a 1927 textbook on personality psychology—arguably the first in the field—observed that most of us pay too much attention to the external expressions of people we come into contact with—to their "charm and bearing," in his words. For Roback, it was the *inner* personality—an individual's hidden thoughts and desires—that was most critical to understanding the person, and this could be revealed only over time, after we'd come to know someone on an intimate level. To understand people as best we can, we must be willing to delve into the inner person as well—and I'll cover that, too.

The understanding we develop of personality, in turn, can serve as a guidance system for our own lives. Each of us relies on a certain degree of self-guidance that is well learned and automatic, an autopilot that gives rise to our often quick evaluations of others—liking someone at a first meeting, or steering clear of a street peddler who is belligerent to passersby. Personal intelligence contributes most, however, to the conscious thinking we do about personality.

The guidance we exert over our lives is analogous in some ways to other systems that benefit from sophisticated control. It isn't too fanciful to remark, for example, that both our lives and a space mission involve disciplined exploration and travel to a desired destination. A spacecraft itself has many guidance systems on board—automatic systems for craft orientation and course correction. This is like the automatic reactions we possess as part of our evolutionary heritage to respond quickly to people. In addition to automatic systems, a spacecraft needs the oversight of human beings—an astronaut on board or a specialist at Mission Control—who can step in when an issue arises. Our personal intelligence provides such opportunities to oversee our own trajectory and guide ourselves through the hard spots to what we hope will be a successful mission.

Howard Gardner once suggested that intelligences could be identified in those cases where cultures valued them. But it is also the case that scientists can identify intelligences that cultures have under-appreciated or overlooked so as to ensure that those abilities are valued as they should be. By uncovering an ability such as personal intelligence, we can more fairly value people who possess such skills and appreciate their contributions to our world. It may turn out that people high in personal intelligence, relative to others, are more highly motivated themselves, better able to guide others in their lives, and can relate in more helpful ways to other people as circumstances demand. If so, their skills might contribute in a crucial manner to the better functioning of society.

2

CLUES TO OURSELVES: CONCEALED AND REVEALED

We seek clues from our environment about the people around us—a tendency that likely began deep in our evolutionary past. Many clues as to who we are can only be found deep within us, private and seemingly unobservable to others. Yet as hidden and unknowable as we might sometimes wish to be, we give off traces of ourselves. Think of personality as a geographical region on a map surrounded by four neighboring regions with which it engages in a form of trade. An overview of these areas can give us a preview of where the clues are.

Below personality are the brain and body.* All of personality's processes emerge from a functioning brain, and so we are inextricably bound with keeping our brains and bodies healthy, and the brains and bodies must, in turn, perform sufficiently for our personalities to operate.

On that same map is the region of the person's "setting" to the lower right. Shakespeare penned "All the world's a stage," and the setting is like a stage set—the place we act in the ongoing drama we live:

---

*I have laid out this map, and description, in keeping with the "personality systems framework"—one standard view of personality that describes personality's relationship to the systems with which it interacts. In this visualization, smaller systems (e.g., neurons) are below, larger systems (e.g., social groups) above; systems within personality are to the left; those outside the person are to the right. Time occupies a third dimension. The rationale for this model of personality's location can be found in my 2005 article on the systems framework in *American Psychologist* and in a recent exposition, with Allen, in the 2013 special issue of *Review of General Psychology* on the unification of psychology.

dressed in whatever costume we need to get by there—and with any props we need. We go to the beach in a swimsuit, with sunscreen, a picnic lunch, and a change of clothes; we go to work in dress-casual clothes and with a briefcase.

Returning to the map, personality engages with the psychological situation to the right, influences the situation, and is influenced in return. A situation involves a coherent set of actions we carry out that have a shared meaning in our community. "Walking down the street to our destination" is a situation, as is "building a cabinet," "attending a bridal shower," and "interviewing for a job." We communicate in these instances using our facility with language, our facial expressions, bodily posture, and even our skin (e.g., blushing). We influence these situations by acting on them: we use our hands and arms to manipulate tools—screwdrivers, hammers, and glue—to build a cabinet in a woodworking shop. Or we use good posture, pleasant manners, and a firm handshake at a job interview at a local firm. And the situations impact us in return—the owner of the cabinet shop tells us to follow the safety rules; the firm where we'll interview tells us the time and place to arrive for the meeting.

Finally, above us on this map are the groups to which we belong: our families, communities, the groups of fans we root with for our basketball teams. Although our memberships in our ethnic or age groups are fixed, we can switch our memberships in other groups such as our high school glee clubs or even our nationalities. We follow the codes of the groups to which we belong and, if we are lucky, draw some psychological sustenance from them—support from like-minded people.

Personality's job is to do business with each neighboring area: to manage the individual's physical health and safety (in the case of the brain and body), to find decent settings to be in, to engage in situations so as to get things done, and to draw on group alliances for protection, companionship, and a sense of identity. To get these jobs done, personality must act in each realm—and as we act, the signs of our behavior become visible in the neighboring regions. People who observe us can pick up signs as to our health or stress levels from our faces and bodies; they read signals about our social status from our settings, such as the neighborhoods in which we live or whether we shop at Walmart or Neiman Marcus. And they gauge us according to the skills and the social interactions we exhibit across the myriad situations we face each day. Other people pick up on our backgrounds and attitudes from the groups to which we belong and our relationships to those groups. Like it or not, in other words, our personalities leave behind clues—behavioral traces—to who we are in each of these realms.

Each of us is like a detective when we want to understand another person, searching these regions for clues that reveal an individual's intentions. A real-life detective can help illustrate some of the information we search out. During an interview, Phil Panzarella, a detective with the New York City Police Department, recounted apprehending a suspect I'll call Jones. Panzarella used clues about the suspect from each of the four areas I just described to apprehend the man.

Panzarella had a good idea of his suspect's behavior across several key situations from the previous day. According to the police report, the alleged perpetrator had been in an argument, was chased by the police, was arrested, and had spent some time in a hospital. If most of us were in such situations, I'll wager we would try to end our argument peacefully, would cooperate with the police officer who arrested us, and would generally welcome any medical assistance at a hospital—that's just how we work. Jones's behavior was different, however, and provided a not-so-subtle look at who he was. To conclude his argument, he shot his adversary; fearing the police, he stole a car to get away, ran a roadblock, and crashed into another car, killing a sidewalk vendor. Then Jones jumped from the car and swam across a creek, and when two police officers on the other side arrested him, he assaulted them as well. The officers brought him in. Then Jones complained of chest pain in the police station, was transferred to a hospital, and escaped. This is highly consistent behavior across situations: mortally dangerous and self-serving, and including the intention of preserving one's freedom at any cost—lots of clues there, and not too hard to spot.

Panzarella also knew something about the groups to which

Jones belonged—in particular about Jones's family and relationships. After his escape, Jones called both his mother and his girlfriend and visited his mother's home; when the police arrived he fled through neighborhood backyards, so Jones knew the police had been watching his home since. Therefore, Panzarella knew Jones was temporarily cut off from some of his key social supports—his mother and a friend.

The setting, broadly speaking, was a precinct in New York City—its streets, businesses, homes, and people. Early the morning after Jones fled from his mother's home, Panzarella and a second detective were in a police cruiser when they saw the suspect walking out of an alleyway. The detectives' car (another aspect of the setting) gave Panzarella and his partner a considerable advantage over Jones, who was on foot.

Panzarella appraised an additional area relevant to Jones's personality: his physical condition. It was still dark and the detective could tell from the way Jones walked from the alley that he was tired—and he appeared wet as well.

Panzarella put these clues together to make a prediction about Jones's mental state: that a part of him was ready to give up. The last thing Panzarella wanted to do was to unnecessarily threaten Jones, which might reenergize him. So, after explaining his plan to his partner, the detectives drove slowly up alongside Jones as he walked. Panzarella rolled down his car window and called to Jones by name, "You know, you're really breaking my balls here tonight. For Christ's sake, I could have been home in bed. I could have had a cocktail or two with the guys. Hey, stop fucking around and get in the car, all right?" And they stopped the car.

After a moment or two, Jones turned, opened the police car door, and said, "Officer, there's a jacket in the backseat." Panzarella moved his jacket and Jones got in. Panzarella shared a Slurpee from 7-Eleven with him, and explained apologetically that he would have to handcuff him and take him back to the police station. Jones agreed, and he was booked—peacefully—at the precinct station.

Some people are better than others at using clues to anticipate how a person might behave, and Panzarella's skill was unusually good in this instance. In fact, Panzarella's captain expressed initial disbelief that the arrest could have unfolded so peacefully after the suspect's earlier violence—until he heard the story independently from Panzarella's partner and from the suspect himself. As Panzarella put it, you need to develop "a feel" for the particular person and conditions under which to arrest someone: "Detectives have been taking people off the street for years, without getting hurt, only because they're smarter than the individuals they apprehend. If you plan it right and you play the cards, it is to your advantage."

We may not be police detectives, but that doesn't stop us from seeking clues to predict what the people around us will do. Consider the signals from a person's physical bearing. We often begin collecting information about a person from a variety of his physical attributes that are biologically based. At the plainest end of the spectrum, we sort people into demographic categories such as male, female, children, and adults. Qualities such as sex and age are sufficiently important to reflect not only our physical qualities but also groups to which people belong: the young are typically school students, the old are often retired. And we are likely to make use of broad demographic information as we perceive others. We guess that an eighth-grader from Washington, D.C., who wears a Nationals baseball cap will happily talk about baseball, and that an adult who is carrying an NPR tote bag will be more interested in current events than the NASCAR race we were at over the weekend—although we keep in mind that we are using averages and will frequently need to correct our suppositions.

People who use clues about an individual's gender, life stage, and other demographics may improve their accuracy in understanding those around them. Karyn Lewis and her colleagues at the University of Oregon found that people who used such knowledge about new mothers were, in fact, more accurate in perceiving them. The researchers first collected people's everyday beliefs about what new mothers think, and then asked an initial group of participants which of the written-out thoughts were most common among women caring for their newborns. The participants believed new mothers frequently reflected on "how exhausting it is to have a newborn baby and how challenging it was to find time for myself," and were less apt to be "feeling sad—as if the pre-baby me has been lost"—although new mothers can experience either, of course.

The researchers next video-recorded fourteen women after the birth of their first child. The recording was stopped at regular intervals, and at each point, the new mothers wrote down their thoughts leading up to that moment. Next, the researchers asked a new set of participant observers what the new mothers were thinking at the stop points in the videos. The participants were unaware of the earlier-identified "common thoughts." Nonetheless, those who drew on ideas similar to the common list of thoughts, believing, for example, that a video-recorded mother believed "her baby is her top priority now and she has less time for herself," were more accurate at predicting what the mothers reported thinking than those who did not employ such everyday knowledge of mothers.

Mixing in a bit of general knowledge about a group—new mothers or eleven-year-old baseball fans—in other words, provides clues to what a group member might be thinking, but we are wise to hold our theories lightly and to revise our opinions quickly if people don't fit our preconceptions. Few of us would like to be viewed as a "typical new mother" or "typical eleven-year-old," and we ourselves would be regarded as rigid if we insisted on seeing other people only through such a lens. So, although we use knowledge about age and sex, we nimbly shift gears if, after asking our eighth-grader how the Nationals are doing, he replies he is wearing his brother's baseball cap and doesn't follow sports, or if our NPR tote-bagger is a mechanic who listens to *Car Talk* and attends NASCAR races.

Sometimes physical characteristics speak more directly to personality. Professor Ian Penton-Voak of the University of Bristol and his colleagues have studied how people recognize personality traits such as extraversion and conscientiousness from faces. Early researchers in physiognomy tried to connect personality traits to individual facial features such as the size of an individual's eyes or the shape of her mouth, nose, or ears; this didn't work too well. Contemporary

researchers such as Penton-Voak have shifted to studying facial configurations: they study the overall appearance of a person's face, including not only its specific features but also how the mouth, nose,
ears, and other parts are positioned relative to one another. Penton-
Voak and colleagues demonstrated that everyday perceivers can use
these holistic configurations to read traits from faces.

For example, Penton-Voak and his team took photographs of the
faces of 146 men and 148 women. Each of the individuals who were
photographed filled out measures of a few of their traits, including
extraversion, openness, and emotionality. Independent raters then
looked at their photographs and tried to estimate the men's and
women's traits from their pictures. These observers were successful
in identifying the self-evaluated traits of the target individuals in
the photographs at levels meaningfully above chance, using only the
information from their faces—a finding demonstrating Penton-Voak's
claim.

To study the phenomenon further, Penton-Voak then distilled a
type of face that more clearly represented a particular trait. The research team first identified the fifteen men and fifteen women who
scored most extremely on each of the ten traits they studied: the
most extreme extraverts, the most extreme introverts, the most extremely open people, and the most extremely closed people, and so
on through the traits.

For every group of fifteen extreme scorers, Penton-Voak and his
colleagues mapped the key features of each person's face, one by
one. Starting with an individual's photograph, they superimposed
gridlines and charted the X and Y coordinates (as if on graph paper) of such key points as where the person's eyebrows began and
ended, the sides of their eyes, nostrils, and so forth. From this information, they developed a composite image of an extreme male
extravert, an extreme female extravert, and so on through the remaining groups.

To my eye, for example, the composite face of the extraverted
male has a pleasant look to it, with a bit of suppressed mirth around
the lips, calm eyes, and an overall impression of vigor and energy.
The composite neurotic male face, by comparison, has a slightly

downturned mouth, with a possibly brooding lower lip and eyes that are slightly tired and unfocused, and gives off an overall serious aspect—even, perhaps, a sense of persevering through pain. The composite extraverted woman has a calm mouth and lips, with the hint of a smile and rounded eyes that seem wider and clearer than in some of the other composites, and these are set in a larger-seeming face, giving an overall impression of considerable strength.

As a final step, the researchers asked a new group of participants to evaluate each of the ten composite male faces and ten composite female faces. This new group could reliably identify, for example, that the agreeable-woman composite did in fact express agreeableness, and the composite "neurotic" face of the most emotionally unstable men really reflected their neuroticism.

Researchers also distinguish between individuals with "baby-faced" appearances—relatively round faces, large foreheads, round eyes, and small noses—who are perceived as gentler, kinder, and less dominant than others. Such baby-faced people (and those with baby-like voices as well) do report more intimacy in their social interactions than others, show a greater willingness to share their thoughts and feelings, and are less aggressive than those with faces that appear to be more mature. When Alexander Todorov of Princeton University displayed portraits of political candidates who ran against one another for Congress, participants were asked to rate their competence based on their facial appearance alone (if a participant recognized a candidate, the response was excluded). Between opponents, the candidate with the face more suggestive of competence—an attribute related to mature faces rather than baby faces—won their House or Senate race 70 percent of the time.

Researchers are also beginning to examine the possible causal links between certain traits and facial features. For example, circulating testosterone may affect both one's behavior and one's face. Researchers believe that testosterone promotes both greater assertiveness in men and their greater interest in objects relative to their interest in people. James M. Dabbs of Georgia State University and his colleagues have found relationships between testosterone (measured from saliva) and career choice: laborers, machine operators, and factory workers were higher in testosterone when compared with professional managers and technical staff. In other comparisons, actors and football players were higher in testosterone than ministers, and trial lawyers were higher than lawyers who prefer research and client interactions. Ian Penton-Voak, who examined trait recognition from faces, has found that men with higher levels of circulating testosterone also have faces that are perceived by independent raters as more masculine. Not surprisingly, high levels of estrogen may influence both the faces and behaviors of women: Miriam Law Smith of the University of St. Andrews and her colleagues reported evidence that higher levels of estrogen in young women who had not yet had children were related both to the perceived femininity of their faces (as rated by independent judges) and the women's stated desire to have more children when compared with matched control women with lower levels of estrogen.

These are fascinating and provocative findings for sure—and as psychologists learn more about these physiognomic relationships, we all will confront clearer understandings of what our faces say about us. However, although real relationships are being revealed, they are probabilistic ones—remember that each of Penton-Voak's images of a person with, say, extraversion are based on composites of fifteen people at the extremes of that dimension. Facial features express more than one quality at a time, so a masculine face may appear somewhat different for an introvert than for an extravert. There are, in other words, many factors that influence a person's appearance. An individual also may possess a masculine-appearing face owing to family characteristics rather than actual levels of testosterone. Finally, diet, illness, cultural influences—and hairstyle and makeup—may modify the appearance of a certain face. So it is worth treating our impressions lightly—and that is true as well for all the clues I will describe here. It is only as we detect consistent or clear clues that we might ratchet up the confidence level of our appraisals.

The clues we look for also come from a person's surroundings.

We leave behind clues to ourselves in our offices, bedrooms, medicine cabinets, and online—our various settings. Samuel Gosling and his colleagues at the University of Texas, Austin, studied clues to personality found in the offices of ninety-four professionals in real estate, advertising, architecture, and banking. To create a "standard of correctness" for what the office dweller's personality was like, Gosling asked the occupants of each office—who I'll also refer to as the targets—and two other people who knew them to fill out personality questionnaires about them. Gosling and his colleagues considered the average of the personality profiles to best reflect the target's actual characteristics. Next, the researchers took groups of up to five undergraduate observers to the occupant's office while he or she was away, to judge the occupant's personality. The observers individually rated the target's personality by using any clues they found in the office. They noticed sound levels and lighting, sniffed odors, and examined the colorfulness, cleanliness, costliness, organization, and stylishness (among other qualities) of the office to make their estimates. When the observers' judgments were compared with the aforementioned average personality profile for the office dwellers, the observers had some success: they correctly guessed that more decorated, cheerful, and colorful offices reflected their occupants' extraversion and that organized, neat, less cluttered offices reflected their occupants' conscientiousness; they also correctly surmised that decorated, stylish, and unconventional offices reflected an occupant's openness.

Building on these findings, Gosling sent observers to eighty-three bedrooms in dormitories, apartments, and private houses near a West Coast public university. This time, seven observers visited each room and from their observations were able to estimate the extraversion, agreeableness, conscientiousness, and other qualities of the occupant, all at statistically significant levels, using a similar pattern of clues as before.

Although the observers were successful in their perceptions overall, Gosling believes they could have done better. For example, many observers concluded that if a bedroom had a lot of art, the occupant was politically liberal, but this belief is mistaken—both liberals and conservatives like art. The judges could have done better had they known that sports equipment often reflects conservatism.

We also detect clues to personality from how people behave in situations such as making an introduction, negotiating a deal, or visiting members of the community. Researchers sometimes simulate such social encounters in the lab to study the clues that people use in particular situations. At the beginning of a lecture course in psychology, for example, seventy-three students at the University of Mainz in Germany entered a large room with desks aligned in rows. As they passed through the door, a research assistant handed each person a random seat assignment. Once the students were seated, the rightmost person of the first row was asked to stand, move to a marked spot on the floor, and provide a brief introduction of who she was while she was being videotaped. The video was stopped, and all the students evaluated her as to her leadership and authority, sense of superiority, and self-entitlement, among other qualities, and finally, how much they liked her. Then everyone in her row shifted seats to the right and the just-finished student took the empty seat on the left. A second student then introduced himself, and the whole procedure was repeated; when the first row was finished, the researchers moved on to the second row and so on. Welcome to the world of "personality judgments at zero acquaintance," where the purpose is to understand how people perceive the personalities of those they've just met—and sometimes, their levels of accuracy and the bases for their judgments.

In this case the researchers were interested in a seemingly paradoxical finding—that people especially like narcissistic individuals more than other people when they first meet them. That was what the researchers found here—the students especially liked their peers whom they (and the targets themselves) perceived to be more entitled than the others (entitled people indicated, on surveys, "I insist on getting the respect that is due me"). In fact, the students were attracted to their narcissistic classmates' often neat and fashionable dress, self-assured physical movements, charming facial expressions, and sense of humor. This study and others like it make clear that people are good at judging visible characteristics of a person—although in this instance, their liking for the target people might not be such a good idea (liking for narcissists falls off as people get to know them better).

Knowledge of people's personalities has been analyzed for a long time, of course. More than two thousand years ago, the ancient Greeks already knew how to sort out their various character types. The philosopher Theophrastus, the director of the Lyceum in Athens after Aristotle, outlined more than a dozen of them, including the "Talkative" man, who, as Theophrastus put it, would

> sit down close beside somebody he does not know, and begin talk with a eulogy of his own life, and then relate a dream he had the night before, and after that tell dish by dish what he had for supper . . . he will remark that we are by no means the men we were, and . . . there's a ship of strangers in town . . . And if you let him go on he will never stop.

Researchers have wondered whether some people—like Theophrastus—are more accurate than others in observing people. The University of California's Riverside Accuracy Project is a two-decades-long project directed by Professor David Funder and devoted to examining how we perceive and assess one another. Tera Letzring of Idaho State University has tried to identify the distinguishing characteristics of the best judges of personality who have passed through the project. In one analysis, she examined data from 142 ethnically diverse participants who were videotaped interacting in groups of three. During part of their fifty-minute-or-longer interactions, participants followed instructions to talk about whatever they liked so as to get to know one another well. Later, their behavior was coded by independent raters who viewed the videos. Each of the 142 participants was both a judge of the others in the group and served as a target of others' judgments.

Funder and his colleagues created an overall personality profile for each target to serve as an accuracy criterion. The profile drew on the targets' ratings of themselves, ratings of them by acquaintances, and evaluations by clinical psychologists who interviewed each participant for an hour and then assessed their personalities. The most accurate judges evaluated the targets in a way that closely matched their overall profile; the least accurate failed to see what everyone else had.

Letzring found that the most accurate judges, relative to the others, spoke more comfortably about their own accomplishments as well as the accomplishments of their family members and their housemates; these same top judges also engaged in more eye contact with other members of the group, expressed warmth toward them, seemed interested, and appeared to enjoy their interactions with others. The accurate judges also described themselves on personality scales as being sympathetic and considerate. Acquaintances regarded them as more agreeable, and as possessing "a clear-cut internally consistent personality."

Letzring described the least accurate judges quite differently. They seemed socially ill at ease and needy and often asked either for advice or reassurance or felt self-conscious. Some of these lesser-skilled judges described themselves as relatively domineering and vindictive, scored highly on a scale of narcissism, and were described by acquaintances as anxious, exploitative, or both. And indeed they were evaluated as behaving in ways that undermined, sabotaged, or obstructed their group's getting-to-know-you process. The results from the study indicate that good judges have better and more equal relationships with others whereas poor judges are more self-preoccupied, disagreeable, manipulative, and exploitative.

I believe the good judges in the Riverside Accuracy Project are also likely to be higher in personal intelligence than the bad judges. Letzring's best judges were warm and interested in others; likewise, high scorers on our Test of Personal Intelligence are also more agreeable and open than others, and endorse the importance of discussing problems and understanding others. Leitzring's worst judges seemed uncaring and calculating at times. The respondents who scored lowest on the TOPI also scored higher than others on scales of narcissism and grandiosity. The Riverside Accuracy Project began well before David Caruso, Abigail Panter, and I developed the TOPI, but these similarities between the good judges and high

TOPI scorers suggest that personal intelligence may contribute to at least some of the best judges' skills.

There is yet another area we can check for information about people: the groups to which they belong. For example, studies have found that people's membership in political groups may be a consequence of their personalities, in part. Young conservatives are happier than young liberals: they have a greater sense of personal control over events, are more optimistic, generally believe in the fairness of the world, and hold transcendent moral beliefs—according to research by Barry Schlenker and his colleagues of the University of Florida, who surveyed a large group of southeastern college students. Generally, liberals are more open to others' perspectives, are more empathic, and are more creative problem-solvers; they also are risk-takers compared with their conservative brethren, who are more conscientious. And according to Jacob Hirsch and his colleagues, if you want to be treated reliably, decently, and well, visit a conservative; but if you are searching for understanding and stimulating conversation, talk to a liberal.

Belonging to athletic teams also says something about us. Those students who participate in college football, basketball, soccer, and lacrosse are high in the personality trait of "activity level," as measured by the Zuckerman-Kuhlman personality scale. High-activity people prefer to be doing things in their leisure time (and, conversely, have a hard time sitting around). These individuals have high energy and are most happy engaging in hard physical work. Club membership also provides clues to personality: among adolescents, those who regularly attend club meetings in a youth organization, or a sports, religious, or political club, have better health and mental well-being relative to their peers who do without such regular memberships— findings replicated across six countries.

Psychologists sometimes refer to the regions neighboring personality—the brain and body, the setting, situations, and groups to which a person belongs—as the individual's life space, and any portion of those surroundings may contain clues to who we are. But are there also holistic patterns of information identifiable across this life space that tell us about a person? Marc Brackett, Kevin Carlsmith, Heather Chabot, and I wondered if we could identify broad patterns of clues across all these areas at once. To do so, we used a questionnaire of massive size and a mathematical technique that can identify patterns in responses to many questions. In our most recent study, Brackett and his colleagues asked participants 1,073 questions about their life spaces—from their physical qualities to group memberships. The participants responded by telling us hundreds of details about their lives—from their heights and weights, to what was in their medicine cabinets and refrigerators, to what their dwelling spaces looked like, to how many times they spoke to friends in a week, to the groups they belonged to.

Several holistic patterns emerged, each involving dozens of small clues that depicted specific lifestyles. Some students lived what we called a positive social lifestyles. They were—at the very specific level we measured—more likely than their peers to own tablecloths and glassware, to take vitamins regularly, and to keep family mementos nearby; they interacted regularly with their mothers, and a bit less so with their fathers.* We believe these students appeared nurturing, social, and warm to those who knew them. Another group of participants lived an athletic lifestyle: these students were physically larger than others, owned team-related sports equipment and posters, and wore clothing that expressed their affiliations with schools and teams; they also had more interactions with their fathers than was typical. They were less likely to belong to school organizations such as bands and choirs, and less likely to smoke than others.

Yet another group of students exhibited a pattern of alcohol and drug use, judging from their lifestyle expressions. These students possessed alcohol and illegal drugs and had experienced fewer-than-usual interactions with high school friends, while reporting more relationship conflicts than others. Yet another group

*Because each lifestyle was represented by an overall pattern of possessions, activities, and memberships, few individuals fit the profile exactly; rather, some people fit the profile well—exhibiting a large number of the specifics—and others exhibited few or none of the relevant indicators.

of students exhibited the pattern of a "Solitary Media Consumer," owning many books, movies, and musical recordings; spending a great deal of time reading, watching movies, and listening to music and relatively less time in interactions with others. Many students exhibited blended patterns of expressions: for example, combining an athletic lifestyle with a positive social lifestyle; others were high in positive social orientation but also in alcohol and drug use.

As we suspected, no single aspect of a person's life—no single tablecloth or bottle of wine or hockey stick by itself—decisively marked someone as exhibiting a given personality pattern; rather, a bottle of wine in the kitchen signaled a nurturant social life if it was paired with candlesticks, tableclothes, and positive interactions; the same wine bottle paired with ashtrays, hash pipes, and conflicts with friends reflected an involvement with drugs. To read a person's life space, in other words, it helps to draw on dozens of life expressions from the individual—from her living space, to her weekly social life, to her groups—and to develop an overall picture of what those expressions collectively imply about the person.

Searching a person's overall life space by looking at the regions around personality not only provides a foundation for understanding other people, but also can tell us about ourselves. Daryl Bem proposed a theory in 1967 that we learn about ourselves more or less identically to how we learn about other people: by carefully observing ourselves as we act in the world. For example, if we know a friend went to six movies over the past month, we would guess he liked movies. As Bem saw it, if that same friend wanted to know how much he liked movies, he might recall the same six movies, too, and conclude, "I sure must like movies because I go to them a lot."

Bem illustrated the effect of watching ourselves on our self-understanding in several ingenious experiments. In one, he first trained participants to tell the truth when a colored light was on and to tell lies in the presence of another light. This way, participants learned that they made true statements when the "truth light" was on; false ones when the "false light" was on. In a second phase of the experiment, Bem instructed the same participants to state that magazine cartoons were either very funny or not at all humorous;

they were told that either the "truth" or "falsity" lights would flash on while they were speaking, but to ignore them, as the lights weren't relevant to the new task. The experimenters showed participants only cartoons that they earlier had rated as neutral, so the participants, by following the instructions, always stated falsehoods whether they claimed that the cartoons were either very funny or not. But the students' attitudes about the cartoons changed at the end of the study. Later on, they reported being more amused by cartoons they had said were funny if the "truth" light was on compared with when the "false" light was on. They also reported finding a cartoon less funny if the "truth" light was on when they reported it was not at all humorous. That is, the "truth" light provided them with a signal to believe in what they were saying—even though they had been told that the light was irrelevant to the study.

Edward Deci of the University of Rochester conducted another kind of experiment that illustrates how we watch ourselves "as if" from the outside. When people are paid to perform a task, Deci showed, they conclude they are less motivated to carry it out than if they perform the task for free. In one study, Deci asked students to work on a Parker Brothers puzzle called Soma that many people find fun; it involves putting three-dimensional puzzle pieces together to form various shapes. The participants in Deci's study played with Soma on three successive days. In the second day's session, the control group played with the puzzle normally, but members of the experimental group were paid a dollar for their play. The dollar payment provided an additional rationale for their play over and above their inner enjoyment. After being paid, those in the experimental group reported that they enjoyed the game less, and the experimenters observed that they spent less time on the puzzle in the third day's session than those who were never paid to play. Deci concluded that the experimental participants observed their monetary reward, and that reward crowded out their sense of enjoying the game. Deci's message is that we need to make sure that clues from our world don't distract us from our genuine feelings about a task at hand. Knowing we really enjoy doing something is a valuable asset, and we don't want to forget about it just because other rewards are present. Those of us with higher personal intelligence, I suspect, are better than others at reminding ourselves of our inner feelings amid confusing or contrary outer conditions.

We also learn about who we are through the eyes of others. Charles H. Cooley, a sociologist at the University of Michigan in the early twentieth century, introduced a theory of the "looking-glass self," by which he meant that we imagine ourselves as others see us, changing our self-image according to others' perceptions and paying special attention to the beliefs about us held by authority figures. For example, when Ogden Nash was a young poet, he learned about his talents through the eyes of others. Early in his career, Nash had hoped to write serious poetry and short stories and other fiction. Even so, he sometimes composed humorous poems to entertain his friends, jotting them down on scrap paper and tossing them on colleagues' desks. At first, he regarded his light verse as inconsequential. After an editor at *The New Yorker* informed him they would publish a humorous piece of his, he still didn't realize how good it was, remarking in a letter to his fiancée that the magazine would "run the asinine verses week after next." Another time, he wrote a brief satirical poem just to annoy a friend—who submitted it to a newspaper, where it was published at the beginning of a prominent New York literary column. Gradually, Nash came to appreciate that people liked his humor. Once he did, he went on to amuse a large part of America in the 1950s and 1960s with such witticisms as "Candy is dandy but liquor is quicker" and "Why did the Lord give us agility if not to evade responsibility?"

Yet some people may be relatively insensitive to such feedback. Tucker Max, author of the satirical memoir *I Hope They Serve Beer in Hell*, has acknowledged, "I am not very adept at picking up subtle social clues," and provided this self-description on his website: "I get excessively drunk at inappropriate times, disregard social norms, indulge every whim, ignore the consequences of my actions, mock idiots and posers, sleep with more women than is safe or reasonable, and just generally act like a raging dickhead." But Max redeems himself, he says: "I do contribute to humanity in one very important way. I share my adventures with the world."

In a droll personal account, Max described his time as a summer associate at a prestigious Silicon Valley law firm. He introduced himself at orientation by remarking that he was "out all night and I couldn't see anything because my contacts had fallen out when I was hooking up with some random girl." The firm's hiring partner spoke to Max in private about the reputation he was developing as the "party guy," but Max dismissed the significance of the conversation. When the partner called him into a private meeting a second time over concern about his attitude, the partner added, to be more balanced, that the quality of his work was good. Max remarked, "I took this as carte blanche to keep doing what I was doing (As long as my work was good, that's all that matters, right?)." Forging ahead, Max attended the firm's charity auction and afterward sent an e-mail account of his bids on items he could not afford, the behavior of the associates, and his use of profanity, while drunk, in front of most of the firm. After his e-mail spread across a number of law firms, the partners gave Max the choice of withdrawing from the summer program or being fired.

Perhaps Max was, as he described himself, relatively unskilled at recognizing what other people were thinking about him; or maybe, as he speculated elsewhere, Max did understand the hiring partner's warnings but chose to ignore them because he no longer wanted to be a lawyer and didn't mind getting fired (and the story added to his already-remarkable reputation). By itself, such stories can tell us that someone disregards clues to personality, but not why—whether the person missed the cues, misinterpreted them, or chose to put them aside.

As Max's experience suggested, reputations can reflect accurate information about us. Cameron Anderson and Aiwa Shirako of the University of California, Berkeley, studied MBA students enrolled in a six-week negotiation class. The students often discussed one another both in and outside of class. During several weeks of the course, each student negotiated with another class member in a role-playing exercise. Both members of the pair rated each other as to their cooperativeness and ability to integrate their different needs in the negotiation (both these attributes are important to a business reputation), and the outcome of the negotiation was recorded. At the end of the course, the students were asked to nominate those class members who were highest in cooperativeness. The students' actual behavior in the earlier negotiations did indeed contribute to their reputations over the time of the course. The best-known students affected their reputations more through their behavior, and were more likely than others to be nominated as the most cooperative, or alternatively as the most selfish, aggressive, or dishonest. Compared with the less-well-known students, these best-known individuals also possessed reputations that more accurately reflected how they had behaved during the negotiations.

Most of us do keep track of what others think. Even narcissistic people, who believe that they are more intelligent and gifted than those around them, know that other people often view them as less intelligent and less special than their own self-estimate, according to research by Erika Carlson and colleagues at Washington University in St. Louis. The authors speculated that narcissists may view others as "too dim" to truly understand them and choose to behave with authentic arrogance rather than with inauthentic humility.

So understanding how others think about us can contribute to our self-knowledge, but there are other sources of understanding we can access as well. The philosopher Brie Gertler points out that introspection is the only method we can use to directly sense our feelings and thoughts. Only we can access the inner warmth of our genuine happiness, and it is only our interior self that hears a private voice urging us on during a competition. Only our selves are able to track our inner mental states. Personality—and the conscious awareness that is part of it—is the nexus of such information, and introspection allows us to seek such clues from within.

The direct access we have to our motivational urges and feelings is key to knowing who we are. If, for example, we hear a few people at a barbecue mention that they "need to start exercising," it may be impossible to tell from listening to them who actually will exercise and who is just talking the talk. Lippke, Ziegelmann, and Schwarzer of the Free University of Berlin studied possible exercisers among 423 orthopedic rehabilitation patients and distinguished between Non-Intenders and Intenders, among others. According to their research, the Non-Intenders may acknowledge to others that they should really start exercising, but they possess little inner conviction to do anything about it. On surveys they agree with statements such as "I am not thinking about exercising" and "I was thinking about exercising, but I have not yet made up my mind." People in the Intenders group had an inner conversation that was quite different, even though they had not yet begun to exercise. They endorsed statements such as "I have made the decision to restart familiar physical activity soon" and "I will take part in a new physical activity soon." People in both groups believed in the value of exercise, and had considered it in relation to themselves. Only those in the Intender group, however, had organized their thinking around an actual plan to begin—including the time, the place, and the exercise—and they were more likely to begin exercising in the near future, it turned out, relative to the Non-Intender group.

Philosophers refer to these internal messages as "privileged information" that only the individual knows. Reflecting this state of affairs, we accept others' self-reported feelings as a matter of social convention, according to Professor Gertler. If Patty believes she is happy, but others believe she is troubled about something, it is customary to accept Patty's self-depiction nonetheless. If a person is certain of her feelings from looking inward, then the appearance is the same as the reality: pain is pain; pride is pride. We recognize this implicitly in day-to-day interactions. If I say, "I am feeling sleepy," and someone contradicts me—"No, you actually are wide-awake" (and there is no reason to believe I'm insincere or insane)—that someone simply doesn't understand how such statements work. And indeed, the gold standard for psychologists who measure moods and emotions is simply to ask people how they feel. When you introspect about emotions, what you see is what you get. These social customs assume that each of us does in fact possess sufficient personal intelligence to know how we feel, and for the most part that is likely true.

But there are exceptions, and part of reading clues involves attending to possible errors in a person's self-perception. As observers, we may wonder if Patty's unsmiling face, her tired eyes, and her slowed movements—as well as our knowledge that she just broke up with her boyfriend—indicate that she is not as happy as she claims. We may be unlikely to bring up our concerns (except, for example, to check them with a friend who also knows Patty well) because it violates convention to do so. Even when Patty's happiness seems betrayed by that sad expression, if she insists on her good mood, we are socially compelled to take her at her word. That said, we might keep our reservations privately in mind; we might later discover that Patty had been unable to read her own feelings well, or that she was refusing to admit a problem because she didn't want to talk about it.

Introspection's authority is greatest in the realm of emotions, preferences, and intentions; beyond that, its use is limited. For example, we can't know our abilities simply by looking inward. If Patty believes she is smart, but others regard her as rather clueless, who is right? Patty's declaration that she is clever won't carry much weight with her friends if they know that she had difficulty in school, has trouble figuring out how to split a restaurant bill, misuses words when she speaks, and shows no particular prowess at reasoning. Being smart involves external, generally agreed-upon performances.

A key trick to using inner clues—as with other clues—is to know their strengths (good for emotions) and weaknesses (not so good for mental abilities). A classic series of research studies by Timothy Wilson and his colleagues at the University of Virginia makes clear that certain kinds of introspection also work better when we go with our gut. In one of their studies, one of many female participants arrived at a laboratory waiting room and was seated by a research assistant in a chair about ten feet from several posters, three of which depicted animals in fairly humorous situations (in one, a cat balanced on a rope with the caption "Gimme a Break"); two other posters were reproductions of the paintings *Nymphéas* by Monet and *Les Irises, Saint-Rémy* by Van Gogh.

The women in the experimental condition were then asked to write about their reasons for liking or disliking each poster. The research assistant told them they wouldn't need to hand in the form—it was to help them organize their thoughts—and afterward, in fact, the participant saw the researcher put their comments in the trash. Women in a control condition went through the same process, except that they wrote about irrelevant matters such as why they had chosen their major at the university, rather than their reactions to the posters. Next, the research assistant asked participants in both conditions to fill out on a scale how much they liked each poster, and then offered them a "little something extra"—to take home the poster they liked best. Each woman selected her favorite poster.

A couple of weeks later, a research assistant surveyed the participants on how much they liked their choices. Those who had provided reasons for liking or disliking the posters were *less* satisfied with their choices than those who had written about other topics. The researchers concluded that the participants who had explained their reasons for liking the posters had in fact distracted themselves from their true feelings. Wilson and his colleagues have replicated these findings in other studies using various strawberry jams and choices about college courses. In the strawberry jam study, for example, the participants who were forced to explain their jam preferences evaluated the products quite differently from food-tasting experts, whereas the group who had just tasted the jams and stated their preferences without explaining them ranked the jams similarly to how the experts had.

Wilson believes that people who introspect come up with reasons for their feelings, but that those reasons are the most easily verbalized, most socially desirable, and foremost in their minds. The problem is, those easily stated reasons are not likely to be the ones that truly drive their preferences—rather, the real reasons are often inaccessible to introspection. For that reason, being aware of one's gut feelings is a great clue to one's inner self, often leading to better choices.

One key exception to this rule is that if a person is especially expert in an area, then engaging in introspection won't disrupt her optimal choice. For example, students in the poster study who were knowledgeable about art chose posters they were happy with regardless of the condition they were in—their reasons were aligned with their taste.

Knowing small tricks, such as looking all around a person for relevant personality information, weeding out useless clues, and keeping track of our own inner preferences and not trying to explain them too much (unless we are an expert in the area), helps. Getting someone else's opinion can also help—particularly if the other person is insightful—because other people bring a different perspective and can sometimes coax us out of our accustomed biases and errors.

I like a story along these lines recounted by Theodore Reik, a psychoanalyst in New York City who wrote a book published in 1948, about how psychotherapists understand others, titled *Listening with the Third Ear*. Reik recounted the story of a patient he called John who told many lively stories about himself in his therapy but whose treatment was not bringing him much improvement. Reik described John as possessing brilliant intelligence, emotional awareness, and nice manners, but as nonetheless unable to apply himself successfully to his career or to his relationships.

One day, John recounted that he had seen his friend Jill again and, as was his habit, began entertaining her with his storytelling. She listened patiently at first, but after a while she grew frustrated with him and gently scolded him, pointing out that he was telling his stories to impress her again, but he didn't need to do that because it wasn't like they "met yesterday." Jill was perceptive enough to realize that John's charming entertainment interfered with the possibilities for a more intimate kind of conversation.

Upon hearing this story, Reik understood something about John that he had missed: John had been dazzling both him and Jill by offering his anecdotes, and at the same time avoiding his inner thoughts and feelings. The pattern was slowing John's progress—both romantic and therapeutic. Reik was particularly impressed with Jill's ability to read the clues to John's personality:

Who had taught her the fine art of psychological observation and discernment? You do not learn such things in the psychology department at Smith or Vassar. I was ready to believe . . . [she] . . . was smart enough, but it was not her intelligence that had spoken like that. It was her heart that had told her.

Or, perhaps, her personal intelligence.

3

THE PEOPLE OUT THERE

In the kitchen, we hear the banter between a new friend who has invited us to brunch and some of her crowd. We hear the mew of the cat and the sound of a spoon hitting a pot as brunch is prepared. We wonder if this new group we're spending time with will accept us—and we're still making up our mind about them. We smell the coffee and hear the oil and water sputter in the frying pan as the eggs cook. We watch as our host brings food to table, trying to discern her expression; we accept the offer of eggs and toast; and as we start to eat, we feel the warmth of the coffee cup in our hands and the texture of the toast as we hold it. Our senses convey this information so seamlessly that it feels as if we are taking it all in exactly as it happens.

But in fact, we're responding to sensory excerpts of reality: our eyes convert visible light into electrochemical impulses that allow us to register objects according to their outlines; our ears translate sound waves to vibrations, using the bones of our inner ears, and from there to neural impulses, and our perceptual system fills in the blanks, creating a vivid-seeming representation of what exists around us. But the rich continuity of our perceptions is illusory in certain ways: everything is mediated through our senses. Our knowledge of the people out there—and everything else—is incomplete, as our own errors in perception and other people's viewpoints remind us.

For example, our thoughts of these new people are provisional:

Who are they, really? Do they truly like us—and we them? Our inner representation of them is what we think is accurate—but our construction of what is going on and the reality can be two different things. There is no golden bridge from the inner to the outer world. We are faced with the dual reality of what we believe to be happening, and what is actually there.

In his 1943 book *The Nature of Explanation*, the Scottish philosopher and psychologist Kenneth Craik argued that we discover real people and other objects that exist in the outer world and then translate them into inner mental representations—mental models—and behave on the basis of those models. A fundamental reality of the mind, he wrote, is "its power to parallel or model external events." Thinking with these mental models is cheaper, faster, and more convenient than operating first in the real world. He drew an analogy to the shipbuilders who designed "the *Queen Mary* . . . with the aid of a model in a tank"—to anticipate how the real ship would behave, so that some weakness in the final product wouldn't take them by surprise. Similarly, we try to model how people will react to us before we carry out important behaviors. One of the fundamental purposes of memory is to hold and operate on these models of the outside people—and to use them for planning.

Generally speaking, the more accurate our mental models of people, the better we'll know how to interact with them. If, back in the kitchen, two of the new crowd had begun a relationship the night before without letting anyone know, our models of them would be off the mark. As a consequence, our social conduct may work against us—for example, if we tell one member of the new couple something critical about the other.

Forty years after Craik's prescient argument, research in social cognition emerged in part to explain the ways we represent other people in our minds. Two founders of this field, Susan T. Fiske and Shelley E. Taylor, wrote of the many challenges we face in trying to understand someone—our preconceived notions, stereotypes, and weaknesses of memory among them. Those challenges acknowledged, we do manage to establish models of other people that often help us, as I'll describe. To begin with, though, Fiske and Taylor also pointed out that we sometimes behave like "cognitive misers" toward other people, saving our attention for key people in our lives. We don't need to spend much time understanding the people who slip quickly in and out of our lives with little consequence: the man in the beret waiting next to us at the bus stop or a fellow customer who darts in front of us for a carton of milk in the dairy aisle.

At other times, however, we encounter people with whom we are likely to interact for the long term; our overall well-being may depend crucially on how easily and positively we can relate to them. So as to promote good interactions with a given individual, we apply our personal intelligence to the clues we have gathered about him, weave them into a likeness of the actual individual, and approach the person based on our inner simulations of his traits, motives, and life stories. Naturally, our decisions will be better if our model is good.

As an example, shortly after President John F. Kennedy took office in 1961, he studied the personality of Nikita Khrushchev, the premier of the Soviet Union, whom he had arranged to meet in Vienna in order to establish agreements between the two nations. In the early 1960s, the Cold War pitted Communist nations against capitalist ones and the world's leaders stared down the possibility of nuclear war. According to one biographer's account, to study the Soviet leader, "Kennedy prepared meticulously, searching for clues to Khrushchev's character, personality and thoughts. He trimmed appointments, creating more time for solitude and study." Kennedy's developing description of Khrushchev was "of a crude, opinionated peasant. Often deliberately unpredictable, he was 'a mischievous charmer one moment and a loud bully the next,' an expert in the use of power with an inclination to gamble. Although a doctrinaire Marxist, he willingly bargained."

Kennedy decided he would impress the Soviet leader with his knowledge of foreign relations, discussing policy issues one-on-one with him, rather than referring policy questions to his secretary of state, as had his predecessor, President Eisenhower. In this way Kennedy hoped to exhibit his confidence, knowledge of international relations, and personal charm and charisma.

Even when we do our best to size up another person, however, we may miss the mark in several key ways. Given our tendency to brush ambiguities aside, we may be overconfident in our assessments and fail to anticipate how people might react to *us*. Kennedy's advisers, Dean Rusk and George Kennan, warned the new president, in fact, to meet the Soviet premier only after specific policy agreements could be reached in private between the two nations. But Kennedy disagreed and held the meeting as soon as he could. In this and other calculations, some have argued that the president overestimated the allure of his own charms and underestimated the power of Khrushchev's beliefs and the lengths to which Khrushchev would go to dominate an opponent.

After three days of meetings, Kennedy, a decorated PT boat commander during World War II, told James Reston of *The New York Times* that his exchange with Khrushchev was the "roughest thing in my life." He added, "He just beat the hell out of me," and concluded that he had appeared weak, exacerbating the two nation's troubles. Paul Nitze, the assistant secretary of defense at the time, characterized the three days of meetings between the two leaders as "Just a disaster." But perhaps not all was lost: Kennedy later concluded that what he had learned from the meeting helped him to navigate his next challenge: his successful defense of West Berlin during the Soviet challenges to its control. The president believed that his understanding—his mental model of Khrushchev, in our terms—had become more accurate as a consequence of their meeting, and with it, Kennedy's effectiveness as a leader had improved.

One of our challenges in understanding others—and especially our friends, family, and colleagues, on whom our welfare depends—is that we have automatic reactions to the people around us. These reactions are a function of our agreeableness, openness, and other traits, of course, but they are also shaped by what we learned about people when we were children—lessons that may still influence us today. Early in our lives we construct models of our parents, family members, and friends; our feelings toward these people in our formative years serve as a template for intuitions we have about new

individuals who seem to resemble them in our adult lives. Sometimes our childhood learning will serve us well, but at other times we
may use the wrong lessons from when we were young, and misper-
ceive the individual we're trying to get to know. Possessing strong
personal intelligence means, ultimately, that we can appreciate how
those earlier people in our lives affect our present thinking about
the individuals we now know—and adjust for any biases we recognize in our reactions.

To illustrate the ways in which early learning about people influences our later interactions, Michael Kraus and Serena Chen, of UC
Berkeley, asked participants at the outset of a study to describe a
person they knew well and who was important to them, labeled
the "significant other." Such significant others could be mothers,
fathers, stepparents, or an influential teacher. Kraus and Chen then
asked the participants to describe positive and negative qualities of
the individual, and how they had behaved toward the person. At the
end of this initial research phase, the participants were asked to
browse a catalog of two hundred photos of faces and to identify one
that closely resembled their significant other.

Two weeks later, the participants were called back for what they
were told was an unrelated study. The researchers told them that
the university had begun a new "buddy program" to support recently enrolled students and that they would meet their buddy in a
short while. Each student was shown a picture of their buddy-to-be,
as well as a few statements about their buddy's personality that are
true of most people, such as "At times she is extraverted, affable,
and sociable, while at other times she is introverted, wary, and reserved." Then the researchers asked the students to describe what
they thought of their buddy.

The participants in the experimental group were shown pictures
of their buddy's face that resembled the face of their significant
other—indirectly cueing their inner model of the earlier significant
person as a template for their new buddy. Those in the control group
saw a picture similar to somebody else's significant other, which
was less likely to cue any particular inner template for them. The
participants in the experimental condition, relative to the controls,

perceived their new buddies to be more like their significant others, evaluated their buddies more positively, and expected to behave with their buddies in a way that they would with their significant others.

Sigmund Freud first suggested that people create mental representations of their parents and relatives and then apply those models to the new individuals they meet. He believed that people transfer the qualities of the earlier person in their life to the new person—often without knowing it and sometimes jumping to quite erroneous conclusions about the new individual. Freud first described such a case of transference (as he labeled it) in a young woman who was seeing him in therapy. The young woman unexpectedly told Freud during a session that she wanted him to kiss her: "She was horrified at [the suggestion], spent a sleepless night, and at the next session, though she did not refuse to be treated, was quite useless for work."

Over the subsequent sessions with Freud, the young woman talked more about her idea of Freud's kissing her and then recalled having wished, "many years earlier . . . that the man she was talking to at the time might boldly take the initiative and give her a kiss." Freud concluded that the young woman had transferred her emotional relationship from the earlier man to himself.

Guided by Freud's ideas, a group of psychotherapists began a landmark study of transference in therapy situations, beginning in the 1970s. Professors and psychotherapists Merton Gill and Irwin Hoffman asked psychologically trained judges to listen to the transcripts of therapy patients and to describe the relationship themes that the clients expressed during their sessions. The judges identified a group of themes for each patient, and although they worked through the transcripts independently, they nevertheless agreed with one another far more than would be expected by chance—supporting the idea that there were detectable regularities in the patients' perceptions. The patient's "core conflictual relationship themes," as these researchers called them, can be thought of as a person's inner estimate of how a relationship with another person will proceed.

As an example, one young man's model of relationships emphasized how he became frustrated when someone was wasting his
time, and he didn't feel able to address it. In one session, the young
man complained about a new acquaintance:

> [He] was keeping me from reading and . . . I really fucking
> resented it a lot . . . You know, among my friends, they're
> respecting . . . But you know, with a guy like this [clears
> throat], he's just in another world totally from that. And you
> know, he would be insulted and that kind of shit. You know
> it was kind of a hassle.

A few sessions later, the same young man considered whether he
was wasting the therapist's time:

> Well, now I'm getting that same feeling that, you know, I'm
> sort of talking about worthless shit. Because, and you know,
> my basis for thinking that is the fact that you haven't said
> anything. Jeez, we go through this nonsense every session,
> it's just amazing to me, I'm sort of ashamed that my mind
> isn't a little more creative.

Researchers in the area had found that an inner model like this one
devoted to time-wasting will repeat itself in many aspects of an
individual's life—including, in a nod to Freud's broader psychoanalytic theory, appearing in one's dreams.

Shortly after I began my graduate training in psychology, I
learned just how powerful these mental models of transference can
be. I was a classroom assistant in a school for children with special
needs when I was befriended by a shy six-year-old girl I'll call Tricia.
During playtime, I sat by the blocks and Tricia would gradually
make her way across the room and begin to play with the blocks or
crayons, and we would talk in very simple terms: saying hello and
asking how each other's day was. The teacher was very glad to see
this relationship begin, because Tricia had trouble making friends
and relating to adults. Tricia and I had repeated this pattern once a

week for several weeks when, one day, I came in and Tricia, who by this time could be counted on to join me right away, avoided me in a very pointed fashion.

The play period ended and I joined the teacher to lead a group sing-along. Afterward, the teacher and I considered why Tricia was avoiding me. Unable to answer that question ourselves, I asked Tricia if something was wrong. She answered, "You're wearing a belt today." (I often dressed in blue jeans at that time and apparently had not bothered to put on a belt before then.) "Yes, I am," I said, agreeing with her about the belt. She then asked, "And who do you hit with your belt?" My heart sank: Tricia must have seen a man strike a child with a belt: quite possibly her own father hit her. She had befriended me as an adult man who did not wear a belt and therefore might be safe to play with, but when I did wear one, I triggered her reaction that grown men hit little girls. I told her that I didn't hit anyone with my belt, that I thought doing so was wrong, and that I just happened to be more dressed up because I had a special meeting later that day. That seemed to mollify her a bit. After that, Tricia and I played again over the remaining weeks of the semester—and I began to realize that I had seen a bit of transference firsthand. The mental model that Tricia had formed was that all adult men who wear belts hit children with them. I slipped through her belief system at first by neglecting to wear a belt, but when I did, I triggered her model.

Part of developing our self-knowledge as adults is to recognize the key models we use repeatedly to understand people, and how they can become triggered automatically. A first step is to watch for recurring beliefs we have about people, particularly those thoughts that don't seem entirely reasonable. Our friends may help us spot these reactions when they tell us someone isn't the way we think (and we recognize we've made the same error before). Therapists are also trained to spot such biases. Devon and Noah Rosenbaum, for example, were a couple in their mid-forties who had a number of complaints about their marriage of fifteen years—some of which seemed a consequence of mental templates they had acquired in their youth. One of their complaints had to do with the fact that when Noah told his wife he loved her, Devon brushed him off. Devon acknowledged to her husband, "It sounds stupid, but it does scare me when you say you love me." Devon's model of men who loved her was fraught with a fear of betrayal. When she was a young girl, her father doted on her, tucked her into bed, and told her he loved her. After her mother and father divorced, her father re-married and his behavior changed abruptly: he would pass her on the streets of their town, doting on a younger daughter from his new marriage rather than on her, and she felt dismissed. When Noah told Devon he loved her, Devon couldn't help but anticipate the same betrayal that she had earlier experienced with her father. Although Noah may not always have communicated his love as best he could, Devon's model introduced unwelcome noise into their communication. She was overlooking the decency and sincerity of Noah's commitment to her.

Obviously, none of us choose our parents, relatives, or earliest teachers. Consequently, we end up with an education about the people around us that is haphazard: experience rarely follows a well-worked-out lesson plan. We expect new people we encounter to think like the people we knew earlier, and are surprised when they exhibit their own distinct patterns.* Having learned about a kindly but distant father at an early age, we may be very good at identifying a similar person when we come into contact with him. We also run the likelihood, however, of misjudging other people who remind us of him but are in fact quite different.

Knowing the templates of significant others that we formed as children helps us to identify our biases when we interact with people and to gain a clearer understanding of the actual personalities around us. The most highly skilled perceivers among us are able to

---

*An interesting consequence of this phenomenon is that if our parents were, for example, near average in a great number of areas—that is, sharing in common a great number of attributes with many other people—we will expect other people to behave near average as well, making our predictions mostly accurate (because in the absence of any other information, predicting average behavior will be most accurate). By comparison, those among us whose parents are unusual in many ways may be more apt to mispredict others. Yet the redeeming value of that misprediction is that we learn early that there may be some advantage to expecting the unusual; for one thing, we recognize early on that people differ from what we expect.

factor in how their earlier-learned reactions affect their expectations of the new people they meet. We can all become better perceivers by having some sense of our own inner expectations and how they might go awry at times; we can do this by carefully checking our reactions to people to see if we exhibit consistent biases in our expectations of others.

In addition to our built-in models of others, we can intentionally represent new kinds of people in ways that may help us anticipate what they'll do. Since the beginning of recorded history, philosophers have often directed their attention toward methods for understanding people. In Chapter 1, I briefly mentioned Ptahhotep, whose "Instruction of the Vizier Ptahhotep" dated to about 2450 BCE; Ptahhotep's advice includes studying personality:

> If you are investigating / the character of a colleague,
> . . . Conduct your business with him alone . . .
> If he talks too freely about what he has seen,
> Or if he does something at which you are taken aback,
> Nevertheless be amiable with him and remain silent.
> Do not turn your face away (from him),
> But be cautious about revealing anything to him.

I think of such instruction as a first level of personality-centered education used to guide people in how to understand and behave toward one another. Similarly, another historical figure already mentioned, the Greek philosopher Theophrastus, laid out certain character descriptions by the second century BCE so that "our children will be the better for it . . . It will help them to choose the best people to know and be with, and they will have something to aim at." Early writers already recognized that we could instruct ourselves by studying people, admiring some, and learning from them.

Halfway around the world in ancient China at roughly the same time, Confucius reasoned much like a contemporary psychologist when he explained the importance of gathering diverse observations when appraising others. A young man named Yu who studied with him had promised to do a great deal but slept too much and got too little done. Confucius explained: "There was a time when I used to listen to what people said and trusted that they would act accordingly, but now I listen to what they say and watch what they do."

With this example, Confucius illustrated the multifaceted nature of information about people, and how a wise observer compares people's claims with their actions. No doubt Confucius watched his student pretty carefully after that.

Our skill in representing the people around us is in part a product of our inner templates—the models we have acquired by watching others; our skill also includes pointers passed down through folk wisdom from the likes of Ptahhotep and Confucius that have been repeated through the ages because they capture basic truths about personality. To these, we can add new skills based on contemporary research. And combining these sources, we draw on groups of techniques we are most skilled at—reading faces or understanding traits, or deciphering intentions, to understand another person. I would characterize our capacity to draw on these different approaches as *a toolbox model* of understanding others. Each tool helps us to unlock a person's secrets and to predict her behavior.

Certain psychologists are widely admired among their colleagues for their seeming ability to unlock key aspects of a personality. Their special skills can serve as a road map to what those with high levels of personal intelligence do—and guide the rest of us as well. Professors Jerry Wiggins, of the University of British Columbia, and Krista Trobst, of York University, provided a unique window into how these top-tier assessment professionals actually work. In 1999, Wiggins and Trobst identified an Albuquerque lawyer, Madeline G., who volunteered to participate in a highly unusual psychological mission: to have her personality evaluated by five of the best personality assessment teams in the United States, with each team focusing on different tools to understand her personality—from her interpersonal behaviors, to her traits, to her life story.

Each team assessed Madeline without knowledge of what the others knew or had written about her. As part of the study, Madeline traveled by jet, first to Yale University to take a battery of tests including the Rorschach inkblots and the Wechsler Adult Intelligence Scale (WAIS), and then flew to Northwestern University for a biographical interview, and then back home, where she completed additional psychological tests for the remaining three assessment teams. Professors Wiggins and Trobst also collected information about Madeline from her friends and acquaintances in Albuquerque, so as to provide an everyday description of what she was like.

A key tool that most of us use to understand people is to monitor how they look and act at a given moment. This tool served as a starting point for the Yale assessment team, consisting of Professors Rebecca Behrends and Sidney Blatt. Shortly after Madeline's arrival at Yale, Behrends called the hotel and asked Madeline to come to the lab the next morning at 8:30. Behrends observed that Madeline protested that she had plans to go out that night and such an early time "was not what she had in mind at all!" When the Yale team member explained that they had only one morning together and the shortened time could compromise the assessment, Madeline backed down and agreed to appear as scheduled.

Yet Madeline failed to show up at 8:30 the next morning, and when Behrends called her hotel, Madeline explained apologetically that she had overslept, having failed to receive a wake-up call from the front desk. When Madeline arrived on campus, Behrends and Blatt adjusted the testing protocol and forged ahead, but not before they also took careful note of Madeline's outward appearance:

> When she arrived for the testing session, her short, black, wavy hair was still wet from the shower. She wore a black turtleneck, black pants, and a plain black wristwatch. Her only jewelry was a diamond stud, worn high in the curve of one pierced ear . . . She went on to say with obvious pride that [in her legal career] her "minority status" had been clear from the start, both as a woman and as a Navajo Indian. She has high cheekbones and strong features . . . Her skin appears medium to light in contrast to her black hair and clothing. She wore just the lightest touch of makeup . . . and

her overall manner and stance can perhaps best be described as rather androgynous. Her gestures are highly expressive, and she inhabits her body fully, in a sensuous, cat-like way.

Madeline's friends in Albuquerque, it turned out, had also remarked on her sensuousness, telling the study organizers that she was "apt to making sexually suggestive remarks and to flaunt her own considerable sexuality," and that she especially liked to do so "with individuals who are made uncomfortable by such actions, playfully mocking their prudishness."

As the testing at Yale got under way, Madeline took the WAIS, the Rorschach inkblots, for which she told Rebecca Behrends what she saw in the images, and the Thematic Apperception Test, for which a test-taker is asked to tell a story for each of a series of pictures. As Behrends administered the tests, she kept up an ongoing conversation with Madeline to experience her firsthand, to learn about her childhood and to make observations that would later be combined with information from the test results. For example, Behrends noticed that Madeline often tried to wrest control from her so as to ensure she was an equal collaborator, and yet she also could appear apologetic and play the role of a good child. The Yale team's assessment of Madeline drew on both these interpersonal observations and the test results.

The Rorschach test that Behrends and others employ, for example, asks people to look at inkblots and report on what they see; the test provides a standardized way of listening to a person construct subjective meanings from ambiguous stimuli—the inkblots. It is analogous to listening to a friend describe what he sees in a cloud, or the sense he makes of a partly overheard conversation. There is a lively debate as to how well the Rorschach functions as a measure; my own opinion is that knowing something about a person's construction of meaning under these conditions can be informative. Blatt and Behrends regarded most of what Madeline perceived in the Rorschach cards as psychologically normal, in that the images she described fitted what the inkblots actually looked like fairly

well. For example, when Madeline saw a blot that looked like a butterfly to most people, she saw a butterfly too—a majestic butterfly
out for a flight. At other times, however, Madeline inserted unusual
emotional materials into her perceptions, and these potentially reflected some of her inner concerns. On one inkblot she saw a monster breathing fire where many people commonly perceive such
monsters, but she also saw someone being burned by the fire, which
is an uncommon and vivid response. The researchers conjectured
that this emotional response might be a lingering effect of her
victimization as a child.

Another tool we use to understand a person is the life story—
the individual's autobiography. This was the focus of Professor Dan
McAdams, whom Madeline next traveled to see at Northwestern
University, in Evanston, Illinois. McAdams focuses on studying the
stories people tell about themselves, which he regards as central to
what we know about someone when we know them intimately. Mc-
Adams met with Madeline for three hours and during that time
drew out portions of her life as she perceived it.

To attain an autobiography, McAdams asks a person to think
about her life story as if it were the chapters of a book. From those
chapters, he hopes to hear about a number of key scenes, including
her earliest memories, the high points, the low points, and the turning points. He also asks his interviewees about their values and
the possible future chapters of their lives, as well as to identify any
themes they perceive in their stories. McAdams also collects a few
pieces of demographic information, which helps him to understand
an individual's setting and the groups to which she belongs. Madeline, he learned, worked as a defense attorney making more than
$70,000 annually, and was legally single but had been in a commit-
ted relationship with a college professor for six years in what she
referred to as her common-law marriage.

Madeline divided her life into three large sections for McAdams:
"Childhood," "Jail," and "The Present." Madeline was the daughter
of a Navajo couple who lived in a rural New Mexican town; both
her parents suffered from drinking problems. Her account was that
her father often beat her and her siblings—she often showed up to

school severely bruised—and that he was even more violent toward their mother, at one point shooting her. Her mother was hospitalized but survived. The low point in Madeline's life came when she hoped to kill her father but realized that she lacked the strength to do it. She became involved with drugs and alcohol herself, and this led to the second part of her story, in which she spent her teenage years in jail. Her life began to change after her release, when she moved to a prairie town, worked hard at the waitressing jobs available to her, and began community college.

Her life's high point was earning a college degree. After that, she was admitted to an Ivy League university and obtained degrees in social work and the law. Madeline perceived an important turnaround in her life when she obtained her legal degree and was admitted to the bar. She then worked defending Native American clients in civil and criminal cases. She regarded her survival and eventual flourishing as the central themes of her story—a description that McAdams agreed with, adding that her story also echoed "rags-to-riches" narratives, stories of reform, and heroic myths. Such biographical information allows us to understand how a person sees herself and her life's progress.

Another way we understand others is by looking at their motives and intentions. We often care less about whether someone is sociable or solitary than we care about her aims and, ultimately, whether she is "for us or against us." Two of the teams who assessed Madeline—the Yale team (Behrends and Blatt) and the Northwestern team (McAdams)—talked with her and observed her around her intentions (with the additional assistance of psychological testing). McAdams asserted that Madeline was motivated not only by a need to reform herself, but also to gain power. The Yale team similarly emphasized Madeline's need for power in her attempts to wrest control from authority. They also suggested she possessed a desire to be constantly active, and to seek exciting new experiences, and believed that her restlessness served the purpose of distracting herself from feelings of depression and anxiety: "She experiences the nagging question of whether there is something wrong with her," they wrote, "and whether she has really been able to escape and overcome her painful and traumatic past." We might wonder whether her intention to help others was in part to maintain her own self-esteem rather than entirely altruistic.

Serena Chen (of the "significant other" study) examined how frequently we tune in to others' intentions. She and her colleagues conducted a study in which their participants read descriptions of people in the form of an "IF," "THEN," and "BECAUSE." For example "IF a person is at a party," the researchers began, "THEN" "she talks to everyone" (a study participant added), "BECAUSE"? Chen asked. Participants sometimes completed the BECAUSE by mentioning the situation—"Parties are places where people talk"—or by attributing her behavior to a trait, as with "BECAUSE she is sociable." But by far, people complete the BECAUSE clause with an explanation of why someone acted as they did: "BECAUSE she wanted to meet people." The better we know someone, Chen found, the more likely we are to complete the BECAUSE phrases with a specific intention.

Glenn Reeder of Illinois State University has illustrated people's logic in inferring intentions in a series of innovative experiments. In one, participants read about Kimberly, a fictional student who wrote a class essay arguing that NASA ought to undergo a budget cut. Reeder described Kimberly's situation differently to three groups of participants. Participants in the first group learned that Kimberly's instructor told her to express her own beliefs in her essay. These participants concluded that because she was free to express her opinion, Kimberly favored cutting NASA's budget. Participants in the second group read that Kimberly's class assignment had been to argue that NASA ought to have its funds cut. Now participants factored in that Kimberly was obediently following the assignment, and they were less certain about her viewpoint. Participants in the third group read that Kimberly had overheard her professor tell a colleague that he thought NASA ought to have its funding cut. These participants believed that Kimberly expressed her attitude with the ulterior motive of getting a good grade. In other words, participants carefully take into account the pressures on a person—

such as a professor's viewpoint, in this case—and factor those into an individual's behavior to infer her intentions.

We use some variant of this logic to understand a person such as Madeline G. We know that many people who go to jail like Madeline quickly get into trouble with the law after their release. The fact that Madeline instead moved to a small town and worked hard there indicates to us her sincere intent to be law-abiding. Her choice to attend college—and her success there—further supports our impression that she hoped to build a better life. And her decision to focus her legal practice on defending people of disadvantaged circumstances similar to those she had faced as a child increases our respect for her intentions; so we may find ourselves rooting for her. As important as intentions are, they must be integrated with still other facets about a person—for example, a person's traits.

Paul Costa and Ralph Piedmont of the National Institute on Aging were another team who assessed Madeline. These researchers focused on Madeline's social and emotional traits. Psychologists study many different kinds of personality traits, but one set known as the Big Five is widely studied. These five—Neuroticism, Extraversion, Openness, Conscientiousness, and Agreeableness—are among the most common descriptors people use when they describe one another, if studies of the language are any indication. Lew Goldberg, of the Oregon Research Institute, described the Big Five as emerging, historically, from a "lexical hypothesis": the proposition that people's more important characteristics could be identified from the study of relevant words in human languages and, more specifically, by identifying which traits were most represented in our lexicon. In fact, the Big Five approach had its start in 1936, when Gordon Allport and Henry Odbert scoured the English language for a comprehensive list of all its personality-related terms. They found 17,953—including 4,504 trait terms such as *outgoing, lively, risk-taking, anxious*, and *friendly*. Similar lists have been developed in German, Italian, and Chinese.

To get from the 4,504 trait words to five categories, researchers eliminated synonyms and applied mathematical techniques to identify the central ideas among the words. They hypothesized that there existed "big traits"—broad clusters of attributes that are found together in a person—and their research supported that idea.* For example, when people describe themselves on long lists of trait words, it turns out that they tend to naturally identify five or six "big" groups of traits. One such big trait is extraversion: it can be thought of as an umbrella concept that includes specific facets including being outgoing rather than reclusive, talkative not quiet, and lively rather than lethargic.

Madeline took a measure of the Big Five referred to as the NEO-PI-R. On it, she agreed or disagreed with 240 items such as "I generally prefer to go along with others rather than make a fuss," which helped to indicate her agreeableness, and "I get irritated easily," to assess her neuroticism (negative emotionality). Her partner filled out the same items for Madeline, but for him the agreeableness item read, "This person generally prefers to go along with others . . ." Based on averaging her own and her partner's responses, one of Madeline's most noticeable big traits—where she was well above average—was extraversion. Drawing on studies of other such extraverts, Costa and Piedmont suggested:

> She is active and energetic . . . She prefers large parties and events to more intimate gatherings, and is often a group leader . . . She is typically forceful, energetic, and fast-paced in style, and cheerful and enthusiastic . . .

Madeline was also highly disagreeable. Drawing on studies of people who are similarly low in agreeableness, the team concluded that she

---

*A bit more technically, each of the Big Five is considered to be a psychological dimension, anchored at either end by opposite trait terms: "extraversion-introversion," "neuroticism–emotional stability," and so forth.

is characteristically suspicious of other people and skeptical of others' ideas and opinions. She can be callous in her feelings, and her attitudes are tough-minded in most situations . . . Although antagonistic people are generally not well liked by others, they are often respected for their critical independence, and their emotional toughness and competitiveness.

Because this particular set of traits was selected from our common parlance, many of us can recognize and understand some of these traits—particularly extraversion, agreeableness, and openness—by careful observation. Professionals may employ psychological tests that provide them a bit of extra precision, but we have the advantage of observing people in our everyday lives.

Yet as good as some of us are at picking out people's traits, we are not all equal. Neil Christiansen and his colleagues at Central Michigan University asked participants to take a multiple-choice test that measured their ability to understand personality traits. For example, one of their questions asked:

Coworkers who tend to express skepticism and cynicism are also likely to:
a. Have difficulty imagining things
b. Get upset easily
c. Dominate most interactions
d. Exhibit condescending behavior

The best answer here is "d": people who are skeptical and cynical are more likely to treat others with condescension, relative to other people. Some skeptics do, no doubt, get upset easily (alternative "b"), and not all skeptics talk down to others. That said, "d" is most likely to be correct according to extensive psychological testing across diverse groups of people. Test-takers who answered correctly also were more likely to understand that if you ran into "an athlete you know who was largely responsible for his team losing in a recent game," exhibiting empathy would be helpful.

The participants in Christiansen's study then watched a

videotape of a job interviewee and tried to predict how the applicant had described himself on a personality scale. The participants who were better at estimating the applicant's self-description also had higher scores on Christiansen and his colleagues' test—that is, a knowledge of traits is related to understanding other people, whether a friend, a family member, or a stranger in a video.

Aaron Pincus and Michael Gurtman were another expert team who examined Madeline G.'s traits, with an emphasis on her relationships with other people. When these researchers looked over Madeline's reports and those of her romantic partner, they were struck by how highly nurturing Madeline viewed herself as being, including being warm and agreeable, whereas her partner viewed her as quite coldhearted, arrogant, and calculating. The assessors warned that "Madeline and her partner are likely to butt heads about this at some point, and its resolution will be critical to the stability of their relationship."

The teams who considered Madeline also examined her capacity for self-control. Our lives are often easier when we are around people with a good level of self-possession—who can control their disappointments and hostility and express such feelings constructively. Costa and Piedmont put some of Madeline's traits in a "to be controlled" column, including Madeline's need for excitement and impulsiveness and her disagreeableness. Next, they placed other traits in the "helps with self-control" column, including her trait of openness, which included her flexibility and ability to respond to challenges creatively, and her positive emotionality. The assessors then weighed the "to be controlled" column against Madeline's "helps with control" column, and were cautiously optimistic about how well she could manage herself.

Dan McAdams, who studied Madeline's life story, also referred to her ability for self-control, and expressed a similarly optimistic outlook as to her future—although he was concerned that her life could darken significantly in the short term. Madeline's transition from an abusive childhood to an Ivy League school was enough to lead McAdams and several of the teams including the Yale group to conclude she had excellent self-control as an adult. Even given a possible setback, McAdams said, it would be hard to imagine that her life would return to the depths of her youth; rather, "the protagonist in this narrative is simply too strong now."

These different approaches to studying a person—focusing on interpersonal expressions, inkblot perceptions, autobiographical stories, traits, intentions, and self-control—represent a group of methods used by experts for understanding people, but we can also apply many of these ideas ourselves as we try to comprehend others. And, in fact, we employ many tools for understanding people that parallel what the experts used to understand Madeline.

But by themselves, each tool we use might represent an isolated skill, with some people being good at understanding traits and others good at understanding intentions. The theory of personal intelligence, however, regards these skills as going together—as related to one another in a coherent pattern. David Caruso, A. T. Panter, and I wanted to understand whether skills like these were part of overall personal intelligence. In the terminology of psychological science, we tested whether personal intelligence could be regarded as a new "latent variable." A latent variable is a psychological attribute that, although it cannot be directly seen, is inferred from the visible features of a person we can measure: in the present case from a group of *indicators*—specifically, the relevant abilities at problem-solving about personality that make up the tool kit.

Caruso, Panter, and I developed the TOPI to measure such skills as detecting cues about people, understanding traits, and evaluating a person's goals. In 2012, we reported a successful attempt to model personal intelligence from such indicator abilities. We had administered the TOPI to three samples of several hundred people each. We used a mathematical technique called factor analysis, which can detect the presence of a latent variable in observed data. If a unitary personal intelligence were present, then people who were good at one specific ability would be good at the others, and conversely, people who were challenged in one area of ability would be challenged in the others, generally speaking. (The pattern allows for exceptions; for example, most people are somewhat better at certain skills than others.)

Across our three studies, individuals who better understood which traits went together also scored higher on identifying clues to personality and in understanding which of a person's goals could go together without contradicting one another (and so on through other areas of understanding). So skill at using one tool correlated positively with skill at using another. People apparently draw on a common ability when solving many different kinds of problems regarding personality. A specialist in traits is also likely to be above average at interpreting a person's autobiographical memories (and vice versa). This makes sense because each of these areas of understanding a person's character likely informs the others.

Beyond that, we don't know if any of us integrate these diverse observations into a unified picture of a person or whether we leave our observations unintegrated. Surely we sometimes interpret a person by thinking of traits alone, or by selecting a snippet of a life story, and then decide that we have enough understanding of the individual. Our sense of knowing a person may be just a "felt sense" that coexists with dozens of small techniques that allow us to understand the person's motives and to anticipate their behaviors. Regardless, some of us are more able to carry out problem-solving across these many areas; others, less so.

And these tools of understanding can be very helpful. McAdams had noted that Madeline was "on a roll" at the time of her assessment because she perceived her relationship as going well and was about to start a new job, but, he noted, such lucky streaks can come to an end. Shortly after her assessment, Madeline's new job at a law firm didn't work out and she and her partner broke up as well—an issue flagged by Pincus and Gurtman. But she spent the next year beginning a legal practice of her own, which began to thrive.

The project's organizers, Jerry Wiggins and Krista Trobst, believed that Madeline volunteered for their project out of an adventurous spirit, a desire to live life fully, and the considerable enjoyment she took in telling people about herself and her life. The two organizers had hoped to tell Madeline what each team had discovered about her as they received the psychological assessments. Despite Madeline's initial enthusiasm for the project, however, she decided she didn't really want to hear much about the findings at first.

Wiggins and Trobst attributed Madeline's change of heart to a desire to concentrate on her own work—she was quite busy in establishing her own law practice. And, as those researchers saw it, Madeline had participated in the study more for the pleasure and excitement of being studied than for the knowledge that might come of it. Perhaps that was all there was to it. Still, I can readily imagine that she may have been unnerved at the thought of what all those psychologists saw in her. (I would surely be apprehensive under similar circumstances.) Few of us, after all, are entirely comfortable with ourselves, and many of us find at least a few of our attributes downright uncomfortable. Information about ourselves is "hot"—it's hard to hear without reacting in some way: general comments about our character can leave us feeling exposed as private aspects of ourselves become known to others, or we can feel deflated as we realize some of our personal qualities are quite mundane and readily recognized by experts, and there is always the potential we might burn indignant over what we view as unwarranted criticism. Some people regard even a compliment as potentially troubling—it can interfere with our hard-earned equanimity or distract us from our focus, they believe.

During Madeline's final interview, she did ask to hear a bit of the results. In particular, Madeline was curious as to what the Rorschach inkblots had said about her. The study organizers read some of the Yale assessment of her, which couldn't have been entirely easy to hear: the Yale team discussed her vulnerability to depression and her use of excitement-seeking activities to cover it over. Yet the Yale team also had concluded that "Madeline tolerates a great deal in herself. Rather than repress or deny her experience, she lives with the conscious recognition of . . . the legacy of . . . [her] traumatic past"—both of her own victimization and of the angry thoughts it left her with. When the Yale assessment was read to her, Madeline experienced a bit of shock that such private portions of her mental life had been revealed. Nevertheless, she also experienced a deep sense of recognizing herself, a moment of "Wow! Did everyone get me like that?"

Madeline could, in fact, let some of the information into her life—and indeed found it interesting. The multiple assessments of her provide us with a sense of the variety of tools we use to understand a person, and the different inner models we construct from them. Although each of these techniques captures only some of the reality of another person, if we are lucky, the techniques, when combined, clarify our understanding of the individuals in our lives.

But this isn't quite the whole story. Just as we construct mental models of the people "out there," we construct models of what goes on inside us. For example, as Madeline took in the information from the Yale assessment that Trobst read to her, it likely changed her self-concept. These inner representations of ourselves are important to what we know and how we act—as I'll examine in Chapter 4. We may not like everything we learn about ourselves, but sometimes accepting just a bit more about ourselves can help clarify who we are, and having an accurate model of what we want and what we can do may help us guide our lives.

After hearing the Yale University report, Madeline asked whether the other teams had done as well at understanding her. After Trobst answered yes, that the other psychologists had seemed to understand her too, Madeline responded enthusiastically: "I love that. I love the idea of this. That's it! What a great idea this was!"

4

FEELING INFORMATION

Self-knowledge would be easy to attain if our minds were designed solely to create an accurate picture of who we were. Just a glance inward would reveal our need to be loved and respected, the people we care about, and our best qualities. A further look would bring forth the weaknesses we need to cope with such as our lapses in self-control and the gaps in our social skills. And we could take a step back to grasp our overall identity, just as easily as we look in the mirror. It is oh-so-obvious, however, that our minds don't work this way. True, some aspects of our inner lives are hard to escape— mental distress among them. Aside from such inescapable feelings, many of us are out of touch with who we are; we may become preoccupied with other matters, or otherwise end up losing our sense of direction.

It helps to know who we are when it comes time to make decisions and to present ourselves clearly to other people. We construct our identities from the social feedback we receive, from observing our conduct, and from looking inward. But sometimes we coast in an environment if we don't explore ourselves. H. Ray Wooten, a professor of counseling, believes that college athletics programs create this kind of milieu for their star players, who expect others to make decisions for them. Wooten described the plight of a college football player who failed to join the professional ranks after being given several tryouts. His family noticed that the young man withdrew from his friends and teammates as it became clear his professional career was at an end, and they referred him to counseling. Once there, the young man confessed to his counselor, "I don't know what to do. I have let others make all the decisions and look where it got me. I knew the dream was too good to be true." In order to regain his footing, the athlete decided he needed to answer the question "Who am I?"—and that only after he had developed a new and stronger sense of himself apart from his football experience could he make good choices for his future.

Even if we can answer who we are, our self-conception at best approximates the reality of our personality, and just as we can misjudge another person, we can misjudge ourselves. So keeping our model as accurate as possible is helpful; like Wooten's football player, we need to know who we are to find our life's direction. Among the obstacles we face is that our self-concept arises from many diverse information sources, stored in different parts of our memory. According to the cognitive scientist Ulric Neisser, we tuck away information in various pockets of memory; in each area we store information of different kinds, including our global self-concept, our autobiographical memories, and our conscious self in the here and now.

Homer Hickam's recollection of his youth in his memoir *Rocket Boys* highlights examples of these different selves. Hickam chronicled his boyhood in the coal-mining town of Coalwood, West Virginia. As he saw it, his boyhood divided into two parts: "everything that happened before October 5, 1957"—the date the Soviet Union sent *Sputnik* into orbit—"and everything that happened afterward." Hickam possesses, as do all of us, several long-term memory systems. Several of these memory stores—the procedural, semantic, and episodic, among them—contain information relevant to understanding ourselves.

Procedural memory contains instructions for how to carry out actions in the physical world—to tie one's shoelace or drive a car. As the child of a coal mine supervisor, Hickam was a natural target for some of the disgruntled mine workers' sons and he had to learn how to fight, how to protect himself, and when to run. More conventionally, Homer knew how to ride a bike, maintain a paper route, use shop tools to saw through iron pipe, set off fireworks, and get around Coalwood. This procedural knowledge is part of our doing, active self.

Like each of us, Hickam also possessed a semantic memory: a long-term store that contains our general knowledge. Hickam filled his semantic memory in part with knowledge he learned in school. His lower-grade teachers—"the Great Six," as they were known in town—taught him vocabulary, spelling, addition and multiplication tables, geography, and the table of the elements; ultimately his knowledge in these areas became organized without reference to a specific source or event. For example, he could retrieve $9 \times 12 = 108$ from long-term memory without reference to a classroom or teacher from whom he learned it. But some semantic knowledge is more personalized to our lives: the names of the people and streets around which we live—and lists of our own characteristics. Hickam would likely have listed his boyhood qualities as happy, hopeful, imaginative, industrious, clever, intelligent, and tough.

Still a third form of long-term memory is episodic: autobiographical recollections of specific events from our past. As Hickam recalled it, one of the key events of his boyhood was watching *Sputnik* travel across the night sky; afterward, the people of Coalwood congregated at the town store and on their porches to discuss the onset of the space race between the United States and the Soviet Union. Hickam could also recall—again drawing on episodic memory—that he organized his friends around a project to launch a homemade rocket. Following diagrams in *Life*, they jammed explosives from cherry bombs into a tube, attached it to his mother's beloved white picket fence, and ignited it. After a deafening explosion, the fence, but not the rocket, launched into the air and crashed down, burned to embers.

His mother sent him out to wait for her on the back steps. He expected to be chewed out, but she surprised him. Using his nickname, she asked, "Sonny, do you think you could build a real rocket?" When he hemmed and hawed, she expanded on her question. As she saw it, he had no direction to his life up to then; his father didn't think much of him; yet he needed to get out of Coalwood before the coal was all mined: there was no future there. Hickam retrieved all this from his episodic memory, and said that his mother touched his nose and told him: "I-am-counting-on-you . . ." and, referring to his father, "Show him you can do something! Build a rocket!" That's one heck of a life-changing message! Yet it's just one example of the powerful recollections our episodic memories may contain, and that may guide our lives. Hickam would go on to lead his boyhood friends in building rockets and winning science fairs, and would spend a portion of his career working at NASA.

So Hickam's knowledge of himself—like our self-knowledge—draws on his procedural, semantic, and episodic memory stores. And each of these memory stores functions somewhat independently. If we asked Hickam if he was persistent, he could retrieve a list of his attributes from semantic memory—happy, skilled, and yes, persevering—and agree he was persistent. Or, alternatively, he could retrieve a group of episodic memories, such as blowing up his mother's fence, followed by additional attempts at launching rockets until he and his friends succeeded—and from those memories conclude he was persistent. Of these two methods of recall, it's faster and easier for us to retrieve semantic information—and semantic knowledge is more securely stored in our memories, as studies of individuals with brain injuries reveal.

Specific traumas to the brain—such as a hard blow to the head, or a penetrating wound from a projectile—can wipe out almost all of a person's episodic memory, leaving the individual oblivious of earlier life events, and yet semantic memory may remain undisturbed. Endel Tulving of the University of Toronto studied "K.C."* who suffered a motorcycle accident as a young man. K.C. lost *all* of his episodic memories: he recalled nothing of his personal past, and he couldn't form new lasting memories either—his episodic memory was destroyed, yet his semantic memory was relatively intact. As a result of his brain injury, K.C. also underwent a personality change: he went from being a gregarious, thrill-seeking young man who played

---

*Individuals with neurological issues are customarily referred to by initials, whereas individuals in psychotherapy are often referred to with a pseudonym, although there are exceptions in both instances.

cards in bars and traveled to Mardi Gras, to being a subdued, calm, and agreeable person. After the accident, K.C. agreed to describe his personality traits—drawing on his semantic memory—on two separate occasions. To check the accuracy of K.C.'s report, Tulving also asked K.C.'s mother to characterize her son's traits. Not only could K.C. describe his personality, but he characterized it *after the accident* in both instances he was tested. His descriptions matched those of his mother's, indicating the accuracy of his self-perception. Somehow, K.C. was able to revise his self-conception to reflect his personality after the accident, even though his episodic memory was no longer functioning.

K.C.'s case is not unique in this regard. W.J. was a young woman who at the beginning of her second quarter at college suffered a fall that resulted in a concussive blow to her head. After her injury, W.J. couldn't recall a single personal memory from the preceding six months. W.J. was asked to indicate qualities of her personality on two separate occasions, by agreeing or disagreeing as to whether eighty terms described her ("outgoing," "athletic," and so on). She first described herself shortly after the accident. After her memory began to return (it did so completely), she was asked about herself a second time. During her loss of episodic memory, W.J. described herself on the list in ways that agreed with her boyfriend's description (which was used as a test of her accuracy). In addition, her description of herself in college was closer to what her boyfriend perceived than her description of her personality in high school—despite having no memory of anything she had done over her college career. W.J. had somehow noticed changes to her personality during college and had revised her memory of herself, despite her impairments (how W.J. and K.C. did this is unknown). Cases such as K.C.'s and W.J.'s are rare, but their similarities contribute to our confidence that semantic memories of ourselves are stored separately from the episodic memories of our life experiences.

We may think of our episodic memories as recording the past, but portions of memory also contain our imagined futures. Recall from Chapter 3 that the Scottish thinker Kenneth Craik had spoken of how memory simulates the outside world. And indeed, we

construct models in memory to simulate our own possible futures—
and to remember those hypothetical states. Regarding our sense of
self, we imagine who we might become—our *possible selves*, a term
introduced by Hazel Markus of Stanford University to describe the
sometimes vivid representations of who we may desire (or fear) to
become.

Returning to Homer Hickam and his friends, the group's "chief
scientist," Quentin Wilson, constructed a vision of his future self as
he and Hickam walked past the trophy case at Big Creek High School,
then full of football awards. Looking forward to rocket blastoffs,
science fairs, and winning the respect of their classmates, Quentin
told Homer: "Maybe one day we'll have a trophy in here, Sonny, for
our rockets." Future selves guide the people who hold them: Hickam,
Wilson, and their club members went on to conduct successful
launches, for which they won regional attention and science fair
prizes.

There is at least one more form of memory that is deeply integral
to our sense of self, called "working memory." Before I discuss it, it's
worth making a few comments about consciousness, a most mysteri-
ous entity of personality, because we are so closely identified with
this inner awareness and the images and visions that pass through
it—a "stream of consciousness," as William James put it. James, a
founder of American psychology, asked his readers to imagine him
in a lecture hall, and to think about how consciousness binds our
thoughts together:

> My thought belongs with *my* other thoughts, and your
> thought with *your* other thoughts. Whether anywhere in the
> room there be a *mere* thought, we have no way of ascertain-
> ing, for we have no experience of its like. The only states of
> consciousness we naturally deal with are found in personal
> consciousnesses, minds, selves, concrete particular I's and
> you's.
>
> Each of these minds keeps its own thoughts to itself . . .
> Absolute insulation, irreducible pluralism, is the law.

And although our stream of conscious thoughts may be broken temporarily, that stream reliably reconnects to our own pasts: "When Paul and Peter wake up in the same bed and recognize that they have been asleep," James pointed out,

> each one of them mentally reaches back and makes connection but with *one* of the two streams of thought which were broken by the sleeping hours . . . Peter's present instantly finds out Peter's past, and never by mistake knits itself on to that of Paul. Paul's thought in turn is as little liable to go astray.

William James was a master at describing consciousness, but neither he nor anyone else since has figured out how it works. The Australian philosopher David Chalmers has distinguished a "hard" problem of consciousness: that no one knows what it is or how we experience it. The soft problems of consciousness involve what occupies our conscious thoughts, and are so called because they are easier to address. Experts who study consciousness refer to its contents as qualia, and there is widespread agreement (and empirical evidence) that qualia include inner speech, daydreams, emotional experiences, and the like.

Our working memory, containing these qualia, is a short-term holding area directly within the spotlight of our attention, and we draw into it what we're thinking about at a given moment, the changes we perceive in the world around us, and any material we retrieve from our episodic and semantic memories. Psychologists refer to this blend of consciousness and short-term memory in different ways. For William James it was the "I-as-Knower," for Freud it was the conscious ego, and for cognitive psychologists it was—somewhat euphemistically—"executive control." The term "executive control" cleverly sidesteps the mystery of human awareness while gently suggesting that as chief executives of ourselves, nature bestows upon us a gift of awareness—sentience—the consciousness of being alive.

Within our working memory, each thought, image, and feeling

persists long enough for us to perceive them moment by moment as they pass by. When Homer Hickam described how his mother encouraged his interest in rocketry after he had blown up her fence, he beautifully re-created the contents of his working memory—what it felt like for him at the time. It was dusk, he said. He felt his mother's touch as she drew him near to her; he described the events at the periphery of his attention—one of his dogs chasing bats in the yard—and his understanding of her words. Working memory is also a gateway: we can transfer its contents to our long-term memory. Hickam transferred his here-and-now experience of that conversation with his mother to his episodic memory so he could recall it, because it was important to him. He probably did this by reviewing it in his mind multiple times—which promotes the transfer of the conversation (or any other information) to long-term memory.

Another way we use working memory is to introspect. The philosopher Daniel Dennett believed that we look inward first by formulating a question to ourselves. We might ask, for example, "How do I feel right now?" We then access the responses generated by any relevant mental systems. The perceptual system contributes bodily sensations such as a feeling of quickness, lightness, and energy. The emotional system might answer with feelings of warmth and excitement. The cognitive system might characterize our thoughts as optimistic. We then combine the results from the inner systems and label ourselves happy.

But Dennett pointed out that we accept the answers that enter working memory without knowing where the results have come from. Dennett drew an analogy to how we interact with computers: we can type a question into a search engine and a response will appear on a screen, but we have little idea of the processes by which the software arrived at the answer. In much the same way, we may feel lighthearted and energetic but we don't know how our minds produced those inner perceptions. We may be conscious of happy thoughts but have no idea how those ideas got there. Many of these processes take place automatically and outside of our awareness, delivering just an executive summary—"We feel good"—to working memory. A great deal of what goes on in the mind occurs in subsystems to which our consciousness simply has no access.

Most of what we store in memory lies dormant until retrieved by a specific catalyst—a need to know the capital of New York State, or the status of our relationship with our cousin in San Francisco. A memory—if called upon—may emerge into consciousness much like an underground stream channeled beneath a city's streets will emerge into the daylight of a park. Even after shifting into view, an idea may disappear or be replaced by another as the spotlight of attention veers this way and that. For example, we are often challenged to concentrate on a given project at work. We may push ourselves to focus on the task at hand, but our attention is overcome by the latest gossip among our colleagues, and a few minutes later we catch ourselves, realize that time's passed, and admonish ourselves for becoming distracted.

One chief difference between our self-conception and the models we construct of other people is that we live our own model—we embody it, own it, and act on it. In fact, we recruit different sets of neural areas to think about ourselves than we do to think about another person. The portions of our self-concept that we feel—the pain and the joy—convey felt or hot information. How we deal with this felt information will determine the qualities we accept about ourselves. If we can't tolerate the feelings necessary to recognize an unpleasant part of ourself—or if we can't access the feelings to begin with—the models we construct are likely to go awry.

To function well, people higher in personal intelligence track this hot, felt information and sift through it, knowing when their feelings are more or less trustworthy, and accepting any information that may be relevant to their self-image. They go on to make choices that "feel better" relative to their traits, values, and goals. These individuals better sense when a decision feels right and will bring them pleasure, or feels wrong and could injure their self-regard. When people lose access to this hot information, as they can in certain forms of brain injuries, they lose a key part of themselves.

The neuroscientist Antonio Damasio believes that people with injuries to ventral and medial sectors of their frontal lobes end up unable to feel what's right for them. Damasio remarked that many of these patients possess "an overall intelligence within expectations, given their sociocultural background," but they are unable to make good choices or to organize their future lives. He continued, "They never construct an appropriate theory about their persons, or about their person's social role . . . They are bereft of a theory of their own mind and of the mind of those with whom they interact." He believes this comes about because reasoning gets separated, in some way, from the emotions, sensations, and urges that people normally experience as part of their consciousness. His patient "Elliot" had a portion of his right frontal cortex incapacitated, after a tumor known as a meningioma was removed from that brain region in a surgical procedure. Elliot could still solve almost any intellectual problem, but he no longer seemed to care whether he made good decisions or bad. After correctly solving a series of social problems, he remarked on his dilemma, "And after all this, I still wouldn't know what to do!"

In our normally functioning mental lives, we *feel* information about ourselves. We anticipate that an upcoming conversation with our friend will be easy and entertaining, or full of conflict and differences of opinion. Either way, we forecast how the event will influence us in order to make good choices regarding our conduct, even if anticipating how we might act causes us anxiety: that anxiety can help focus our attention on the best way to behave.

Our conscious selves confront hot information all the time, including humbling feedback, our own self-doubt and disappointments, and kind words, caring thoughts, and praise. We care deeply about it all: mental pain can be every bit as depleting as the physical kind, if not more so. Ethan Kross and his colleagues studied the sadness that comes from feeling unwanted by asking a group of study participants to bring in photographs of a love interest who had recently rejected them. The researchers then scanned the participants' brains as they looked at the pictures of their lost loves. The participants' pain responses began in the areas of the brain associated with psychological pain, and then spread to the physical pain areas, a pattern that suggests that mental pain is intense and sometimes indistinguishable from the physical variety. Our language reflects this idea as well, as when we talk of a broken heart, a person who is a pain in the neck, or a piece of news that gave us a kick in the butt. It turns out, in fact, that acetaminophen, the key ingredient in Tylenol, not only acts on physical pain but also ameliorates the intense hurt of social rejection. Beyond brain studies, the tragedy of the many young people who commit suicide each year—it is the third leading cause of death among adolescents in the United States—reminds us that psychological suffering can seem unbearable at times.

Our minds deal with hot information in special ways, often engaging self-protective thought—mental defenses and coping—to deal with it. Most of us exhibit natural buffers to hot information that distort our thinking in positive directions. The "better-than-average" effect, for example, describes people's beliefs that they are superior to others on their personally valued characteristics. At Ohio University, Mark Alicke and his colleagues asked college students whether they were more or less creative than their classmates. Students believed they were more creative than average, as well as higher than average on a dozen other positive qualities. Alicke and his team also found evidence that students were motivated to protect their positive beliefs about themselves: told that they actually received a low score on a test of creativity, many students then estimated that the average student actually scored lower on the same test than was the case.

We take responsibility for positive events in our lives, and regard matters that go wrong as outside our control—thereby enhancing our self-esteem. For example, when a group of colleagues at work is provided with positive feedback, its members believe that they have contributed to the group's success; when the group is provided with negative feedback, its members lay the responsibility for the poor performance at the feet of their partners rather than themselves.

The complexity of the social information around us makes it all too easy to deceive ourselves, especially if we are unskilled at evaluating other people and their reactions to us. As we receive feedback—be it criticism, teasing, or the formal assessment of a performance appraisal—we consider the source from which the feed-back comes and try to gauge its accuracy. We regard some people as relatively accurate at summing up our qualities, and others as less so. Even our most perceptive friends, we notice, criticize us too harshly at times when they are frustrated with us (although even then their criticisms may be accurate). People who can't sort low- from high-quality feedback are at a special disadvantage because they don't know what feedback about themselves to take seriously. Amid their uncertainty, they may latch onto the praise they hear, and disregard the more negative remarks as likely falsehoods, relegating them to the shadows of their awareness. In the end, they subsist with a personally satisfying but unrealistic representation of who they are.

Freud described the painful ideas that undermine our self-conception as "ego-threatening." Painful ideas include thoughts that society at large finds unacceptable—so we deplore them too, and learn to condemn them as members of our community. Consider the following: More than 91 percent of men and 84 percent of women among several thousand responders to an international survey indicated that they wanted to kill someone else at some time in their lives. Conservative estimates are that 22 percent of married men and 12 percent of married women have had affairs. We try to hide thoughts and actions from others, and we help other people avoid their own shortcomings by looking the other way when they exhibit their weaknesses. As a consequence, few of us recognize the prevalence of these tendencies—we are like the students in Bertram Forer's research study back in Chapter 1, who hadn't realized that some self-evaluations weren't unique to them but applied to nearly any-one. Similarly, we fail to comprehend how universal our most hu-miliating thoughts really can be. Defended in this way, we can get on with our lives, maintain our beliefs that we are good, moral people, and live with a bit less anguish.

Freud cataloged a number of practices we use to avoid ego-threat and referred to them as mechanisms of fending off, or *Abwehr-mechanismen*. Denial is one such defense; rationalization, another.

A physician whose gravely ill patient died because of her error may rationalize that the death was "a blessing in disguise" to convince herself that she doesn't need to disclose her mistake to the family. Many of us in a similarly fraught situation may come up with similar reasons to hide errors we've made. Another defense, sublimation, channels troublesome private desires into socially useful activities, as when a person who is preoccupied with aggressive thoughts becomes a butcher or helps to choreograph fight scenes in a video game. We can arrange these, from the more immature defenses, which involve the largest distortions, to the mature ones, which best preserve the facts. Denial involves the outright rejection of reality and is characterized as immature. Rationalization is intermediate—it's superficially logical but requires erroneous explanations of our actions. And sublimation is mature in channeling our demons into proactive paths—for example, placing our aggressive impulses in the service of society.

Freud explained that some people choose more mature defenses than others because they have more "ego strength"—they can tolerate painful challenges to their self-images better than others—and he regarded biological factors as determining this mental power. Personal-intelligence theory suggests another factor, however: individuals who are lower in personal intelligence are less able to reason about themselves and are consequently more likely to think unrealistically as they face hot information; their looser grip on the facts about themselves tempts them to employ positive distortions. Like all of us, they want to feel good about themselves, and they find it easier to avoid challenging facts about their behavior because their self-conceptions are already off the mark. By contrast, people higher in personal intelligence construct more accurate self-concepts because of their clearer appraisal of what is accurate or not; their models may include less positive views of themselves but better fit the relevant facts.

Defensive people not only possess distorted views of themselves, they also hold odd attitudes about other people, as indicated on self-report measures of mental defenses. Self-report scales of defensiveness don't ask test-takers "Are you defensive?" or "How defensive are you?" of course, because the whole point is that people don't recognize their own distorted thinking. Rather, these tests ask responders to agree or disagree with various attitudes about people.

One of the most widely used tests of this kind is the Bond Defense Style Questionnaire. On the Bond scale, people who employ immature defenses endorse items such as "I often feel superior to people I work with" and "People are either good or bad." The traditional explanation of why defensive people endorse items such as "I often feel superior" is that they don't want to acknowledge their own limitations. Arguing from the theory of personal intelligence, however, I'd say that defensive people endorse such items because they're generally unable to create nuanced, accurate models of themselves, and equally unable to reason accurately about other people—and the Bond scale picks up the distortions. As I see it, this is a simpler alternative explanation. (Both explanations could be true as well, with each effect contributing to a person's low-fidelity beliefs.)

The gold standard for evaluating defensiveness, incidentally, is for a trained clinical interviewer to conduct an interview with an individual and evaluate the interviewee's defensiveness. When clinicians do so and the participant also takes the Bond scale, there is some agreement between the two assessment techniques. I'll review some of the research soon. Before doing so, it's worth looking further at the relationship between low personal intelligence and distorted thinking.

Jayne Allen, a doctoral student in my lab, found some evidence that people who think in distorted terms about other people lack a general understanding of how personality works. Allen asked college students about everyday moments when they suddenly realized, "Aha, now I've just learned something about my friend's personality!" One kind of story told by the participants went like this: "Carli," who had just entered college, kept agreeing to everything everyone else wanted her to do—she was a bit of a pushover. Her friend "Mike" had known her from high school, and he began to notice that she seemed to be going too far to please other people. This insight about Carli finally clicked for Mike when he saw her on a bus because she had loaned her car to someone she hardly knew.

Allen created fifteen stories representative of those that a first group of participants had told her—and these new stories became the center of a novel measure: she followed each anecdote with a list of possible lessons a person might draw from the incident. In the story about Carli, the alternatives included both the fairly accurate idea that Carli "seemed to want to please everyone she knew," as well as the less accurate interpretations that "college made Carli nicer" or that Carli "liked everyone else more than Mike." Another less accurate conclusion was "People only do favors because they want something in return"—a sort of black-and-white thinking reminiscent of the Bond-scale items.

Allen found that there was a group of people who were far more likely to draw inaccurate lessons from these stories than others. These individuals missed the most plausible-sounding lessons from a character's behavior, and instead endorsed alternatives reflecting black-and-white thinking or other distortions. Compared with their classmates who drew more reasoned conclusions, these same biased learners also scored low on a short form of the TOPI; her finding directly links their general distortions to low personal intelligence.

More evidence that people who misinterpret social situations are higher in defensiveness (and possibly lower in personal intelligence) comes from work by Phoebe Cramer of Williams College. Cramer developed a method of studying defense mechanisms using the Thematic Apperception Test, or TAT. To take the TAT, a test-taker looks through a set of pictures and for each one tells a story with a beginning, middle, and end. Cramer relies on the idea that people find some of the pictures she uses to be potentially threatening, and these test-takers may avoid some of what they see by altering it in unrealistic ways or ignoring it altogether.

Cramer has developed a scoring system for defensiveness that she applies to the stories children and adolescents tell. For example, a young test-taker might be shown a sketch of two boys, one of whom is sitting on the floor playing with some LEGO bricks while the other is standing with his arms folded and a frown on his face (this is similar to a TAT card but not an actual one). If a child responded to the picture with "The two children are playing together

and having fun," it would be scored as reflecting denial, an immature defense because it omits the key information that one child is
visibly dissatisfied. An older child might respond, "The one standing
is going to pick up some LEGOs and throw them at the boy who is
playing," a response that would be scored at an intermediate level of
defense because negative impulses are added to the story, but in
unrealistic ways that don't fit the older child's more patient disap-
proval. A mature level of defense is linked to a more realistic story:
"The child playing with blocks isn't sharing very nicely and the other
boy is mad and doesn't want to play with him." A child's defense level
is determined from a series of such responses over multiple cards.

Cramer finds that denial stories on the TAT are common among
children between five and ten years of age. As they enter their teens,
most kids use more mature defenses. Cramer finds that adolescents
who employ more mature defenses are more socially competent,
exhibit better self-control, and possess more clearly defined identities than those who use less mature defenses. Those children who
continue to use immature defenses on the TAT into the preteen
years exhibit more instability, tantrums, lying, and jealousy than
their peers, and if they continue to use such immature defenses, they
may become young adults who are unstable and egotistical, and lack
clear thinking. I wonder if some of Cramer's young participants lack
the personal intelligence to correctly interpret the stories, and this
in turn leaves them more open to picking and choosing the information they do understand, omitting the more complex parts such as
the boy's crossed arms and frown, because leaving them out is easier
than the challenge of fitting them in.

Earlier, I mentioned that trained clinical psychologists can identify defenses through in-depth interviews. George Vaillant, of Harvard Medical School's Laboratory of Adult Development, is part of
a team that has followed the lives of men and women of diverse backgrounds in the Boston area. In one investigation, specially trained
clinical social workers interviewed 307 men, then forty-seven years
of age, who had been studied by the Adult Development program
for more than thirty years since junior high school, in inner-city
Boston schools. The interviewers paid particular attention to the

men's current defensive styles. Some of the middle-aged men described themselves with apparent accuracy; others could not depict themselves clearly. One middle-aged participant had completed his schooling through the ninth grade and worked as a security guard. He described himself as coming from a close-knit family, although his complete interview suggested otherwise. His parents had recently remarried each other after a divorce twenty-five years earlier, and they remained two thousand miles away from their son. He also remarked that he was not particularly close to any one relative and that "they are all the same—cousins, aunts, and everybody." He and his wife had no children. He also said he got along with people and wanted to help them. When asked more about it, he said he struck up conversations with people on park benches. He added that he had no particular best friend and said he did not need other people. The man's depiction of himself as coming from a close family and getting along with people seemed off the mark.

Contrast that with a second study participant, also with a ninth-grade education—but whose self-description seemed far more consistent with the facts. This man told the interviewers that when he was angry or upset he tried to "take things in stride." When he was upset, he tried to hide his worries so as to appear calm "at least on the outside"—and he believed he was so convincing that many people at his workplace regarded him as having no emotions. Although he presented an easygoing exterior, he knew his own feelings, which requires accurate self-perception. He explained that he dealt with being upset as he did because "I want to make sure I know what I am hollering about before I start hollering." When he was genuinely worried, he talked matters over with his wife, or if he was angry he played music until he cooled off. He acknowledged that he argued at times if the alternative meant looking weak or losing face.

Vaillant's work shows that accurate self-perception matters to important life outcomes. When the same group of forty-seven-year-olds reached sixty-five years of age, Vaillant and his team assessed them again. The men who were physically healthy at the first assessment and who employed more mature defenses than the rest reported greater physical well-being fifteen years later. Even after controlling for education, those with more adaptive defenses exhibited better psychosocial adjustment, greater marital satisfaction, and more joy in living relative to their classmates who used less mature defense mechanisms; the less defensive group also ended up earning more, suggesting that their better attunement to themselves contributed to their professional performance.

Another advantage of an accurate self-view is that we're more likely to know how other people see us—leading to fewer interpersonal surprises. Thomas Oltmanns and Eric Turkheimer studied the correspondence between people's self-conceptions and their peers' assessments of them. The researchers surveyed a large number of air force recruits who trained together, as well as college freshmen who lived together. Both samples were divided into small groups of peers who knew one another well. Each person's self-perception was compared with how others in their group saw them.

The researchers classified their participants into those who exhibited certain psychiatric symptoms consistent with narcissistic, sociopathic, borderline, or dysthymic (chronic depressive outlook) disorders of personality. Participants who exhibited symptoms of dysthymia saw themselves as others saw them—as somewhat negative and depressed. People with borderline-like symptoms were similarly accurate in understanding that other people saw them as emotional and manipulative. But people in the two other groups saw themselves quite unlike how others evaluated them. The narcissistic-like group believed they were gregarious and cool, whereas others viewed them as conceited, vain, and taking advantage of other people. The sociopathic-symptom group, who dismissed others' rights and expressed an unusual willingness to break rules, saw themselves as angry because they had been treated unjustly. Those who knew them agreed they were angry and also described them as suspicious to the point of paranoia.

A. T. Panter, David Caruso, and I have found that people who exhibit narcissistic symptoms also score less well on the TOPI compared with respondents without such symptoms, providing some independent confirmation of the idea that narcissists lack the skill to accurately evaluate personality. And the accuracy with which we see ourselves is important. In Oltmanns and Turkheimer's studies, those with less accurate models of themselves paid a price: military recruits who perceived themselves as cool but were regarded by their peers as vain, self-centered, and exploitative were discharged for rule infractions at a rate that was well above average. Such individuals were breaking both written and unwritten rules of group conduct, and their military service was terminated as a consequence.

People with high personal intelligence are more competent than others when it comes to creating an accurate self-appraisal. They recognize and (to a degree) accept their own imperfections: their humor and helpfulness to others assist them to manage hot, painful information, and to weave it into their self-conceptions where warranted, and they realize that others share flaws along with them. Over time, this may support their making better personal choices.

The journalist David Carr recounts a remarkable story that illustrates both his sophisticated reasoning about personality and his capacity to cope with his own psychological pain, and it illustrates the advantages of being open to personal information that can be especially hard to accept. Carr had begun his professional career as a reporter in Minneapolis in the 1980s. Toward the end of the decade, he was arrested and jailed multiple times owing to his abuse of alcohol and crack cocaine. As his addictions grew worse, he began seeing a woman who was a local drug dealer, and during this low point in their lives she became pregnant and gave birth to twin daughters. Carr's employers and family urged him to seek treatment for his addiction and he did, but he quickly relapsed.

I believe that personal intelligence (as with any intelligence) can be present among people with personal difficulties—including among those of us who experience problems with drugs and alcohol. Under the right circumstances, people with this intelligence can use it to guide them in their struggles—whether with substance abuse or some other mental or personal challenge. Because good life choices unfold over time, personal intelligence can take a long time to works its effects, but ultimately it can help a person grow toward a healthier life.

After Carr's several unsuccessful attempts at rehabilitation, he tried again and was finally able to maintain a state of sobriety for a prolonged period of his life. As he recounts it, he drew motivation from a growing sense that his daughters needed him and that he might be their best hope for a parent. As Carr maintained his drug-free state, he began to turn his life around. He gained custody of his daughters, and in the 1990s he became the editor of the *Twin Cities Reader*, an alternative newspaper in the Minneapolis area. From there, he was hired as the editor of the *Washington City Paper* in the nation's capital and became a contributing writer for *The Atlantic Monthly* and *New York* magazine. He then moved to *The New York Times*.

The next part of Carr's story intersects with the idea of developing an accurate model of oneself. Sometime after joining *The New York Times*, Carr took a leave to write a memoir. Regarding his knowledge of personality, Carr had noticed that many addicts described their recoveries as turning on a "key conversation" with a friend or an authority figure who helped them attain sobriety. Carr was skeptical about whether so many addicts could recall a single life-changing conversation seemingly word for word at a time when their brains were presumably addled by drugs. He concluded that these were many-times-told tales that, although often recounted with sincerity, were unlikely to represent the actuality of what happened.

So Carr investigated his life using the tools he had learned as a journalist. Video recorder in hand, Carr interviewed those in Minneapolis and elsewhere who had known him, sometimes employing a detective to help find them. He also collected and read court documents about his brushes with the law, obtained the clinical notes from the hospital records surrounding the birth of his twins, and reviewed letters from his earlier life. He wrote that the experience "has been like crawling over broken glass in the dark. I hit women, scared children, assaulted strangers, and chronically lied and gamed to stay high. I read about That Guy with the same sense of disgust that almost anyone would. What. An. Asshole."

Yet by the time of his memoir, he could face the hot information about himself without too much flinching. Part of personal intelligence is putting this information together, synthesizing it, and extracting from it understanding and reconciliation. Carr's project required him to rethink his self-conception. He was, as he described himself during those years, "a complicated asset as a friend: a guy who presented significant upsides—when it was fun, it was really fun," but he had a dangerous and threatening side as well, often pushing people well past their comfort zones. This sort of accuracy and nuance in self-modeling is a hallmark of personal intelligence.

Intelligences enable people to reason about a matter at hand: to see ideas from different angles, and to draw on good answers to problems. Carr shared with his readers some of his reasoning about how he ought to present himself. If, he said, he described himself as "a fat thug who beat up women and sold bad coke," few people would be interested in knowing him, though he acknowledged this was part of his story. But, he argued, what if instead he presented his story this way: "I was a recovered addict who obtained custody of my twin girls, got us off welfare, and raised them by myself, even though I had a little touch of cancer? Now we're talking." He copes in many ways. He keeps his earlier self at arm's length, for one: Carr's life story includes two guys, as he describes it: his earlier carousing, addicted self, and his present responsible self. Accounting for his earlier self while writing his personal history, he says, "I often feel I have very little in common with him." Although Carr keeps his two selves separate to a degree, he also maintains a connection to the earlier reality of his life, saying that the distance between his two selves is part of what kept him writing his memoir—to describe that earlier guy "until he turns into this guy." Reading between the lines, one of Carr's purposes in undertaking his research must have been to visit and to reconcile, where possible, with those in his life he felt he had hurt; acknowledging his faults helped him make amends to others—and to himself.

Research by Roy Baumeister and others suggests that people with moderate self-esteem who question themselves from time to time tend to behave in relatively ethical ways. By contrast, people with unrealistically high self-esteem are less likely to question themselves and are more prone to cross over key moral boundaries. More than two thousand years ago, the Greek philosopher Plato anticipated this finding when he argued that people who exaggerated their own abilities and consequently lorded it over others could learn to behave more equitably by first developing their self-knowledge and learning to acknowledge their own weaknesses.

Personal intelligence is all about processing personality-relevant, often hot information. That means, alas, taking the heat from feedback and recognizing a broad spectrum of one's own inner motives and feelings, which are likely to be socially undesirable at times, and accepting the good and bad parts of our reputations.

If we use the tools available to us, we can create a more accurate self-image. We're apt to think things over before getting angry and expressing it. We are more likely to use humor to defuse tough situations, to identify with others, and, as a consequence, to help others. The tools I've discussed so far, from recognizing traits to handling hot information, contribute to our ability to accurately model ourselves and other people; and accumulating evidence associates better skills in these areas with higher levels of well-being. Yet personality, like other complex systems such as the weather, the economy, and politics, can't be fully understood by a single coherent model. These tools of understanding penetrate the mysteries of our psychological being only so far.

5

A GUIDE TO MAKING CHOICES

Over our lifetimes we make thousands of decisions that influence our well-being. Experts in decision-making often recommend a strategic approach that involves framing the problem, gathering the facts, combining opinions from various stakeholders, weighing pros and cons, and identifying the better alternative. Their perspectives are useful and thoughtful, but sometimes we face two possibilities that are both reasonable, and we want to decide which option is best for *us*. Whether we face a mundane choice of which restaurant to eat at, or the selection of a partner for a crucial relationship, there may be a distinct advantage to factoring in our personality—to matching our inner needs to the outer alternatives available to us. We draw on our personal intelligence to do so, and if we find the choices that are right for us, we can enhance the quality of our lives.

There are many decisions for which we wisely put our own needs aside. When we make expert decisions, we intentionally keep ourselves out of the equation because we don't want our personal desires to influence what we are doing: a bank officer sets a borrowing rate by following impartial rules designed to arrive at a supportable decision; a physician makes a reasoned judgment when she reads a medical test and determines her patient's blood pressure is too high; and a teacher evaluates students' responses to a short-answer test question according to the facts the students can produce. In such cases, we express our personalities through our expertise, and we know to let our reasoning run its course independently of our transient moods, thoughts, or other distractions.

We also sideline our needs for decisions that are relatively impersonal as we see them: many of us don't care much about which bank we use for our checking account so long as the bank is reasonably fair and efficient, or which brand of television we end up with so long as it is of a decent quality. These choices involve information that is "cool" in the sense of standing apart from our personal concerns.

And yet another group of decisions we make are so habitual that we're hardly aware of them. We choose Crest toothpaste at the drugstore and Hellman's mayonnaise in the supermarket, and prefer Tide to Cheer detergent. We acknowledge that our preference may be little more than a historical accident—our parents preferred these products—and competing products might be just as good. True, our personality might be involved in these decisions in small ways—Tide might remind us of a happy family moment at times—yet inconsequentially so.

But there is another kind of decision we make that affects us deeply: a decision that we realize expresses something important about us, or that determines a key part of our future—such as whether to move abroad to take a new job that will mean sacrificing a promising new relationship, or instead to stay where we are, with a more limited professional future. In 1897, William James described the challenge of deciding between mutually exclusive alternatives. One option, he wrote,

> shall forevermore become impossible, while the other shall become reality . . . Both alternatives are steadily held in view, and in the very act of murdering the vanquished possibility the chooser realizes in that instant he is making himself lose. It is deliberately driving a thorn into one's flesh; and the sense of *inward effort* with which the act is accompanied is . . . an altogether peculiar sort of mental phenomenon.

Linda Greenlaw, a fishing boat captain and author, describes a striking example of this effortful decision-making in her memoir *The Hungry Ocean*. In the 1990s, Greenlaw captained the F/V *Hannah Boden*, a deep sea fishing boat. She highlights the challenges her sailors faced in signing on for a thirty-day swordfishing trip along the Grand Banks: the trip meant dangerous and hard work, enforced sobriety, and loneliness. In September 1991, as the boat left the harbor of Gloucester, Massachusetts, she sighed with relief, thinking it was "too far for anyone to jump" and swim to shore. Then her attention turned to herself and the unmet wishes she would relinquish to make the trip. She kept the ship's radio off so she couldn't call home until after she was steaming from the harbor, and as she spread out her navigational charts, she reported, "I quickly forced from my head the depressing reality of no romantic attention." She reflected on her desires for a husband, a house full of children, and a quieter job, and yet she could not let go of the sea.

These are the kinds of decisions we are personally invested in. We reserve time to think about them, weigh the alternatives carefully, and imagine how we will fare once we have chosen an alternative, because we will live the outcome. If we don't know who we are and who we want to be, or if we fail to connect our identity to the choices we face, we may make decisions that lead us to the wrong job, or to an unpleasant place to live, or toward a troubling relationship—initiating an uncomfortable period of our life.

Each of us varies in our capacity to know our true desires. Rebecca Schlegel and her colleagues at the University of Missouri, Columbia, distinguish between our "true" inner selves, and how we behave more generally. Schlegel defines our true selves as consisting of the characteristics we privately believe we possess and share only with our closest friends, but that we would feel uncomfortable expressing in many other social situations. For example, we might privately regard ourselves as highly competitive, but try to avoid the appearance of competing with others in public. Schlegel asked participants in one study to list ten traits that reflected their "true inner" qualities and ten that described their actual outer behavior.

Next she asked her participants to click on "me" or "not me" in response to a series of traits flashed on a computer screen, some of which the participants had listed earlier. Schlegel hypothesized that the quicker the participants identified their true inner traits as "me," the more connected they were to their authentic qualities. In fact, participants who most rapidly selected their true traits reported more meaningful lives and better psychological well-being relative to other participants.

Schlegel also examined how knowledge of one's true self can promote decision-making. She and her colleagues asked students to rate their satisfaction with their choices of university, their college major, and whether to live in a fraternity, a sorority, or the Corps of Cadets (a large group on campus). Students with a stronger sense of their true selves were, on the whole, happier with their decisions.

Yet we often feel pressured to let go of our private self-knowledge in the face of social pressures. Even our most basic perceptions can be distorted by the beliefs of those around us. In a classic 1955 study on conformity, Solomon Asch of the University of Pennsylvania examined how social groups can disrupt personal knowledge. Participants were told they would be engaging in a study about visual perception. A young man was chosen to sit at a table with six to eight other people. The young man and the rest of the group were shown two cards. One card had a single line on it and the other card had three lines; of the three lines, one was equal in length to the line on the first card, and the other two lines clearly were not. The group's task was simply to choose which line of the three matched the one on the first card.

The experimenter showed the young man and the rest of the group the first pair of cards; one by one, each of them called out his selection, all agreeing in this instance as to which line matched the original, and concluding with the young man, who chose the same line as the rest of the group. A second round proceeded in the same way and the participants seemed prepared to do the best job they could at this fairly easy task. On the third round, the students stated their choices, but the young man, whose turn was last, looked increasingly surprised at everyone else's answer; he disagreed with all the rest about the correct line, choosing a different line as the only one that (to him) plainly matched the target. On the next trial, the young man disagreed again, this time looking worried and self-doubting. And on many subsequent trials, he reluctantly gave in to the majority—often showing signs of anxiety and dismay.

The experiment held a surprising twist: everyone seated around the table was a confederate of the researcher except the dissenting participant, and all had been instructed to choose the same plainly wrong answer beginning with the third trial. Each time the young man dissented, he was forced to express his correct perception in the face of a group who uniformly contradicted him, and it was so hard to keep this up that most participants ended up joining the group and suppressing their obviously correct choice.

When we feel the pressure from social groups or other authorities to conform, we may lose a sense of authoring our own choices. Edward Deci and Richard Ryan of the University of Rochester have studied our feelings about *owning* the decisions we make: they find that people who best control their own choices (or feel they do) possess higher levels of well-being than others. Say you are a firefighter hoping for a promotion to battalion chief. You may also have been thinking of attending college in your off hours, and you know it could improve your chances for a promotion. You may feel less motivated if you hear your chief has just made an advanced degree a requirement for a promotion. Your own enjoyment of returning to school might feel diminished, as you could no longer point with pride to your personal motivation to educate yourself—others might believe you were doing it solely for the promotion. (To counteract that feeling, Deci and Ryan might advise you to remember your interest in attending college before the rule was instituted.) Baltimore firefighters heard news of just that requirement in 2012 from their chief, James S. Clack. Although the chief's new policy was enlightened, it felt imposed from above to many employees, and many objected for that and other reasons. (One local union representative opined: "You can't fight fire with books.")

Deci and Ryan view each of our choices as existing along a continuum of ownership, from those that are forced on us by our parents, supervisors, and groups, at one extreme, to those that emerge from our own desires and preferences, at the other. People who are driven solely by outside forces are "externally regulated," in their terms. Such individuals carry out a task because they are told to. In fact, the ways we choose begin early in life. For example, Ryan and James Connell surveyed third-through-sixth-graders about why they studied in school. Some young students were already feeling externally controlled, explaining that they were doing their schoolwork "Because I'll get in trouble if I don't" or "So that the teacher won't yell at me."

We take a small step toward greater inner direction by imagining an authority figure and what that person would say to convince us to perform a task (called "introjected regulation"). At this level of motivation, we want to prove ourselves—and we begin to wonder why the goal is important to others. But the goal still belongs to the authority, not us, and our motivation remains more externally than internally directed. In Ryan and Connell's study of grade-schoolers, those with introjected regulation said they wanted to learn because "I want other students to think I'm smart" and because "I want people to like me."

Our parents are a key source of external motivation when we are young. For example, Press Maravich, a highly regarded college basketball coach, tried to motivate his young son Pete to play basketball by carefully planning out how he would hook him on the sport. When Pete was two years old, Press gave him a Christmas gift of a basketball—but Pete didn't take the hint at that young age. As Pete entered elementary school, Press shot baskets behind the house while his son watched, inviting his son to toss the ball with him. Pete was drawn in this time. Pete himself remarked that Press "knew any son would want to copy his father and if his calculations were correct, I would be drawn into the sport he worshipped." If Pete played basketball as a child because he sensed his father wanted him to, he would have been motivated by introjected regulation. And when our motivation is introjected, we remain directed by external figures.

Deci and Ryan view our motivation as becoming more inner-directed as we internalize the values of other people and decide to live by them ourselves ("identified regulation"). In these cases, we consciously value what we are doing, and regard our own actions as important to us. The children in Ryan and Connell's study who were internalizing the values of their teachers said they studied because "I want to understand the subject."

By the time he was nine, Pete wanted to learn more, and had worked through forty basketball exercises that his father had developed for him. The great basketball coach John Wooden encountered Pete at this time: the boy could dribble blindfolded, spin the basketball on his fingers, and throw the ball one way while looking another. Wooden—not prone to overstatement—said, "I saw him do things . . . I didn't think anybody could do." But Wooden felt compelled to ask Press to what end he had trained his boy that way, to which Press replied, "He's going to be the first million-dollar pro." Wooden recalled warning Press that he was putting too much pressure on his son. When Pete was a grown man, Press did acknowledge that he had gone overboard at times, explaining that he and his relatives were an emotional group with feelings that were "hard, very hard, to contain."

But Press continued to advocate for basketball throughout Pete's youth. As Pete's interest in sports broadened, he asked his father to practice baseball with him. On one of those occasions, Press accidentally hit a ball that struck his son's forehead, knocking him off his feet. Seizing the opportunity, Press told Pete that he himself had been "hit by a baseball once," and that he ended up in the hospital as a result. "That's why I stuck with basketball." And later, when his son tried out for football, Press arranged for the coach to let his son quarterback the team during practice—Pete was still inexperienced and small enough in stature that the other players creamed him; Pete quit soon afterward.

By junior high, Pete's basketball practice sometimes began at 6:00 a.m. and extended after school until 9:00 p.m. When Pete's math teacher complained about the quality of his homework, his father showed up and told her that Pete's homework wasn't very important. When his teacher objected that the seventh-grader has "got to get out of school first," Press replied, "Don't worry about that. I'll see to it that he gets into college and gets to be a basketball star."

Soon thereafter, Press accepted a job as the basketball coach at Clemson University and moved there with his family. Pete increasingly appreciated the benefits of playing basketball as he saw how his skills brought him recognition from other students. By high school, other players would sometimes break off playing their pick-up games and simply stare at him because he was so good. Pete used to wait after school until six in the evening to play his high school basketball coach, Don Carver, so as to improve his game. They'd play one-on-one, the best of eleven baskets. Pete was by then 5 feet 8 and 120 pounds; his coach was 6 feet 4 and 220 pounds. His coach recounted that they won equal numbers of these practice competitions, adding: "And I wasn't going to give him anything, because I wanted him to get better." Yet the external pressures continued: as Pete prepared for college, he thought he might want to play for West Virginia, which had expressed interest in recruiting him. Press, who by this time was coaching basketball at LSU, insisted on coaching his son's college game—telling him to either sign a letter of intent to play for LSU or "don't ever come home again."

Pete had a brilliant basketball career at LSU—but had a tumultuous career as a professional league player afterward. "Pistol Pete," as he was known by then, attracted basketball fans wherever he played, but although he had developed into a stellar player, he didn't always find it satisfying. He struggled with depression and a lack of motivation, and sometimes drank heavily. He famously dismissed his young self as a "basketball android," and adhered to extreme beliefs about flying saucers, healthful diets, and alternative medicine. To be sure, Pete faced challenges as a player that had little to do with his motivation: his unique style of play was far ahead of its time and it often put off coaches (although it would dominate the game of basketball just a decade later). After turning pro and playing for the New Orleans Jazz, Pete scored 68 points one night against the opposing team and received an ovation from his fans. He couldn't help but focus on the approval of others, acknowledging at the time:

"All I could think of were the expectations of the New Orleans fans, the club owners, the coach, the players, my dad, and worst of all, myself . . . I figured the only way I would continue to be accepted by the public would be to score sixty-eight points again and again."

Deci and Ryan believe that those who act chiefly in response to the demands and rules of other people will experience stress, gradually lose energy, and feel uncommitted toward their goals. By contrast, we begin our lives as inherently curious, motivated, and active, and will remain so as adults under the right conditions. The "right conditions," they argued, are those that allow individuals to recognize their own desires and to choose socially permissible activities that fulfill them. People who do this successfully, Deci and Ryan asserted, will be more genuinely motivated and better enjoy the activities they engage in.

That acknowledged, the Maravich family experienced happy times as well. Press and Pete maintained a close relationship and Pete gradually became the more influential partner. And, in 1987, "Pistol Pete" was elected to the Basketball Hall of Fame. He brought his own sons to the All-Star weekend in Seattle and introduced them to a then-up-and-coming player named Michael Jordan.

On the basketball court Jordan epitomized Deci and Ryan's idea of autonomous motivation as well as anyone could. According to the researchers, such motives emerge from our authentic inner desires; as we allow our genuine motives to be expressed we feel *joy*. Michael Jordan's father was a supervisor at General Electric and his mother was a teller at a bank; neither was very tall, and so basketball was not a focus for them as Michael grew up. Jordan played several different school sports and decided on basketball because it was something he liked—plus, he had grown unexpectedly tall. Jordan excelled at the sport and ultimately signed with the Chicago Bulls in 1984. The Bulls' standard contract included a clause that prohibited its athletes from playing basketball during the off-season, to protect them from injuries. Jordan remarked: "There was no way I could live with that kind of restriction. I needed to play. Not only had I always found comfort on the court, but I used the summer to improve." So the Bulls added a clause to Jordan's contract allowing him to play year-round that he referred to as the "Love of the Game Clause." And Jordan exulted that he could "do what I always had done. I could play the game of basketball without consequence." The rest is basketball history.

Personal intelligence involves reasoning about our mental lives with a set of principles that are in many instances universal. But is intrinsic motivation valued universally, or is it desirable only in Western societies where cultural teachings emphasize self-direction and in-dividualism? Researchers studied autonomous motivation among college-age students in Korea, the United States, Russia, and Turkey to see whether such autonomy was as important in societies that emphasized collectivism as in those that emphasized individualism. The team was led by Valery Chirkov of the University of Saskatche-wan and Richard Ryan of the University of Rochester.

Consistent with other research, the Korean college students viewed themselves as highest in collectivistic attitudes relative to the other groups, endorsing survey items such as "Family members should stick together no matter what sacrifices are required"; stu-dents in the United States viewed themselves as the most indivi-dualistic, endorsing attitudes such as "It is important that I do my job better than others," and those in Russia and Turkey were in between.

That said, respondents from any single nation varied in their preferences for individualistic versus collectivist values, with some students believing it was best "to depend on oneself rather than on others"—an individualistic notion—whereas others hoped "to maintain harmony within any group that one belongs to"—a collec-tivist view. Within both collectivistic and individualistic societies, some people were more autonomously motivated than others. Ex-amining just the collectivist respondents, for example, some said they took care of their families because they "feel free in choosing it and doing it, and responsible for the outcomes," whereas others took care of their families, "because someone else insists that I do it." So intrinsic motivation certainly existed in collectivistic societies, and in all four nations studied, those individuals who felt the most intrinsically motivated had higher well-being—relatively better emotional states and better life satisfaction.

One reason we benefit from making our own choices is that we know our preferences better than other people—and that helps us find social environments we're comfortable with. Researchers at the University of California, Riverside, track the environments we select using the Riverside Situational Q-Sort, or RSQ, a list of descriptions that apply to the situations in which we find ourselves. For example, if Kristen spent an evening at home with her friends, judges might describe her gathering with the RSQ descriptors "involves competition," "simple/clear-cut," and "allows expression of charm." By contrast, making dinner for herself and her boyfriend involves "a job needs to be done," "allows for immediate gratification," and "includes sensuous stimuli."

It turns out that we select the situations we like on the basis of our personalities. Ryne Sherman of Florida Atlantic University and his colleagues followed 202 undergraduates for several weeks using the RSQ. The researchers also measured the students on several of their traits including extraversion and other members of the Big Five (which I went over in Chapter 3). Extraverts more commonly chose situations that were described as "talking is permitted, invited, or conventionally expected," and people who were open to experience preferred situations that involved excitement and novelty. The better they fitted their personalities to the situation, the greater their psychological health.

We also make decisions by picking alternatives we believe other people like us would prefer. Professors Paula Niedenthal, Nancy Cantor, and John Kihlstrom asked participants who lived in dormitories at the time to rate the kinds of people who would be happy and comfortable living in an apartment, a single-sex dormitory, a rented house, or another alternative. Different types of people preferred each kind of housing; those who preferred dormitories were studious, task-focused, and enjoyed group living. Those who preferred apartments were more independent, assertive, and outgoing.

Participants' personalities matched their rank order of the kinds of housing they would prefer. This matching was especially strong for participants with more "distinctive" personalities—those who had described themselves as possessing only a few carefully chosen personality qualities and who had rejected the rest of the self-descriptions as not applicable.

Follow-up studies have found that people who, for example, prefer restaurants serving foreign cuisine over restaurants serving more familiar foods described their outlook as "unconventional, friendly, intelligent, and spontaneous," whereas those who preferred family dining characterized themselves as "practical, responsible, loyal, and polite." Similar research indicates that teenagers are more apt to become smokers if their personalities are similar to other smokers—somewhat unhealthy and nervous but also "acting big," liking groups, and more interested in the opposite sex than average—and, in another study, college students who resembled grad students in their responsible attitudes toward school were more apt to become graduate students themselves.

Among the most important decisions people make in their lives concern who to have a close relationship with, be it a friend, a partner, or a spouse. Surveys of married couples confirm that people typically choose partners who are similar to themselves, especially in regard to religious background, traditionalism, intelligence, and socioemotional qualities such as extraversion and agreeableness. Our mental models of significant others—which often influence us in ways we're unaware of—likely contribute to this matching effect as well. Loving feelings arise more often when a new person reminds us of someone we have loved in the past—perhaps automatically eliciting an echo of our early love of our parents and their love for us (as I discussed in Chapter 3).

For example, Professor Glenn Geher of the State University of New York at New Paltz asked undergraduates who were involved in romantic relationships at the time to describe the personalities of their partners. With the students' permission, Geher then contacted their parents and asked the parents about their own personalities. Geher found that his sample of students chose opposite-sex romantic partners with personality traits that resembled their opposite-sex parent more than would be expected by chance alone, even after controlling for the students' own trait profiles; in other words, people who remind us of a parent may awaken our feelings of love.

And we tend to marry people who are similar to ourselves. This preference for similar others occurs both within cultures that teach that people should marry others like themselves, such as in China, and in cultures where a number of people believe that opposites attract, such as in the United States. Of course, each of us has myriad attributes, including our age, religion or lack thereof, ethnicity, maturity level, self-control, extraversion, and many more. For that reason, no couple can match themselves on *all* their qualities; matching is a matter of degree. That said, studies indicate that among couples who marry, those who are the most similar have easier and longer marriages than others.

This "similarity effect" can have a drawback, of course. Some of our key mental models of people are based on our significant others when we were young—parents and other caretakers. If the important people in our lives had psychological difficulties, our mental models may prepare us to love similarly troubled people as an adult. Adult children of alcoholics provide a much-studied example of this phenomenon. Evidence suggests that they have a greater likelihood of marrying alcoholics themselves, as well as to be at somewhat greater risk for other relationship issues such as partner abuse. As expected, given the love between parent and child and the possibility of genetic transmission of risk factors, the adult children of alcoholics are also at greater risk than others for becoming alcoholics themselves. Yet self-knowledge may assist in breaking the cycle of such troubled relationships: the glory of falling in love is also likely to be a wake-up call to consider their partners' habits when it comes to drinking. The adult children of parents with other difficulties (be they schizophrenia, depression, or anger control) may experience the same wake-up call. It doesn't mean the worst will happen. A couple with similar histories of alcoholism, for example, may never experience any difficulties, or, if they do, may mutually support each other's sobriety. My point here is that being aware of the risk can help us to make choices and to cope with whatever comes next. (An interesting question is whether people might also pair up on the basis of physical health issues).

Those who come from families with psychologically healthy parents are at an apparent advantage here—the wind is at their backs in terms of finding another person who is mentally healthy to spend time with. Married couples are more likely to sustain their relationship if they had parents with good marriages, and if the couples share good emotional health, moderate self-esteem and calmness, and good interpersonal skills. (The longevity of a marriage is also related to being older at the time of marriage, and having a more educated male partner.)

The rest of us can apply some personal intelligence here by being alert to findings about repeating unhealthy patterns in new relationships, and, when we fall in love, by thinking about the history of our potential partner. This isn't always easy. Our tendency to overgeneralize our significant others' qualities to new people can also lead us to imagine that new people share more characteristics of our significant others than they do. In other words, we run the additional risk of *mistakenly* attributing old issues to new people we meet. Accurate perceptions require honing our appraisals of other people over time and regularly checking on the validity of our evaluations. Personal intelligence may promote our awareness of these factors and allow us to navigate issues around the mental models we form of others by checking our perceptions, observing and asking questions of someone new to our lives, getting help from impartial and insightful friends, or calling on the aid of a psychotherapist for particularly thorny problems.

We might wonder why we should be so rational. Why not indulge our feelings without further thought? When others object to our decisions, we think to ourselves, "I'll follow my heart and deal with the consequences." Although we might seem bullheaded to others, this proposition isn't so unreasonable from the standpoint of personal intelligence—because satisfying our inner needs is a part of good functioning. The problem comes in living with decisions and their consequences. Our present decisions hold our future selves hostage, and however joyous it is sometimes to fulfill our inner wishes come what may, it is wisdom incarnate to be kind to our future selves.

When we're caught between two choices, it's sometimes because two different mental systems are working in partial independence of one another and are giving us two different answers. For example, when a young adult considers becoming engaged, she may feel good about her ability to express her feelings with her prospective partner, and feel good about her emotional self-control, but less certain this is the right time for her to commit to a long-term relationship.

Matters are not any simpler when we choose a friend or a partner: we can match our selves with another person only up to a point. Once we form a relationship, we'll need to cope with differences in personalities no matter how "similar" we may be. Struggling with these differences can lead to positive outcomes if we use them as an opportunity to learn coping strategies ourselves, including compromise with our partner. When we encounter two people who are very different from each other but somehow stay together, their success may reflect many strengths they learned in getting along: how to cope as a couple, how to negotiate constructively, and how to frame the other partner's qualities to emphasize his or her best features. Partners like these can teach each other a lot over time.

Many marriages are made without much regard to the similarity of the partners' personalities. A case in point involves a group of marriages formed within the Reverend Sun Myung Moon's Unification Church. The Reverend Moon viewed marriage as integral to his religion and he personally married, renewed the vows of, and blessed more than one million marriages over his lifetime.

Reverend Moon eliminated some of the customary romancing that potential marriage partners go through. Specifically, he often took on the role of an international matchmaker, pairing men and women who had never met before and marrying thousands of them within days of their first encounter. In doing so, he set in motion what scientists refer to as a natural experiment—so-called because the intervention the researchers study is brought about by external "natural" forces—in this instance, Reverend Moon's matchmaking—as opposed to interventions set in motion by the scientists themselves.

Let's suppose that the Reverend Moon matched these thousands of couples so quickly that his choices were more or less random. Acknowledging that all the couples had personalities that led them to follow Moon, let's further suppose the members were quite diverse (some didn't even speak the same language at the time they were married). As it turned out, the married participants expressed the same levels of marital satisfaction as a community control group, according to Marc Galanter of New York University, who followed the new couples for four years after their marriages. To help the marriages succeed, middle-echelon members of the church often assisted the couples to learn coping strategies. The *Washington Post* reporter Michelle Boorstein interviewed some of those insta-couples years after Galanter's study. Many church members acknowledged the challenges they faced in their relationships. As one man put it, the support from the church was a factor, but "when you're in the kitchen duking it out . . . we fight just like atheists." Another member of a couple said they used "old-fashioned patience and secular self-help books" to make it through. So couples with differences can learn to live together. But similarity between members of a pair may make for an easier time of it.

Another kind of decision in which we try to find a match for ourselves is in our choice of a career. According to a theory developed by John Holland in the mid-twentieth century, every occupation attracts its own specific personality type. Holland divided occupations into six groups based on the personality types that were drawn to them: Realistic, Investigative, Artistic, Social, Enterprising, and Conventional. Social occupations, for example, include nurses, counselors, teachers, athletics trainers, and dental hygienists. People who work in those fields are usually helpful, friendly, and trustworthy and prefer to interact with others.

Nurses, for example, describe their outlook as altruistic, with many stating that a key motivating factor in their work is to bring about a change for the better in someone's life. A study of female staff nurses in the *British Journal of Nursing* indicated that nurses were more outgoing, agreeable, emotionally stable, and conscientious compared with women in other professions. Assuming the nurses' self-perceptions are reasonably accurate, they set a high standard of conduct that only some of us could meet. I suspect almost no amount of supervision will turn an introverted, disagreeable, and careless person into a good nurse without the employee's willingness to change the basics of his or her personality over the long term.

Holland arranged his careers around a hexagon, with similar careers near one another, and opposite careers across from each other. Across from the Social occupations—indicating that their interests were most different—were people in the Realistic occupations, including carpenters, locksmiths, farmers, and firefighters. These individuals enjoy hands-on, practical jobs such as working with plants, animals, and mechanical objects. They're more interested in motors, water systems, and crops—things—relative to people in social occupations like nursing and teaching, who are more interested in people.

A slight turn around the hexagon from the Realistic careers reveals the Investigative occupations, which include computer science professionals, medical researchers, physicians, and engineers. Individuals in these jobs prefer to analyze data, to problem-solve, and to research. And still another turn reveals the Artistic group: advertising copywriters, graphic designers, performing artists, and interior designers. These individuals are creative themselves and prefer to work at unstructured creative tasks; they can be unconventional and are less governed by social customs and rules than are other people.

People are happiest when they have matched their own interests to the occupational group that suits them best. There are, however, a few key qualifications. For one, happy people are generally happy regardless of their career; unhappy people less so. So although the closer people fit with their career, the more their happiness will improve, the match won't account for a person's absolute level of happiness, which is determined by many other factors, from genetics to cognitive style to positive experiences.

Because people do seek to improve their well-being through their choices, Holland's theory helps explain how people choose their line of work—and research bears out the theory. At the University of Southern Queensland in Australia, Lynette Sutherland and her colleagues examined how well 154 adults had matched their personalities to their occupations: those with the closest matches exhibited lower levels of stress compared with their colleagues who were less well matched. Moti Assouline and Elchanan Meir at the Hebrew University of Jerusalem reviewed forty-one such studies and concluded that better matches more often led to better job satisfaction—making those choices highly important to a person over the long term. So we will often be able to improve our well-being by matching our personalities to the jobs we take on, as well as to the people with whom we have relationships.

Whether we are trying to fit ourselves into a relationship or a career, it's not like fitting a plug into a socket—we are more multi-faceted than that. It's more like fitting a tuba into a duffel bag: the tuba has many different-shaped parts (like each of our personalities): mouthpiece and mouthpiece pipe, valves and valve pipes, and the bell from which the sound emerges. As such, we need to push and pull a bit, and stretch our container as well from time to time. Luckily, if we don't choose right the first time, we often have a second chance. David Oleski and Linda Subich of the University of Akron studied forty-two adults who had returned to school to begin a new career. Most of those switching careers chose new occupations that more closely matched their personalities than had their initial line of work. The better the congruence with their new work, the more job satisfaction they experienced.

So we make our choices and hope to arrive at a good fit; and if obstacles arise, we adjust. Ludwig van Beethoven's musical career, for example, illustrates some of the give-and-take necessary. Beethoven viewed his commitment to music as self-authored. His talent was so obvious, both to himself and to others, that at a very young age he became heralded as the next Mozart. Beethoven was like the creative and innovative people Holland described in Artistic occupations, albeit to an extreme at times. The composer had little use for social niceties or conventions; he behaved abruptly and unsociably with others, and was uninterested in everyday housekeeping: his apartment was so unkempt as to become a matter of gossip among those who had seen it. The musician's hard work, commitment, and talent brought him many successes but he nonetheless suffered both physical and mental hardships—a reminder that even if we make a good choice, life can deal us a tough hand to play and we should be prepared to cope with our challenges.

By 1802, at age thirty-one, Beethoven faced the unmistakable fact that he was becoming deaf and that there would be no medical miracle that could preserve his hearing. On a professional level, he feared the threat to his life as a composer; on a more personal level, he already was known as a disagreeable person, and he feared that his increasing impairment would erect a further social barrier to others that would accentuate his reputation as "malevolent, stubborn, misanthropic." Beethoven wrote of his deepening mental pain and acknowledged that "a little more of that [pain] and I would have been at the point of taking my own life." Yet the autonomy and purpose he experienced as a musician sustained him. He also wrote, "It seemed to me impossible to leave the world until I had produced all the works that I felt the urge to compose." Beethoven kept his affliction largely secret for years thereafter.

Twenty-two years later, on May 7, 1824, Beethoven conducted the premiere of his Ninth Symphony in the beautiful Kärntnertortheater of Vienna. In the fourth movement, instruments strain toward something close to speech. This is followed by a baritone soloist who proclaims, "Oh, Friends, not these tones! Let us instead tune our voices more pleasantly and joyfully." Shortly thereafter, the choir sings an idealistic message of spiritual love and, at another level, perhaps a note of gratitude from Beethoven to those who had sustained him over the years, expressed as a quote from Schiller's poem "Ode to Joy." The choir recites: "You millions, I embrace you / This kiss goes to the whole world; / Brothers—above the starry canopy / A beloved father must surely dwell."

The musicians, knowing of Beethoven's hearing loss, had agreed to follow the rhythms of Beethoven's colleague Ignaz Umlauf, who stood discreetly to one side of the theater, counting time. In a short while, Beethoven's hearing loss was revealed to the public for the first time, including to the royal family. After the final notes of the performance, the composer stood facing the orchestra and studying his score, unaware of the audience reaction until the singer Caroline Unger touched his sleeve and motioned to him to turn so that he could see the audience and their tumultuous applause; he bowed.

Beethoven's biographer Lewis Lockwood wrote of musical masterworks that "they are created . . . by individuals carrying out specific imaginative purposes . . . [from] deeply rooted elements in the creative individual's personality." From the onset of Beethoven's hearing disability to this moment some twenty years later, the composer's choices had allowed him to prevail over a fearful time and to attain a new maturity of outlook and greatness of spirit. Many psychologists regard Beethoven's coping throughout this time as a testament to the possibilities of personal growth—growth that was made possible, in part, by his inner motivation to pursue musical composition, and through it, to express his gratitude toward others.

We use our personal intelligence to understand our intrinsic needs and other mental traits, and to fit those to the situations, people, and careers we choose in life. By doing so, we make big life decisions that help us develop from our present selves to what we hope to become in the future. Although making a decision by listing the impersonal, publicly available pros and cons of each alternative might work well in some kinds of choices, personal intelligence taps the hot information of our inner desires and reasons; we then know how to channel our needs into a social outlet that fits our nature. This kind of decision-making emphasizes using self-knowledge to fit our talents, abilities, and social preferences into well-tailored relationships with other people and with the world of work. Those of us who can recognize our most important inner desires—and who can think accurately about others—will have a leg up when it comes to facing serious obstacles in our paths. By reasoning about the consequences of our choices, we act as stewards of our selves who must live, in the future, with the decisions we make today. And if a decision we make doesn't fully work out—we don't like our new job, or we're having doubts about our fiancée—we must be ready to cope as best we can with the decisions we've made, and to revise them or to change ourselves.

6

GROWING UP WITH PERSONAL INTELLIGENCE

Our babies—our newly minted descendants—entrance us with their smiles, gazes, and coos. At the same time, those babies are also learning about the surrounding world: evolutionary selection has prepared them to observe other people in order to begin understanding the personalities of those around them. Five-month-olds already recognize that adults reach for a spoon to eat, and that children reach for a push toy to roll it. By ten months old, most infants understand that adults—larger people—are more socially commanding than smaller people. To demonstrate this, researchers show infants a cartoon clip of a small character and a large character who march toward each other. If the smaller character steps aside for the larger one, the infants watch calmly, but if the larger character steps aside for the smaller one, the babies exhibit surprise at the social interaction—indicated by a prolonged gaze.

Children continue learning about the people around them as they head into preschool, and they begin to diverge from one another when it comes to their skills at comprehending people. By middle school, many children have developed a good understanding of personality but a few lag behind their classmates in reading their peers and authority figures. And on the road to adulthood, older teens differ markedly from one another in their skill levels, as indicated by their scores on the Test of Personal Intelligence (TOPI).

The TOPI is made up of 134 multiple-choice questions about perceiving people, the meaning of traits, establishing goals, and other personality-related information. The most current version is designed for those seventeen years of age or older. For each correct answer, a person receives one point. So someone with no insight into himself and others who guesses on every question would select the right answer by chance one out of four times and get about 25 percent correct on the test. The more questions a person answers correctly—with the correct answers identified by personality research—the more points she accrues.

I recently examined a study of 384 test-takers whose perfor-mance on the TOPI varied from 24 percent correct—just below chance guessing—to 95 percent correct overall—with most per-forming at levels in between. The distribution of the scores contains a clue as to where such variability comes from: If personal intelli-gence were caused by, say, just one gene, there would be two levels of performance. If you lacked the gene, you would guess your way through the test at about 25 percent, and if you had it, you would answer all the questions correctly. If we add a second, equivalent cause of the ability—for example, exposure to a schoolteacher who talked insightfully about personality—then there would be three levels of performance: Those who lacked the gene and lacked the teacher could only guess at the answers. Others would have either the gene or the insightful teacher and would score at, say, 65 per-cent correct; and those who had both would score close to 100 per-cent correct. In fact, however, scores on the TOPI are distributed like a bell curve rather than divided into two or three discrete score levels. That bell-like distribution of scores points to the idea that personal intelligence is determined by many factors, some likely to be genetic, others environmental.

Psychologists often look to twins to figure out how much of an outcome is due to genetic causes and how much is due to the envi-ronment. The classical model of twin genetics states that monozy-gotic (identical) twins share 100 percent of their genetic material in common, dizygotic (fraternal) twins and other biological siblings share on average 50 percent of their genetic material in common, and second-degree relatives such as cousins share 25 percent. Sci-entists using the classical model make a further assumption that the family environment is similar for identical twins, fraternal twins, and other siblings, insofar as those influences might affect a particular trait. This is called the equal-environment assumption. If genetic influences are involved, two people who share more genes in common—such as identical twins relative to cousins—ought to be more similar to each other on a given characteristic.

As it turns out, identical twins are more similar than siblings and second-degree relatives for many traits, including general intelligence, extraversion, and openness, which argues for a genetic influence in each case. Using the classical twin model, scientists have estimated that genetic influences on general intelligence account for roughly 60 percent of a person's intellectual difference from average. So if a person had an IQ 30 points above the average of 100, then roughly 60 percent of those points (18 out of 30) would be due to genetic influences. That leaves about 40 percent of the influence as environmental or genetic-environmental interactions. Because no twin studies have included personal intelligence yet, it seems prudent to employ a starting estimate of 50 percent—a middle value—for the level of genetic contribution, and to adjust upward or downward from there as evidence comes in.

Genes don't affect our behavior directly: rather, they influence our mental lives by shaping the structures of our brains, or by affecting the level of neurotransmitters or hormones that in turn influence our behavior. We use many different brain areas to reason about ourselves and other people. I discussed brain areas associated with memory for one's own traits in Chapter 4, but there are other known regions involved with understanding our mental lives. In the 1980s, for example, researchers began to study how macaque monkeys—a close anatomical relative to human beings—made sense of body movements. In particular, they focused on the primate's premotor cortex. This turned out to be a propitious choice: scientists at the University of Parma next found a single brain cell in a macaque's premotor cortex that became active when the monkey observed a person putting food on a table for sharing, or grasping food from another person's hand—the macaque recognized "specific, meaningful hand movements performed by the experimenters," as they put it. This same neuron fired when the monkey itself put food on the table in the same goal-directed way. They called the cell a mirror neuron, because it responded whether the monkey itself performed the action or saw another person exhibiting the intention (like placing out food to share). In humans, such mirror neurons may serve as the basis for an empathic understanding of other people's intentions. Children's genetic inheritance may influence how their brains develop in regard to mirror neurons and other areas important to personal understanding.

Since the discovery of mirror neurons, researchers have identified many additional areas of the brain responsible for interpreting personality. For example, Andrea Heberlein, of the Center for Cognitive Neuroscience of the University of Pennsylvania, identified brain areas responsible for recognizing bodily movements that express personality qualities such as sociability and unfriendliness. To do so, Heberlein asked a trained actor to express a variety of emotional feelings and personality traits while she made point-light recordings of his movements. (Point-light recordings are videos of lights that have been attached to an actor's joints as he walks, runs, and performs other expressive actions in a darkened room.) People who view the videos can't see any cues in the actor's appearance—they see only the lights in motion. Heberlein found that "neurologically normal" judges could agree that some of the videos conveyed personality traits such as outgoingness, shyness, warmth, and unfriendliness, and others conveyed emotions such as happiness, fear, sadness, and anger.

Next, Heberlein and her colleagues showed the videos to a group of patients with various kinds of brain damage. Some of the individuals could recognize personality expressions but not emotional expressions in the point-light videos, and others could recognize emotional expressions but not the expressions of personality. By comparing the locations of the brain damage with each skill, the researchers localized the perception of personality-related movements to a portion of the language center called the left frontal operculum, which is also associated with using verbs and labeling actions. In a second study, the scientists replicated the key role of the language area in personality judgments, using fMRI neuroimaging. These and other brain areas allow developing children to master a number of milestones in understanding personality.

By about a year and a half, most human infants are able to recognize their image in a mirror, suggesting that they have begun to establish an identity. Few other animal species are able to do this at all, and if they can, they typically take much longer developmentally to establish the skill. (The additional species that can recognize themselves include chimpanzees, some other great apes, and elephants.) But recognizing oneself in the mirror is not the same as forming a sense of self; a fully human sense of self includes the ability to recall past events that make up one's autobiography, and this capacity doesn't emerge for most children until just before three years of age. Before that, young children exhibit a lack of longer-term memories about themselves and their experiences. (Freud referred to this as infantile amnesia.)

Professor David Pillemer, a developmental psychologist, studied this phenomenon among children who underwent an emergency evacuation from their preschool: One morning, a popcorn maker had caught fire, triggering a fire alarm. The staff evacuated the children from the different classrooms according to plan and everyone was safe; firefighters arrived and extinguished the fire. Pillemer and his colleagues wondered what the children would remember about the event later in their lives. They arranged to interview the children two weeks after the fire, and then seven years later. At the seven-year follow-up, children who were older than three years of age at the time of the fire could reliably remember where they were, where they evacuated to, and, more generally, what else happened on that day. Children younger than three at the time were far less accurate in their memories. Pillemer and his colleagues had found more evidence that children's brains must mature to three years of age before they can lay down continuous memories of the self.

Other key abilities in understanding personality involve understanding something about how we think and feel. It turns out that parents contribute importantly to their children's understanding of mental states just by speaking with them about desires, feelings, and thoughts. Jenkins, Turrell, and their colleagues studied such conversations by observing thirty-seven mothers and fathers interacting with their two- and four-year-old children, and then followed up two years later. They found that at first children spoke with their parents mostly about desires—using terms such as *want, hope, wish,* and *care* (as in "I don't care")—until about two or three years of age. Between two and three, the young kids began to use a vocabulary of feelings, including words such as *sad, hurt, angry,* and *happy*; and then, about midway through the third year, the children commenced cognitive talk with their parents, using terms such as *think, know, believe, remember,* and *guess.*

The children's "mental talk" reflects the development of what psychologists call their "theory of mind"—the ability to understand the people around them and how they think. A classic measure of a child's theory of mind is the false-belief procedure. To determine whether children understand the idea of mistaken opinions, they are told a story like this: "Emily puts her M&M's in a kitchen cabinet near her chair and heads out to play. While she is gone, mischievous Madison discovers the M&M's there and moves them to a drawer. Later, Emily comes back to get her candy." The children who hear the story are asked where Emily will look for her candy first.

Children of about four years old who hear this story understand that Madison has moved the candy unbeknownst to Emily, and that Emily has a false belief and will look for the candy in the cabinet where she had left it. Children younger than three, however, do not understand that others may have mistaken beliefs: they know from the story that Madison has moved the candy to the drawer and they believe that Emily knows this and will look for her candy in the drawer where Madison has moved it. Older children understand the problem better, but a child's individual ability contributes as well: a few three-year-olds already understand false beliefs and some four-year-olds are delayed in understanding them.

Children who spoke with their parents the most about their desires, feelings, and thoughts were better able to theorize about what other people know and believe on the false-belief task and other, similar problems. Moreover, the difference between children who speak more about mental states and those who don't isn't just a matter of their verbal skills: the relative advantage for the mental-state talkers remained even after the researchers controlled for the children's verbal abilities.

, Simon Baron-Cohen, an expert in autism at the University of Cambridge, believes that we all possess a part of the brain he refers to as a Theory of Mind Module (TOMM), which we use to make educated guesses about what other people are thinking. Evidence for the discrete brain component comes from the fact that four-year-olds with autism have difficulty with the false-belief task: in his studies, they were unable to guess Emily's state of mind, even though they were able to perform at their age level on nonsocial problems. The four-year-olds with autism also showed deficits in these false-belief problems relative to a group of older, intellectually disabled children who were functioning at about a four-year-old level. From this pattern of results, Baron-Cohen concludes that the Theory of Mind Module exists but functions less well among those with autism.

There is evidence that most children can improve their theory of mind by talking with adults about mental states. For example, deaf children of hearing parents are often delayed in acquiring insights into a theory of mind—unless their parents have learned sign language to communicate such concepts to them. And when psychologists studied the Junín Quechua people of Peru, a group of subsistence farmers who share a language that has few words for mental states and who only rarely refer to mental states, the eight-year-olds were delayed in their ability to understand false-belief problems. The same is true for children in similar tribes in New Guinea. Parents who wish to foster their children's personal intelligence, this research suggests, could take the opportunity to speak with them about their wants, desires, emotions, and thoughts when the topics arise.

Alfred Binet, the French psychologist who developed the earliest successful intelligence tests, pointed out that people with greater verbal intelligence learn faster than others over time. Binet was searching for mental tests that would separate students with intellectual disabilities from other children. Initially, he had little success at

his pursuit because some intellectually disabled children (as identified by their teachers) were able to correctly answer questions that
other, ostensibly smarter children could not. Ultimately, Binet recognized a pattern that was groundbreaking at the time, although it may
seem obvious today. He noticed that it was the older, intellectually
disabled children in particular who could solve some of the problems
that their younger peers could not; that is, a child's age was important
to the problems he or she could solve, as well as the child's intelligence. With this insight, Binet began to assess children's problem-
solving in relation to their age. All children grow smarter as they
grow older, he saw, but some do so faster than others.

Children not only improve their understanding of people's inner
states of beliefs as they grow older, they also begin to identify the
key traits that distinguish us from one another, as illustrated in a
study by Rebecca Eder of the University of California at Davis. Using
a three-foot hand puppet, Eder interviewed three-and-a-half-year-
old children and found that they already could describe themselves
in traitlike terms. When asked, "Tell me how you usually have been
in school?" The children replied: "I have been good" or "Shy." These
same children distinguished such traitlike concepts from their more
specific behaviors. For example, when asked, "Tell me what you
did in school today," they responded with specific activities. In a
follow-up study, Eder further examined how well her young children could understand traits. This time she told the children that
two three-foot-long puppets, now in a puppet theater, were "writing
a story about kids your age . . . They are going to tell you about
themselves and then you tell them about yourself. Are you ready?"

The two puppets described themselves as opposite on a given
trait. For example, Puppet 1 described his level of caution by saying,
"I don't climb things that are high," whereas Puppet 2 would say, "I
climb really high things." In one instance, a conversation among
the puppets and the child around social dominance unfolded
this way:

Puppet 1: My friends tell me what to do.
Child: Mine don't.

Puppet 2: I tell my friends what to do.
Child: I do too. I like to boss them around.

Even three-and-a-half-year-olds, it turned out, gave highly similar answers about their traits over a one-month period, indicating that they had established stable self-concepts. Eder argued that minimally, "these children possessed an elaborate self-concept enabling them to recognize behaviors and emotions as being consistent or inconsistent with their self-concept."

Children are not only able to apply trait labels to themselves, they also understand the specific meanings of traits. Nicola Yuill and Anna Pearson of the University of Sussex read stories to three- to seven-year-old children and asked them to name a trait that described a story's main character. In one story, Mary kept her toys to herself and ate up all the sweets without sharing them. Children were able to label Mary as selfish (as opposed to untruthful) far more than at chance levels. Similarly, after a story about Tommy, who made his friends giggle, they understood that he was a bit of a show-off.

The children were also able to use the information to predict how others might feel: children in Yuille's study who recognized that Mary was selfish further understood that she would be unhappy if she had to share her computer with other children; they also knew that Mary's selfishness wasn't helpful to predict whether she would want to participate in a fun run. Children could perform better than chance by three years old and reached high levels of accuracy by five years of age and beyond.

Regarding self-knowledge, Sarah Burton and Peter Mitchell of the University of Nottingham asked five-, seven-, and ten-year-old children questions such as "Who knows best what you are thinking?" and "Who knows best what you want for your birthday?" Five-year-olds typically told the researchers that parents and teachers knew best what they were thinking and what they wanted for their birthdays. By seven years of age, however, most children realized that their own mothers understood their preferences better than other children's mothers or their teachers, and moreover that they themselves often knew what they wanted best. In other words, a powerful growth curve was evident in how these and similar questions were answered.

Children who learn more quickly about personality put it to use in understanding their peers. Researchers at Leiden University examined children's use of personality traits in social decision-making. First, they asked each child (in private) who they most and least wanted to play with. Based on the responses, the researchers divided the four- to six-year-old children into popular, average, and socially rejected children. Next, they told children a story about John, who had been playing with blocks, putting them together to make as tall a tower as he could. And while he played, another boy approached, described in one condition as "patient and nice" and in another as "often bossy." The children were then asked to guess what the new boy would do. Many of the popular children predicted that the nice boy would want to play with John, but the bossy boy might knock down his tower. Children of average or socially rejected popularity, however, were less logical in their reasoning, guessing that the "bossy" child would play nicely and the "patient and nice" boy would knock down the tower. Perhaps the popular kids became that way by better understanding their classmates and by choosing kind children as their friends. And less popular children may unwittingly spend more time with domineering or troubled classmates because they understand their peers less well.

Knowing the ins and outs of the young people around them can be crucial to a child's well-being. Geoffrey Canada grew up amid the increasing violence in New York City in the 1970s and 1980s, and became versed both in surviving the puzzles of family life and the dangers on the street. One day his two older brothers, then five and six years old, returned home and told their mother that a neighborhood child had stolen the five-year-old's jacket. Geoffrey watched as his mother commanded his brothers to find the boy and demand the jacket back, even if it involved fighting the child for it. Reluctantly, his brothers did as they were told and succeeded in reclaiming the jacket. Geoffrey was impressed but he found violence repugnant. He decided that if someone ever took his jacket, he would tell his mother he'd lost it instead, because a child who told the truth in that circumstance "might be in danger of getting your face punched in by some boy on the streets of New York."

Canada thought long and hard about peaceful solutions to problems and with the help of his brothers was able to minimize the number of fights he engaged in as a consequence, although when he absolutely had to fight other boys, he did so. Canada went on to attend the Harvard School of Education, and eventually founded the Harlem Children's Zone, a service organization devoted to providing comprehensive support to children's development and education. Canada was challenged by the violence he witnessed to think about personality and conflict—and he succeeded in knowing himself and using his self-knowledge to promote his own survival as well as to help a new generation of children grow up with greater safety.

Although there are many resilient children in the world who can learn about their personality on their own, psychologists also believe that certain environments foster such self-discovery better than others. For example, researchers studied children's intrinsic motives in the classroom by giving a group of ten- and eleven-year-olds anagram puzzles to play with. After playtime, the researchers either directed the child's attention to his or her performance using controlling and authoritarian comments ("You solved a lot of puzzles!"), or toward their inner experience ("You looked like you were having a good time"). The researchers found that the children who were given performance feedback were less interested in playing with the anagrams and let the teacher choose their next puzzles to play with, whereas those whose attention was directed toward their inner experience preferred to choose their own anagram puzzles. Letting the children find their own way in this instance fostered their willingness and ability to pursue their own interests.

Not all of us face equally easy environments to navigate, of course. Psychologists distinguish between childhood environments that are relatively secure as opposed to those that are more harsh and risky. Children who grow up in more secure environments receive more supervision and protection from their parents, who invest more in each child. Children who grow up in less secure environments— in families disrupted by economic insecurity or by the absence of a parent—tend to exhibit "psychosocial acceleration," a faster type of development: these kids mature physically more quickly than their peers from safer environments and become sexually active at an earlier age. In this case, harshness may act as a kind of automatic accelerator of maturity to help the person cope with insecure environments.

Jay Belsky of the University of California, Davis, along with colleagues at the University of Arizona, found such patterns in a large-sample study of children's lives. They analyzed data from 1,364 mothers and their children who were part of the NICHD Study of Early Child Care and Youth. Within the study, risky surroundings were assessed according to the children's environmental harshness and lack of predictability during the first five years of their lives. The researchers labeled the family environment as harsh if the family's income was low relative to its basic needs during that time; and they labeled the family environment as unpredictable to the degree that the parents changed residences or experienced job changes, and according to the number of times the father or other male parental figure left from or reappeared in the family home over the child's first five years. The team followed the families from the children's infancy to their adolescence, examining the age of menarche for the girls and the sexual activity of the adolescents, among other factors. As predicted, girls who faced a harsh and unpredictable environment had their periods earlier than the other girls, and both girls and boys raised in such risky environments had more sexual partners than children reared in more secure homes.

These researchers have suggested that the children in their study adapted to their environments in ways to benefit their own survival and success. Young people whose development is accelerated tend to optimize their survival and reproduction for the short term by maturing and parenting earlier, but risk worse long-term outcomes. By contrast, children with a slower style engage in longer-form planning that arguably allows them to contribute more to their families and society—but at the cost of achieving less in the short term.

Few people would advocate raising children in harsh environments, and besides, children in whom we invest more resources—good parenting, education, and medical care—are more likely to contribute to society on average. So columnists, bloggers, and commentators tend to criticize those who parent under harsh conditions and applaud those who create more secure environments for their offspring. For example, when Nadya Suleman gave birth to octuplets in 2009, all of whom survived, she was dubbed "Octomom" by tabloid headline writers. Suleman's octuplets added eight infants to the six children she already had to raise, for which she had earlier enlisted the help of her mother. Suleman's husband had left her earlier in the marriage and she was unemployed and on public assistance at the time. Columnists and commentators depicted her story as "dysfunctional," "over the top," and "grotesque." One journalist who visited the Suleman home reported that he was bitten by one of her children. Yet some evolutionary psychologists point out that child-rearing such as Suleman's can be understood as an adaptation to her own harsh upbringing.

A contrasting case in 2011 was of Amy Chua, a Harvard law professor and self-labeled "Tiger Mother," who penned a tribute to highly invested mothering. Sometimes serious, sometimes ruefully self-mocking, she explained that Tiger Moms "get in the trenches, putting in long grueling hours personally tutoring, training, interrogating and spying on their kids." Although some Tiger Moms were Chinese mothers, according to Chua they could be of any ethnicity or nationality. In her vivid description of this child-rearing style,

> if a Chinese child gets a B—which would never happen—there would first be a screaming, hair-tearing explosion. The devastated Chinese mother would then get dozens, maybe hundreds of practice tests and work through them with her child for as long as it takes to get the grade up to an A.

Chua's words raised their own controversy—whether she was too demanding and controlling of her children. Writing in *The Atlantic*, the writer and artist Sandra Tsing Loh reflected on her own similar but less extreme child-rearing practice, pleading with her readers not to hate Tiger Moms just because "we're hardworking and successful."

Parents who create secure environments and engage in slow parenting may also possess more socially valued personality characteristics, according to Aurelio Figueredo and his colleagues of the University of Arizona, Tucson. They used data from a large and representative sample of adults who were part of the "Midlife in the United States" (MIDUS) studies. They identified MIDUS survey questions that addressed three areas related to slow-style parenting: self-control, family relationships, and altruism. For example, people who endorsed "I find it helpful to set goals for the near future" reflected self-control, and those who answered the question "How much love and affection did [your mother] give you?" with "A lot" indicated their secure family bonds. Examining responses from more than two thousand parents between twenty-five and seventy-four years of age, the researchers found that the parents who created the most secure, slow-style homes also exhibited better cardiovascular fitness, more physical strength, relative freedom from disease, and more extraversion, conscientiousness, and agreeableness. Although only a few of the slow-style parents were lucky enough to have it all, their average levels on these qualities were higher than those who used accelerated styles of parenting.

Personal intelligence is likely to be expressed in both slow- and accelerated-development homes, but in different ways. Children in secure slow-style homes will be more willing to take the time to explore their interests and to invest in longer-term activities such as their schoolwork with reasonable confidence that their long-term investments will pay off. Children in accelerated-development homes, confronted by relatively starker issues of safety, survival, and reproduction, will see greater advantages in forming relationships

earlier and discounting future payoffs that might come from investing longer-term for a career or a relationship partner—they may
conclude there is little use given the uncertainty of their lives. But
they may also be willing to gamble that they can achieve greater
long-term security for themselves by investing in the future.

And harsh and secure environments are rarely as monolithic as
the research might suggest. Most children's upbringing is likely to
be betwixt and between those two extremes. For example, some
children raised in harsh surroundings who get a taste of safety may
use their personal intelligence to construct a plan to attain a more
stable life as an adult. Other children raised in apparently secure
environments might nonetheless encounter substantial doses of harshness; I'll provide examples shortly. But first, it's worth pointing out
that children growing up in any environment will benefit from discovering a sense of who they are. Once they reach adolescence in
particular, young people become particularly involved in exploring
their identities, according to the mid-twentieth-century psychologist Erik Erikson.

Erikson studied the psychology of adolescents in the public
schools of San Francisco, in schools on the East Coast, and among
Sioux and Yurok teens in Native American schools—an early cross-
cultural comparison. Erikson concluded that young people in all
these environments explored their identities during adolescence in
an attempt to decide who they were. Students in the high schools of
Erikson's time often divided up into different social groups—much
as high school students of today often split into theater kids, stoners,
goths, jocks, and geeks, among others. Erikson's explanation of this
behavior was that the students were trying on various identities to
see which one fit them best. If a teenager failed to attain a clear self-
image, Erikson believed, she might enter an identity crisis, unsure
of her core self, values, and beliefs.

Erikson had experienced such an identity crisis himself: raised
in Europe, he had dropped out of high school and spent several
years drifting aimlessly along the beaches of the Mediterranean,
trying to find some direction in his life. A series of chance encounters
along with guidance from friends eventually steered him to London

and studies with Anna Freud. Ultimately, he developed a theory of psychosocial development that viewed such identity discovery as important to a person's further growth.

A young person with a strong sense of identity may overcome a harsh environment, and personal intelligence may help both with knowing who one is and with navigating other people. Lauralee Summer, an academically gifted student, was a young person who made the transition from a harsh upbringing to a more secure young adulthood. Lauralee's mother was an eccentric who often preferred to endure joblessness and homelessness rather than pursue work, and Lauralee had no contact with her father as she was growing up. Lauralee acted in many ways I associate with personal intelligence. Among them, she recognized the advantage of checking her perceptions of people. For example, in recounting her life story, Lauralee interviewed her mother, explaining, "I may know why she is the way she is, perhaps even more than she herself may understand or speak of. But I must ask her the questions, because I tend to write too much into her silences." By asking her mother to speak for herself about why she had raised Lauralee as she had, she created a richer sense of what her mother had wanted. Among many details, her mother told Lauralee she had raised her hoping most of all she would be happy.

During her childhood, Lauralee and her mother had moved from place to place, barely able to make the rent, or staying in homeless shelters, and sometimes returning to the care of relatives in Oregon. After many difficult years, Lauralee had moved with her mother to a Boston suburb and enrolled as a freshman in Quincy High School. She excelled at Quincy at first, astonishing her fellow students by finishing first in her class at the end of the year. She suffered academic setbacks the next year, and to better meet her needs—which, fortunately, she could recognize—she found a mentor who ran an alternative program in her high school who provided her the freedom to study what she wanted; she began to excel again. On a whim, she joined the men's wrestling team—and although it was unusual, she drew strength from her involvement there.

Ultimately, Lauralee gained admission to Harvard University.

However, she found it challenging to make the transition from her prior insecure environment to the security of life in an Ivy League school. For one, although she encountered an ethnically and geographically diverse student body, unlike her, most of her roommates and classmates had led lives of privilege. Matters came to a head on Parents' Weekend in her first year. Many of her friends' parents flew into Boston to visit their children and take them out for a day of celebration; Lauralee's mother arrived by public transit from a homeless shelter, carrying all of her belongings. "From the moment I met her at the T station," Lauralee recounted, "where she emerged laden down with her duffel bags and layers of clothes, I knew that *my* Parents' Weekend would be a lot different from anyone else's." Her mother was delighted to be there but Lauralee felt ashamed about her family and resented that her mother needed to leave earlier than the other parents to be assured of a bed at her shelter.

Shortly after that, Lauralee fled the comfort of her dormitory and, accompanied by a friend, slept on the street near Harvard, reliving her homeless identity. Reliving that part of her past, she believed, cleared her head so that she could begin to integrate her former life with her new one at Harvard and develop a plan for the future. From then on she improved academically, excelled on the men's wrestling team, and graduated. Since then, she has given back to other students as a teacher in Boston's public schools. For all the chaos of her upbringing, Lauralee had enough freedom, talent, and, I suspect, personal intelligence growing up to discover who she was and to transition from a harsh to a secure environment for herself.

Even an adolescent who seems to come from a secure environment may have been controlled so severely by his parents that he can lose track of who he is. One such young man sought psychotherapy with Ed Deci of the University of Rochester. Deci described his new client as "conventionally dressed," wearing a "bland tie," appearing "inexpressive," even "tired" and "robotlike." The young man often spoke of his father during therapy, and at one point clenched his fist while describing his father's tight authoritarian control over him. When Deci pointed out his fist, his client felt terribly uncomfortable and was unable to concentrate, leading Deci to appreciate just how powerful an authority the young man perceived his father to be. Gradually, the young man was able to discuss his feelings of being controlled by his father and to retrieve some of his younger self, and with it, some of his energy returned as well.

The freedom to explore who we are apart from overly coercive forces fosters our self-awareness. And out of our awareness, we can, if we are lucky, begin to form a sense of purpose. Seana Moran of Stanford University interviewed 270 young people between twelve and twenty-two years of age to understand when children developed a sense of purpose. In sixth grade, more than 60 percent of her sample exhibited "nonpurpose": neither a purpose in life nor engagement in a purpose. Yet a small group of sixth-graders, 16 percent, already exhibited all the signs of having a purpose. This percentage increased substantially among the college-age students. It seems likely that children who heard about life purposes—from their parents, teachers, and reading—and who then thought about their own direction in life were likely to begin to form a sense of personal mission.

Professors John Clausen and Constance Jones observed a group of high school students they believed had more organized, better-developed personalities compared with their peers. They described these students as possessing "planful competence"—a combination of self-confidence, intellectual power, and dependability. Only some teens achieved this planful competence by their senior year. They were described by interviewers as "satisfied with self," "calm, relaxed in manner," and "introspective." They exhibited "high . . . intellectual capacity" and were "dependable and responsible." Those lower in such competencies were "fearful," "self-pitying," "uncomfortable with uncertainty," "conventional," "self-defeating," and "rebellious."

Thirty years later, having reached middle adulthood, the difference between the two groups was still clear: the students who had exhibited planful competence in high school were relatively stable in their personalities, coping well with life stressors, including unexpected occupational changes and marital separation or divorce. By

contrast, those lower in planful competence were more often buf-
feted in life, and when they met obstacles or changed themselves,
the trajectory of their new directions seemed less well planned and
less predictable.

Clausen and Jones's study indicates that children who are more
introspective and planful in high school do better later in their lives.
Would it be possible to teach young people about personality to improve their futures? Joseph Durlak, Roger Weissberg, and their colleagues conducted a meta-analysis of 213 studies of school-based
intervention programs that taught lessons about personality, published between 1955 and 2007 and involving 270,034 students. The
educational programs taught "self-awareness, self-management,
social awareness, relationship skills, and responsible decision making." Durlak and his colleagues' analysis of the programs indicated
that students who were taught about personality-relevant topics, relative to those in the control groups, improved their social skills and
attitudes, had fewer conduct problems, and in some instances performed better academically as well.

We can see, by referring to an earlier study of emotional intelligence in adolescence (there is no parallel study of personal intelligence as of yet), how personal intelligence might help adolescents
engage healthily with other people. Compared with personal intelligence, emotional intelligence involves the more specific ability to
perceive, understand, and reason about emotion; it's a more focused
class of reasoning that centers on a discrete set of feeling states
and the key interactions among them, and may draw on somewhat
different brain areas than does personal intelligence. That acknowledged, research in my lab indicates that people who better
understand emotions have an advantage in understanding personality as well. This shouldn't be surprising, because emotions, along
with motivations, cognitions, self-control, and other qualities, are
part of personality.

Regarding the adolescents, Donna Perkins of the University of
New Hampshire had asked them to write about a time when their
friends had pressured them to do something they were uncomfortable with. Two participants—a young woman and young man—both

had high verbal IQs, but they varied in their ability to understand hot information, focused on emotions in this instance. The young man's skills at reasoning about emotion were relatively weak, and this impacted his social life. He described a conflict that was precipitated when his friends demanded he beat someone up. He reported: "Violence makes me uncomfortable (but I wasn't a pacifist). I love nature and always think about what pain I am causing someone even if I try not to." Although he resisted, his friends compelled him to fight the other student, and "I fought so that I would never harm him." Despite his high verbal abilities and his discussion of the principles of nonviolence, the young man never reported what the fight was about, how or why his friends compelled him to fight, or why these young men remained his friends (if they did). We believe these omissions may reflect that the information was both overly complex and too personally threatening for him to think through: he may have felt too ashamed, too fearful, and too worried about how other people would judge him—and this impeded his reasoning.

By contrast, the young woman who tested high in emotional intelligence provided an account of an experience that was full of details about motives, relationships, and personality. Her friends wanted to sneak into someone's room and paint him while he was asleep. She related:

> It began as joking around ("Wouldn't this be funny? Could you believe it if?"). Then it slowly evolved into dares ("I bet you wouldn't," or "I dare you to"). I felt like it was betraying the trust I had with the other person. I didn't feel right with sneaking up on a sleeping person with no way to defend himself, and . . . I know how little pranks like this could really . . . make them feel like everyone is making fun of them, taking away their dignity . . . [How did you handle it?] Told them straight out that was a degrading thing to do and they shouldn't be so cruel.

Adolescents vary dramatically in their ability to reason about their own and other's personalities. And by the time young people of college age take the Test of Personal Intelligence, they show marked differences in their skill levels. But the differences in their learning have started much earlier in their childhood. Starting by three years of age, children are beginning to understand the states of mind of those around them; as they mature they pick up the language of traits, adjust to their environment, be it harsh or secure, and form the beginning of a sense of identity. Fortified by their learning about personality, they are poised to meet the challenges of adulthood, though some do so better than others. In the next chapter, I'll examine how, as adults, our understanding of personality continues to contribute to our lives.

7

PERSONAL INTELLIGENCE IN ADULTHOOD

I once asked participants in a study which of several "big questions" about personality they found most interesting. "Who am I?" came in second highest—and it's no wonder that questions of our identity are so intriguing: if we truly knew who we were and what our purpose was, it would make our decisions much easier because we'd know which choices fit us best. And these questions have been of interest throughout history, including to teachers of the ancient world. Around 250 BCE, for example, Kohelet (Ecclesiastes), of the Hebrew Bible, asked himself what was the best way to live. Kohelet had devoted himself by turns to scholarship, to pleasure-seeking, to acquiring property, and to religion, all with the hope of deciding "what was best for the children of men to do under the heavens for the few days of their life." Today, just as then, questions like these simply fascinate us.

The first-place winner in my study of interesting big questions related to personality was "What is my future?" This was a good question to be intrigued by, according to the psychologists Philip Zimbardo and John Boyd, who believe that people who wonder about their futures exhibit an especially healthy form of curiosity. Zimbardo and Boyd have studied the degree to which people focus on their past, present, or future—what they refer to as an individual's time perspective. People who live in the present, as opposed to wondering about their future, may enjoy the spontaneity and freedom that such in-the-moment styles allow, and many do quite well living that way, but those who are most present-oriented also have a greater likelihood than others of engaging in risky behaviors such as abusing drugs. By comparison, those of us who focus more on what lies ahead often shape our lives in ways that make good sense for our future.

Planning ahead wouldn't be so interesting, I think, except that many of us really *identify* with our future selves. By "identify," I mean that we care for the individual we will become, and lay the groundwork to make that later version of us as comfortable and successful as possible. People with higher personal intelligence may construct more vivid, elaborated future selves than others, and better take on the stewardship of their present lives, so as to guide themselves toward their goals.

Hal Ersner-Hershfield and his colleagues at Stanford University developed a simple method to record our sense of connection to the later versions of who we are. Participants were shown a continuum of seven pairs of circles. Each pair included one circle labeled "current self" and the other, "future self." On this seven-point scale, the first pair of current- and future-self circles didn't overlap at all, indicating that a person saw little relationship between who she was at present and the person she might become. Each pair overlapped a bit more until the final, seventh pair of selves, which decisively overlapped. Participants selected an alternative along the continuum to indicate how connected they were to their later selves. Some people perceived their present self as separate from their prospective self (the first pair); others chose the most overlapping pair to indicate their strong ties to who they would become.

Among the adults sampled from the San Francisco Bay Area, those who most identified with their future selves had planned their lives with longer-term payoffs in mind: for one, they saved more money and as a consequence had amassed more wealth than others. Ersner-Hershfield concluded that envisioning our future selves and feeling connected to who we will become guides our behaviors in the here and now in ways that will create longer-term rewards in the economic realm of our lives—the focus of the study—but also, more speculatively, in longer-term investments in education and family life.

In theory we can create as many future versions of ourselves as we like, limited only by our imagination. But the more fanciful, whimsical, or wishful visions of ourselves, although useful for brainstorming, may be unhelpful if we lack the personal intelligence to identify those selves we hope to become that are plausible. And to be reasonable, those imagined selves ought to plausibly join together our actual personality of today with our likely circumstances over time, and the person we can realistically hope to grow into.

E. Tory Higgins, a professor at Columbia University, has explored the relationships among several of our most common self-images: he asks participants to list qualities of their actual selves, of the ideal selves they would like to become, and of their "ought" selves—the selves *other* people think they should be. Participants whose actual selves were quite different from their ought selves—signaling that they were failing to meet others' expectations—experienced more agitation and fear, and perceived more threats to themselves. Participants whose actual selves were distant from their ideal selves—who weren't what they wanted to be—were more prone to disappointment and sadness. Although it isn't pleasant to be in those negative states, they can serve as a "heads-up" signal—alerting us to get closer to our goals or to meet others' expectations.

Certain periods of our lives may promote the pursuit of one possible self over another. For example, becoming a new parent is a time to fulfill "oughts" for many of us. New parents who are focused on living up to others' expectations of them during their newborn's first several months may make a more comfortable transition to parenthood than those who are focused on their ideal selves. During those early months of child-rearing, parents who are attuned to society's expectations of them as caretakers may take considerable pleasure in their new role as parents and in fulfilling their own parents' hope for grandchildren. By comparison, new parents who focus on their ideal selves tend to feel dejected as the demands of parenting delay their hoped-for course of development. When the demands of parenting a newborn lessen a bit and parents catch up on their sleep, they can more readily return to the pursuit of their ideal selves as the opportunities emerge.

When we imagine our ideal selves, we often see ourselves fulfilling a life dream, according to Daniel Levinson and his team at Yale University. From the 1960s to the 1980s, they had followed forty men from four occupational groups: blue- and white-collar workers in industry, business executives, academic biologists, and novelists. The team conducted multiple interviews with each man, and studied the biographies of additional public figures as well to round out their data-gathering. A number of the men pursued a dream they formed during high school or college that crystallized their motives moving forward. Levinson and his colleagues observed: "This Dream is usually articulated within an occupational context—for example, becoming a great novelist, winning the Nobel Prize (a common Dream of our biologists), contributing in some way to human welfare, and so on." Looking over the men's lives during the study, Levinson and his colleagues viewed the dream as a directional force that could be ignored only at peril to the person's development, and that would resurface if not attended to. As they put it:

> Major shifts in life direction at subsequent ages are often occasioned by a . . . sense of betrayal or compromise of the Dream. That is, very often in the crises that occur at age 30, 40, or later a major issue is the reactivation of the guiding Dream . . . that goes back to adolescence or the early 20's, and the concern with its failure.

Young people's dreams often include not only who they want to become but also a sense of purpose. After the 2008 economic downturn, students at Harvard Business School asked one of their professors, Clayton Christensen, to give them advice about how to live their lives in the future. Christensen often teaches his classes by analyzing case studies, and in this instance he drew on his own personal history to illustrate the importance of an individual's overall intentions:

When I was a Rhodes scholar, I was in a very demanding academic program, trying to cram an extra year's worth of work into my time at Oxford. I decided to spend an hour every night reading, thinking, and praying about why God put me on this earth. That was a very challenging commitment to keep, because every hour I spent doing that, I wasn't studying applied econometrics. I was conflicted about whether I could really afford to take that time away from my studies, but I stuck with it—and ultimately figured out the purpose of my life. Had I instead spent that hour each day learning the latest techniques for mastering the problems of autocorrelation in regression analysis, I would have badly misspent my life. I apply the tools of econometrics a few times a year, but I apply my knowledge of the purpose of my life every day. It's the single most useful thing I've ever learned.

Christensen allocated his efforts at Oxford across two different pursuits: high achievement in economics, on the one hand, and self-knowledge, on the other. As Christensen implied, we must weigh multiple values in choosing a direction. Two people with different sets of values will use their personal intelligence in different ways and to different effects. And, as observers using our personal intelligence, we familiarize ourselves with the range of values people use to guide their lives, because knowing a person's values helps to explain why they make the choices they do. We can't understand someone who values their family highly if we focus only on their work performance.

Shalom Schwartz of the Hebrew University of Jerusalem worked with an international team of researchers to examine the values that people use around the world. In the survey Schwartz developed, respondents are asked to indicate, for example, how much they are like a man who believes that being creative is important to him, or like a woman who wants people to do what she says. Each question was designed to reflect a specific value. Schwartz and his colleagues believe that respondents for whom "being creative is important" valued self-directed, independent thinking; other respondents who chose "wants people to do what she says" more generally sought opportunities for personal power. The team identified nineteen values, including self-directed thinking and seeking personal power, they thought were recognized around the world. They arranged the values in a circular pattern, constructing classes of similar aspirations out of specific values that neighbor one another.

The four "compass points" of the circle organize these universals. At the north of the compass is a universalistic orientation, which includes tolerance ("He works to promote tolerance and peace") and self-directed thought (or creativity). To the east is an area of hedonism ("Enjoying life's pleasures is important to him") and personal achievement in the eyes of others ("She wants people to admire her achievements"). Moving southeast, one can find dominance ("She wants people to do what she says"). To the south is a belief in the importance of security and safety ("Having order and stability in society is important to her"), and to the west are humility and caring ("He tries always to be responsive to the needs of his family and friends"). Each of us does better if we know which way our inner compass points. Then we can apply our personal intelligence to make sure we are proceeding in tune with what we most care about.

The values we emphasize may lead us to excel in one area of our life and fall short in another. People with personal intelligence are likely better at recognizing such compromises ahead of time—and understanding the trade-offs they prefer for themselves. Ravenna Helson and Sanjay Srivastava studied a number of women who varied in the values they pursued over their lives. The psychologists divided the women into four groups: seekers, conservers, achievers, and "depleteds." The seekers wanted personal growth and to think for themselves (they would be toward the north of Schwartz's compass). The conservers valued tradition, family, security, and hard work (toward the southwest of the compass). The achievers wanted both personal growth and to excel at what they did (covering an area from the north to the east). The fourth group, the depleteds, were so-called because they no longer sought either personal growth or achievement, or much of any other direction.

When the groups were compared, it was the conservers who had the highest well-being. By comparison, the achievers and seekers were about average. Seekers felt most creatively involved on the job, but the achievers were happiest overall with their job security and benefits than people in the other categories. The most striking lesson that emerged from the study concerned the depleted group, who most lacked a purpose: they scored well below the other groups in life satisfaction. Their status indicates how important it is for us to develop and maintain a mentally energized pursuit of what we value in life.

I don't want to leave the impression that we always strictly, rationally choose a value system and then logically deduce the best ways to live our lives from what we prize. That may sometimes be true, but it is equally the case that many of us act first in ways that are consistent with our motives, hopes, and desires, and then learn to describe our actions by selecting a value system that corresponds to what we do. That is, we may reason from our values, but we also pick values that seem to fit our behavior. There's nothing wrong with choosing values we like, because the universal values discussed here all have clearly positive aspects; they exclude unvalued human desires such as to coerce others, or to steal from them, or to harm them. In principle, at least, whatever universal values we choose to follow can contribute both to our own well-being and, more broadly, to society, so long as we apply them thoughtfully.

Clayton Christensen used his religious background to clarify his values and then lived by them. David Brooks, the *New York Times* columnist, admired Christensen's discovery of his purpose but reminded his own readers that the account might be quite a distance from the norm when it comes to young people:

A 24-year-old can't sit down and define the purpose of life in the manner of a school exercise because she is not yet deep enough into the landscape to know herself or her purpose. That young person—or any person—can't see into the future to know what wars, loves, diseases and chances may loom. She may know concepts, like parenthood or old age, but she doesn't really understand their meanings until she is engaged in them.

Young people in their mid-twenties have typically completed their undergraduate degrees, are pursuing work or graduate education, and are trying to establish a sense of direction; psychologists often refer to them as emerging adults. Shmuel Shulman of Bar Ilan University and his colleagues interviewed seventy emerging adults (fifty-three employed) with an average age of twenty-four about their self-knowledge and behavior; they identified three types of maturation among their interviewees. The first group, which the researchers called "Low integrated," seemed unable to reflect on themselves and lacked clarity as to their direction. One participant in that group summarized her present thinking as "Confusion. I do many things to get out of this confusion, but . . . it is mostly . . . confusion and I do not know what will come of it in the end." Members of the second group, labeled "Acting competent/low authenticity," acted so as to please other people rather than having a strong sense of self; said one:

> "My parents, though they are very close to me, they don't really know who I am. I behave, let's say, when I am at my parents' place according to their expectations . . . At other places . . . I act according to the context or according to how they would like to see me."

Members of the last group were integrated and able to discuss themselves clearly, with a sense of who they were and hoped to become. For example, one young man said, "It is possible that some matters could be balanced differently, but basically I feel I am capable of including into my life aspects I want to, and I hope I am able to do it in the future." This group has applied personal intelligence to understanding their personal needs and integrated them in their social activities.

The integrated group is likely to fare better than the low-authenticity group over time. Knowing our own direction—

something personal intelligence facilitates—is elemental over the long term for making decisions. For Levinson, we won't be happy if we achieve someone else's goals on someone else's terms: "It is not a matter of how many rewards one has obtained; it is a matter of the *goodness of fit between the life structure and the self.*"

Once we have a sense of direction, a next level in attaining our goals and fulfilling our purpose is to take steps to meet our aims. Since we were children, most of us have made small choices that guided our activities: we chose our friends and who to spend time with, what games to play, and when to do our homework. As we grew, our decisions influenced larger pieces of our lives: we participated in deciding what classes to take in high school and when to get our driver's license, and chose what our first job should be. As we guided ourselves in these small ways, we honed our skills in deciding what worked for us and what didn't.

To become the people we wish to be, we learn how to plan by setting short-term and intermediate goals. Some people are better at such goal-setting than others—they're better able to choose aims that are consistent with one another and to avoid contradictory pursuits as much as possible. The psychologists Robert Emmons and Laura King refer to our medium-term plans as our "personal strivings," and most of us pursue several of them at a time. Sometimes our strivings are related to one another, as with a young professional who wants to get promoted at work and move to a bigger apartment in a safer area. At other times, our strivings may be more independent of one another but can still be carried out with little conflict, such as in a person who wants to meet new people through present friends and to accept others as they are. But a group of us are prone to set goals that conflict with one another, like the participant in Emmons and King's study who hoped both "to appear more intelligent than I am" and "to always present myself in an honest light"; or another participant of theirs who wanted both "to keep my relationships on a 50-50 basis" and "to dominate, control, and manipulate people and situations." Having the skill to set goals that go well together is a net plus: people with nonconflicting aims experience less inner turmoil and greater overall well-being. Participants also had greater well-being if they perceived that their plans were autonomous rather than being imposed from the outside by parents, teachers, or supervisors.

The Test of Personal Intelligence (TOPI) that I've developed with my colleagues David Caruso and A. T. Panter includes a measure of the ability to reason about specific goals. For example, we ask questions such as:

Which goal would be problematic to meet for most people?
a. To become educated in an area that would satisfy one's curiosity
b. To be adequate and competent in all areas of one's life
c. To make new friends
d. To work hard at one's job

People higher in personal intelligence identify "b" as the troublesome alternative. They recognize the near impossibility for most people of fulfilling such an aim. Option "b" is, in fact, drawn from a list of irrational beliefs compiled by Albert Ellis, the founder of Rational-Emotive Therapy, who studied his clients' illogical lines of thinking, which he believed interfered with their well-being. His clients' undermining ideas, he wrote, frequently included that they "must be perfectly competent, adequate, talented, and intelligent in all possible respects and [that they would be] . . . utterly worthless . . . unless that criterion is met." Because people high in personal intelligence recognize the basics of setting reasonable goals for themselves, they are better able to allocate their energies in useful directions rather than becoming unnecessarily tied up in knots over aims they can't meet.

Strivings create a bridge from our current status to where we want to go. But desiring an aim isn't enough by itself—we also need to attain our goals. As adults, we can use our personal intelligence to map out concrete, definable steps to move from where we are in life to where we wish to be. A team led by Daphna Oyserman of the University of Michigan's Institute for Social Research demonstrated how teaching low-income eighth-graders in a Detroit middle school about their personalities and goals could help them to stay in school and graduate. Although the study focused on eighth-graders, its central points are applicable to adults as well.

The researchers first randomly assigned the eighth-graders to a control or an experimental group; over the equivalent of a high school course, they planned to teach the students in the experimental group to plan concrete steps to help them succeed in school and go to college. Students in the control group, by contrast, enrolled in a course of their choosing from several electives offered by the school.

Most of the kids were looking forward to graduating from high school, according to an assessment by the researchers. But there was a faction of students in the school who communicated very publicly that studying wasn't cool. To counteract that group's negative attitude, the researchers explained to the participants that almost everyone in the experimental and control conditions wanted to graduate and believed it was a good thing to do—thereby legitimizing the students' goals. We ourselves use a variation of this technique whenever we find other people who support the values we do. The eighth-graders were further taught how to connect their current selves to their future image of "me, graduating." To do so, they would need to carry out the steps of attending class, studying, and doing homework. To promote their perseverance, the researchers introduced an "inoculation" to small failures: students were taught that if they didn't do well on a quiz, on an exam, or in a class, it didn't mean they were failures, but rather signaled an opportunity to keep at it. In other words, the students were given a road map for how to connect their present-day selves to future high-school-graduate selves. In a two-year follow-up, the researchers found that the students who obtained the experimental training outperformed the control group by achieving higher grades and exhibiting less problematic behavior.

In the TOPI studies, we also measure whether people know how to connect their present selves to the future. As one example, we used a question like "If Margaret wants to become better at the French horn, how could she see herself in a way that would help her attain the goal?" Some participants realized that "practicing the instrument each day" was a better answer than to "imagine she was performing with the London Philharmonic," because in this instance practice provided a bridge from her present self to the better player she wished to become, whereas imagining performing with the Philharmonic may be inspiring (or intimidating), but it lacks the steps needed to get there. People who understand how to connect with their possible selves in this way score higher on the TOPI, suggesting that those of us high in the ability choose steps that move us toward our life objectives.

Some people are unable to formulate the actions necessary to meet their goals. For example, Sabrina was a thirty-three-year-old call-center worker who had participated in a study by Professor Ranji Devadason of the University of Bristol. Sabrina hoped to seek artistic employment as a set designer, but in an interview for the study, she expressed confusion about how to attain her goals:

> I haven't really got any future plans, I have lots of future hopes, I hope that I'm going to be more focused and more motivated, and yeah, I do plan to do something about that really—about getting more sorted.

Sabrina's hopes by themselves, however, wouldn't help to achieve her dreams—she hadn't worked out the steps. By contrast, a thirty-one-year-old former teacher in the same study planned effectively for her wants and needs. She had left her teaching position to enroll in school for additional training:

> I'd like to get a more interesting and fulfilling job, which is why I'm doing the course that I'm doing in the hope that I'm going to retrain. And I want to earn more money . . . and I want to have more control over my working life . . . so that I can combine my family and work, basically.

Less effective planners such as Sabrina may need to reinvent themselves at a later time, often more than once, and sometimes drastically until they construct a well-worked-out plan to attain the objectives they hope for. Although such reinvention can be exciting, it can nonetheless be costly in terms of time and resources. If we fail to mark out the steps to get where we would like to go, as did Sabrina, or choose a career that simply doesn't fit us, it's best to change course earlier rather than later, according to Levinson and his colleagues. Each year that people like Sabrina stay at their jobs hoping for something better, their desired goals may slip further away. By contrast, the teacher who was shifting careers arguably did so at a young enough age to benefit from the change. But wish as we might to plan, it isn't always clear when we should make a change in our lives: we can't know what our future might bring—and that can leave us facing a choice point with no clear idea as to which of our alternatives is best.

In such uncertain circumstances, argued Charles Lindblom of Yale, we often have little choice but to muddle through, but that can be a good thing. Lindblom was describing the choices of professional administrators but I'll take some liberty with his theory, as I believe it can be applied to everyday life as well. Imagine we encounter a life coach who advised his client, Margaret, to write down her values, goals, and purposes to assist her in making her everyday decisions. Margaret wrote down that she was passionate about her work at her legal firm and especially about the high-profile legal cases she was handling. Next on her list was her family, and her purpose was to support her family by earning money for them. Our life coach then instructed Margaret to make decisions about how long to stay at work and when to be home, based on her preferred values and direction. For example, Margaret decided that she should try to be home by 6:30 p.m. on weekdays, and her husband agreed that if possible he would take their daughter to any after-school appointments that arose during the week. Although Margaret had planned an after-school birthday party for her daughter for which she expected to leave work early, she generally intended to follow the guidelines she had set up with her coach to put achievement first.

Lindblom would argue that the coach's recommendations are not so different from those found in certain self-help books by recognized experts in the field.

But no one really makes decisions that way, Lindblom argues, nor should they. Rather, we think about how we have chosen in the past, consider the alternatives available to us, and maybe discuss them with people we trust; then we select the best choices relevant to the goals at hand. No one can state in absolute terms one value they prefer over another, Lindblom would say; rather, decisions take place in context. Margaret said she had a passion for professional achievement; and when she discovered a flaw in one of her legal arguments, she was ready to devote the hours necessary to fix it—except that it was the morning before her daughter's party. She decided to attend the celebration because she knew how important it was to her nine-year-old and for herself. So she alerted her coworkers on the case and hoped to rework the legal brief later, even though the reduced time would be less than ideal, violating the principle she had worked out with her life coach.

Too much about our decision-making is contextual for us to make much use of abstract principles alone, Lindblom argues. We can't really weigh our need for achievement against family values until a specific choice arises. Moreover, we have only imperfect knowledge of whether the choices we make are right—can Margaret really be sure her choice to leave work for the birthday party was correct? She can't, because she doesn't know how things would have turned out if she had stayed at work—there's no control condition in life! The best she can do is to achieve a consensus, if possible, among her colleagues at work, her daughter, and her family and friends, that her choices seem reasonable and prudent.

Although we may muddle through, we can try to improve our practices, seeking to do things a little bit better than we have in the past—hoping these incremental adjustments move us toward our desired future (perhaps Margaret will decide going forward that weekends work best for birthday parties). I suspect this tinkering approach helps us manage our motives, values, and plans so that they coalesce into a better-functioning system.

•

Whatever strategies we use to plan our lives—clearly formulating plans and choosing by principle, or just muddling through—we rarely will be able to fit ourselves into our environments just so. As Daniel Levinson and his colleagues put it in their study of men's lives:

> In creating an integrated life structure, one can utilize only parts of one's self, and this means that important parts of the self are left out . . . The structure one creates in early adulthood cannot fulfill or reflect all of oneself. Parts of the self are repressed or simply left dormant. At some point the life structure must be enlarged, reformed, or radically restructured in order to express more of the self.

As we proceed with our lives, in other words, we may well want to explore new alternatives along the way to rejuvenate the parts of ourselves that we had neglected earlier. That said, it helps to envision an overall plan.

Earlier, I spoke about using personal intelligence to identify steps we can use to meet our short-term and intermediate goals. We also employ our abilities to fit our goals together into a longer-term plan for our lives—one that takes into account the sweep of our development as adults. That is, we order our goals over our life span—college, graduate training, getting married, having children, or whatever they may be. The sociologist Bernice Neugarten pointed out that members of society hold expectations of what people should have accomplished by certain points in their lives, and we are all bound to live according to those expectations (although some of us may be unable to meet others' expectations or choose not to). Sociologists refer to the schedule by which our life events unfold as our "social clock" pattern. Neugarten believed that people who adhered to a time frame that the people around them understood would experience life as less stressful than those who violated such expectations: "Men and women compare themselves with their friends, siblings, work colleagues, or parents in deciding whether they have made good, but it is always with a time line in mind." Evidence backs up this idea that living "on the clock" is helpful.

Ravenna Helson of the University of California, Berkeley, and her colleagues studied social clock patterns in a longitudinal sample of women born toward the end of the Great Depression. Helson's group graduated from Mills College in the classes of 1958 and 1960. The end of the 1950s was a historical moment of unprecedented uniformity of expectations. At the time, many women looked forward to a long-term marriage and having children (desiring four on average).

Their expectations collided with the imminent social changes of the 1960s brought about by a politically active youth culture, an increasingly assertive civil rights movement, mass opposition to the Vietnam War, and a wave of feminism focused on gender equality. As work opportunities for women opened up, some of the Mills graduates rethought their intentions and chose different life courses. Helson and her colleagues divided the women into three broad groups according to the social clocks they followed, which I'll call the Child and Family Clock, the Professional Clock, and No Social Clock.

Women following the Child and Family Clock got married and began to have children by their early to mid-twenties. Among them, the most common time for the birth of their first child was three years after graduation from college, with a fall-off of first births after six years. There was also a group of "Late Adherents" to this Child and Family Clock, whose children were born later in their twenties through their early thirties. Thirty-nine percent of this group rejoined the workforce later.

Women of the Professional Clock group engaged in an upwardly mobile career by the time they were twenty-eight, with a distinctive set of timing norms. These women undertook specific graduate and professional training, followed by pursuing an "exceedingly articulated" career path within a given occupational domain, emphasizing an ascendance across salary and status levels that continued throughout the women's work life.

Women were assigned to the No Social Clock group if they appeared to follow neither the Child and Family nor Professional Clock. These women were different from the others even at the time they graduated from college. They were lower on self-acceptance and on independence, and reported that they found it generally difficult to follow social norms, even when doing so would bring them advantages.

The women who would later follow the Child and Family and Professional clocks were surprisingly similar to one another in measured personality early on—they exhibited the same empathy, social presence, and well-being. Over time, however, the women's early choices influenced their personalities. Those who followed the Child and Family Clock became more nurturing, warm, and caring. Those who initially followed the Child and Family Clock but shifted from it due to divorce exhibited more autonomy, achievement, and assertiveness than did women who remained in unsatisfying marriages on that clock (and those in troubled marriages who stayed married had lower well-being on average). Those who followed the Professional Clock pattern also grew more in assertiveness; they also exhibited self-assurance, self-acceptance, and more social status and social presence than the others. Those in the No Social Clock group fared less well overall. Although there were a few exceptions who did better as time went on, many suffered interruptions in their employment, felt lonely, and, by their early forties, some often felt depressed and embittered.

Those on a defined social clock—whichever they chose—benefited from the structure it added to their lives. Levinson's study of adult men provides a similar picture of men off the clock—who hadn't quite kept the time periods of adult development in mind. He wrote:

> Still another variant is that of the man who during his 20's lives a rather transient, unsettled life. He then feels a desperate need at around 30 to get more order and stability in his life. It is our tentative hypothesis that if a man does not reach a significant start toward Settling Down by about age

34 his chances of forming a reasonably satisfying life structure, and one that can evolve in his further development,
are quite small.

Whether we follow a career path, or one centered at home, it is important for us to draw on the sustaining energy of our dreams, purposes, and values. Yet sometimes mistakes will be made. Levinson
and his colleagues described the individuals who encountered
difficulty:

> In some cases, the man at around 30 decided that his initial
> occupational choice was not the right one—that it is too
> constraining, or that it is a violation or betrayal of an early
> Dream which now has to be pursued, or that he does not
> have the talent to succeed in it—and he makes a major shift
> in occupation and in life structure, sometimes including
> marriage.

Even if we substantially revise our preliminary decisions as
adults, so long as our changes occur early enough in our life plans
we will be all right, according to Levinson. Being on *some kind of
clock*—following some organization and systematization—seemed
better than to be on none at all. Some systematization—some dynamic personal planning over a significant time period—helped both
Helson's women and Levinson's men succeed.

By the 1990s, college graduates exercised far more self-exploration
than that of the Mills College women or of Levinson's men—
society's social clock has been stretched out longer in the intervening
decades, reflecting the need for more education, coupled with our
increasing longevity. Surveys from the 1990s indicate that during
their mid-twenties, many young people don't yet feel like true adults,
and that they explore many more life possibilities than before: they
move and switch jobs more often, and explore their identities and
their relationships more often. Aspects of the family and work-life
clocks remain, albeit allowing for more time. Syncing our plans to
these clocks can provide helpful ways to systematize our lives.

Part of succeeding on the clocks involves understanding that some goals are so long-term that it's easy to lose track of them—but that we must nonetheless attend to those pursuits. Clayton Christensen believed that we are particularly tempted to give into projects with short-term payoffs because they are more salient, but that succumbing to them can work against us over the longer term. Christensen argued that individuals who have a high need for achievement, including the Harvard Business School students in his classes, are likely to neglect their long-term priorities. It is much easier for them to engage in activities that yield a quick payoff at work:

> You ship a product, finish a design, complete a presentation, close a sale . . . It's really not until 20 years down the road that you can put your hands on your hips and say, "I raised a good son or a good daughter." You can neglect your relationship with your spouse, and on a day-to-day basis, it doesn't seem as if things are deteriorating . . . even though intimate and loving relationships . . . are the most powerful and enduring source of happiness.

Christensen pointed out that many of his Harvard classmates attended reunions "unhappy, divorced, and alienated from their children," and yet he doubted that any of them had set goals to achieve those outcomes. What happened, as he saw it, was that they lost sight of their life purpose and failed to prioritize their relationships. (Some people may express a mirror image of this error, I think: they may become so focused on their immediate needs to be with their family and friends that they fail to achieve sufficiently in their careers to support themselves and others, yielding economic insecurities later on.) Christensen's implication is, plainly, to keep the long-term goals and purposes in mind and to be content with devoting some time to those projects, even if the payoff is not immediate, advice that corresponds well to the idea of identifying with one's future self.

If we have identified a direction that is consistent with our personal needs and goals, we usually have lots of energy to put into it.

Even so, outside challenges may demand more of us than we had imagined. Economic disruptions and threadbare social safety nets may especially call on our energies, as may home, school, or work environments that are especially challenging. Facing such challenges, we may need something extra to make it through: grit. Angela Duckworth and her colleagues at the University of Pennsylvania studied grit among first-year West Point cadets and other groups. She defined grit as a tendency to persevere coupled with a passion to meet one's goals. Test items that measure grit reflect a freedom from distractibility—gritty individuals can't be easily diverted from what they have started. Rather, they expect to overcome setbacks and to conquer important challenges. West Point has highly selective admissions standards, yet some cadets simply don't make it through their grueling first summer there. Grit predicted surviving the program and a cadet's level of achievement in it. Gritty commitment is also found among middle schoolers who make it to the highest levels in spelling-bee competitions, where grit is related to the hours a student devotes to practice, and predicts a student's ultimate performance in the competition.

As we follow our pathways, we continue to educate ourselves about personality. In general, we become increasingly influential adults—our social dominance rises, on average, through our thirties and plateaus in the two decades of our forties and fifties.* As a consequence, our ability to understand others and ourselves continues to increase in importance. The philosopher Plato reminded us that self-knowledge is crucial among people with power, to avoid abusing others (and being disliked in return). One of the best ways we have of learning about ourselves is to ask for feedback.

Not all requests for feedback are equal, according to Susan Ashford and Anne Tsui, who examined the requests made by 387 mid-level managers at a public service organization. For their study,

---

*The study I'm reporting didn't include enough individuals at older ages to draw any conclusions about social dominance in the sixties or beyond.

supervisors, peers, and subordinates all observed a given manager at work and described how he or she asked for feedback; each respondent also reported how well the manager performed. Ashford and Tsui found that some managers telegraph that they don't want accurate appraisals of themselves. They don't want to upset their own beliefs, and so they signal the answer they hope for to their potential critic, saying, "I've done pretty well at this job, haven't I?" Other managers really want to learn. They ask questions such as "How can I improve in this job? Please feel free to criticize my current approach." Managers who are more open about feedback were more highly regarded by their coworkers (and also scored lower on scales of defensiveness). Although these studies were situated at work, we use similar strategies in our everyday lives, asking leading questions such as "I'm a pretty good singer, aren't I?" so as to telegraph that we want support. Compare that with "I am interested in becoming a better singer. Do you have any suggestions for how I could improve?" Getting good feedback is of great value to our conduct whether at work, home, or school.

Our ability to describe who we are to others is also important to our conduct: we use brief descriptions of ourselves when we meet new people at social gatherings, on social media, and at meetings. Stephen Kaye, a leadership specialist, described a business meeting in Springfield, Illinois, in which he listened to people introduce themselves to one another. He characterized them as all sounding alike: "My name is something and I work for someone. Here's my card so you can call me." In the midst of these introductions was one that Kaye genuinely liked: a child who was sitting in the room chimed in, "I am four years old": an introduction that was clear, descriptive, and memorable.

As charming as the four-year-old's exclamation was, though, it's a reminder that most of us take a while to learn how to describe ourselves well—and that some of us are better at it than others. According to Susan Bluck and Tilmann Habermas, when we first begin to put our life stories together as children, we simply recount a sequence of events that seem important to us, like eight-year-old Bill, who was asked to tell the story of who he was. Bill jumped right in: "When I started learning to read and to write, that was important for me, and to calculate," at which point he asked if he could start earlier in his life; when encouraged to do so, he continued that when he was very small,

> I learned to walk . . . And when I first went to school, I was very, very excited.
>   —Should I tell everything I have had in life? [Interviewer: Exactly.] Okay, then I really got lots to tell. Then there was, when I was in the airplane for the first time, I was very afraid, I was excited, and then—or when I was in the hospital, I was a little— . . . I was very, very afraid to have pneumonia—or when I learned to swim, when I wasn't yet able to swim, couldn't swim . . .

Bluck and Habermas say that we learn to describe ourselves at a higher level after we realize that there is a social formula to recounting our lives, and we include key life events in our stories such as births, marriages, and divorces. At a still further level of coherence, we convey the themes of our lives—perhaps our risk-taking, our ability to learn from our mistakes, or how we're a support for our family members—and we begin to recognize the themes that identify us.

Dan McAdams of Northwestern University has been studying our life stories, and he believes that, in the United States, a key plot structure people employ to organize their lives is that of the redemption narrative. This narrative begins with a sense that one is special and is committed to a set of core values. This is followed by personal suffering, and eventually the relief of that suffering. The redemption comes as we move beyond our own struggle to help others. McAdams recounted the example of Rob McGowan, a screenwriter and research participant. McGowan grew up in a West Virginia mining town as one of five children of a gambling, ne'er-do-well father and a mother prone to theatricality—she practiced throwing knives at a picture of their father. Ultimately, the children were assigned to foster care and Rob was fortunate to be placed in a stable home and to be recognized by a teacher for his talents as a writer.

As a young man, Rob moved to New York City and took acting and writing classes; he was hired as a television actor, but also became involved with drugs. In a series of interrelated turning points in his life, he met his future wife, quit the television show on which he worked, and he and his wife-to-be left New York City for the southwestern United States. There he focused on screenwriting and his wife painted. He committed himself to helping the next generation and, after some struggle to have children of their own, his wife and he adopted two children. He devoted himself to his family and to his community. Reviewing the people who had helped him and his family, McGowan concluded that he had learned "how many good people there are in the world." When asked to look back over his story and identify a theme, he answered, "I guess for me if you had to distill it into a nutshell, it would be redemption."

McAdams traces the large number of redemption stories he hears to the cultural belief—stemming from American Transcendentalists such as Ralph Waldo Emerson and Henry David Thoreau—that people are inherently good and should strive for self-reliance. Many of McAdams's more fortunate research participants tell their stories this way—expressing the feeling of being special, overcoming struggles, and then going on to help others.

By comparison, some of us tell tales of an early misfortune from which we never have recovered; we often view parents and authority figures as uncaring or exploitative. Rather than overcoming these setbacks, these adults view themselves as repeating the same troublesome behavior, unable to break the cycle: a middle-aged man recounted that he was unable to commit himself to a wonderful woman—who ultimately left him on that account—and that he had made the same mistake since with new women he met. A woman described how she refused people's offers of help over the course of her life, only to descend into desperate circumstances as time passed. People's stories of themselves—and the themes they express—often contain ready-made prognostications as to their own futures, and we would do well to pay attention to them. Our personal intelligence adds to our ability to listen for these stories and to understand their meanings.

Good personal stories also serve the purpose of inspiring our own activities. We can recall a past event to motivate us in a new situation. For example, when the basketball star Michael Jordan felt he wasn't playing hard enough, he often recalled the time he failed to make the high school basketball team in his sophomore year:

> It was embarrassing, not making that team. They posted the roster and it was there for a long, long time without my name on it. I remember being really mad, too, because there was a guy who made it that really wasn't as good as me . . . Whenever I was working out and got tired and figured I ought to stop, I'd close my eyes and see that list in the locker room without my name on it, and that usually got me going again.

Jordan isn't alone in using such motivating memories. In one study, many individuals reported that self-motivation is a principal factor in why they recall events from their lives, but so is self-improvement: one person recalled certain memories "when I want to learn from my past mistakes," and another said he reminisced so that "when . . . I think about something bad that happened I can learn some lesson from it." People also said they recalled earlier events to gain confidence, make a life choice, or better understand their lives.

Some people use memories of their family history to create a cross-generational drama. As a child, Robert Russa Moton subsisted by working on a plantation just after the Civil War. But his grandmother told him he was descended from a prince who was captured shipside at an African port by traders and sold into slavery upon reaching the United States. Inspired by such stories, and with the support of his parents, Moton worked hard in the local school and ultimately left the plantation and his former life to pursue further education. He became an educator of African-American youth during his adulthood, helping others gain the advantages he had obtained for himself. Having thrived despite the overt racism of the time, Moton went on to inspire others:

> In all the years of my experience I have found that a great deal more is accomplished when one does not permit himself to dwell overmuch upon the difficulties and discouragements which he encounters, but keeps constantly before his mind those forces and influences which make for the removal of the very obstacles which often hamper his progress.

Perhaps the most sophisticated level of recounting our autobiographies involves identifying the pattern of influences that help explain our life stories. As we learn the causes of our behaviors, we have the opportunity to better control ourselves because we can minimize triggers of bad behavior, and seek environments that promote good acts. As we learn about the consequences of our actions over time, in turn, we have a better basis for making choices. We begin to develop a sense of wisdom through appreciating both the impact we have on others and the limits of that impact. Remember a time in your life you thought, did, or said something wise? Researchers have asked people to recall such situations and they have found that wisdom often involves the capacity to empathize with and support others, to assert oneself when necessary, and to develop knowledge and flexibility.

We use our personal intelligence to construct a meaning that knits together our direction, values, and purpose until they coalesce into a meaningful organization of our life. We draw on our feelings and values for direction; we plan over time and fit those plans approximately to a socially comprehensible sequence. Personal intelligence helps us know when to change course, and when to exhibit grit and perseverance. There is enough leeway in how we do this that creating a life story is in many ways like creating a work of art. The shape of our life emerges and the many parts of our personalities may coalesce in surprising ways that we never imagined when we were younger.

The life of the great painter and art instructor Robert Henri provides one example of such a coalescence. Henri was an early-twentieth-century artist whose works today can be found in the Metropolitan Museum of Art and the National Gallery of Art. But he didn't have a future goal to be an artist when he was a child. His father had moved his family to Atlantic City when Henri was still a boy. As his father began to invest in real estate, Henri put himself to work painting "For Sale" signs that included depictions of the properties that his father put on the market. Henri used his skills at painting to help his father; this helpfulness was modest in its scope, but provided the beginning of his life's direction.

During his youth, Henri seemed to follow a muddling-through approach to decision-making—redirecting his activities in small ways as he matured. For example, his friends admired the quality of the "For Sale" signs he painted, and, listening to their feedback, Henri took to heart that he might have some talent, and enrolled in art school in Philadelphia. The school's faculty observed his substantial gifts, and some of them suggested he travel to Paris for further study. With the support of his family, Henri increased his commitment to painting and set sail for France. In Paris, museum curators took note of his exceptional promise; one displayed his paintings at the Luxembourg Museum, an unusual honor for an American. Returning home, Henri attracted the attention of younger illustrators and would-be painters and found himself willingly teaching them.

Shortly after beginning as an art instructor, however, the National Academy of Design rejected his students' works for its 1907 Annual Show. Displaying both grit and a willingness to help others, Henri found an opportunity in this setback: rather than passively accept the disappointment or play cautious politics in the art world, he recommitted himself to his own painting and that of his students. Drawing on his own resources, he organized a show of his seven students' works at a New York gallery, mixing in his own work as well. The show was entitled simply "The Eight." It became an art-world sensation: with its emphasis on paintings of urban settings, real-life portraiture, and inventive styles, many historians mark it as the beginning of modern art in the United States. The exhibition attracted enough visitors to become a commercial success as well.

The art critic Dorothy Grafley spoke of Henri's skill, later in his career, at capturing personalities in his artwork—an interest and ability that I believe reflected his personal intelligence. She wrote that in his portraiture, Henri "participates with vivid imagination in the motivating experiences of his subject [seeking his goal] . . . not in a likeness that someone else desires or dictates, but in character revelation . . ." Each movement of the body expressed a person's psychological meanings: "Henri would catch, in the life of an eyelid, the accent of the nostril . . . deft accents of personality."

Henri's deep understanding of personality helped him not only to shape his own career and artworks, but to unleash the talents of his students. As an instructor, Henri's style was to gently guide his own and others' goals and plans to enhance their well-being. In doing so, he shaped the careers of many of America's next generation of painters, including Edward Hopper and Rockwell Kent. Hopper said of Henri that he "was the most influential teacher I had."

Henri asked his students to paint what they felt and to paint who they were:

> The object of painting a picture is not to make a picture—however unreasonable this may sound. The picture, if a picture results, is a by-product and may be useful, valuable, interesting as a sign of what has passed. The object, which is back of every true work of art, is the attainment of a state of being, a high state of functioning, a more than ordinary moment of existence.

Henri assumed that his students practiced hard to develop their technique—but they needed something more. Perhaps he was expressing the idea that as our personal lives coalesce—as our personalities become organized and highly tuned—great things may come.

8

THE POWER OF PERSONALITY

All our actions—however great or small—emerge from the well-springs of our personalities. And we use our personal intelligence as a guide to how our personalities work. We detect clues about other people, recognize the meaning of traits, and set our goals thoughtfully. My colleagues and I have distilled portions of this problem-solving into a psychological test, and with it, we have confirmed that some of us are better at understanding people than others. Yet as important as our personalities are, each of us is just a small part of the broader world in which we live.

In his work *Leviathan*, the philosopher Thomas Hobbes described a social contract that exists between the individual and society: we each serve society by following its rules and behaving as responsible citizens, and in return we are clothed, fed, and cared for by our families and broader social institutions. Consistent with that vision, we use our personal intelligence to plan our lives: we find a direction we value, create steps to meet our goals, fit our life plan into a social sequence, and tell coherent stories about ourselves, all in the context of our social world. The better we do, the more we bring rewards to ourselves and to society more generally.

And cultural leaders and opinion makers guide our behaviors—with more personal intelligence at some times than at others. Artists create novels or videos that praise some character types while they satirize others. Psychiatrists, through the *Diagnostic and Statistical Manual of Mental Disorders*, draw lines to distinguish normal from abnormal behavior. Human-resource professionals urge us to conform to our workplace's "organizational climate." And, of course, our families have expectations of us (and we have expectations of ourselves). Each of these groups makes claims on our personalities and how we are supposed to behave.

We sometimes use our personal intelligence as a tool to understand the relationships we form with the broader society in which we live. People of the ancient world, from its philosophers to its storytellers, already used personal intelligence to aid society by guiding people in their social relations and rules to live by. For example, the "golden rule," "Treat others as you wish to be treated yourself," is an apotheosis of reasoning with personal intelligence: to formulate that advice, ancient philosophers had to recognize, first, that human beings were enough alike that, if one person viewed a given act as praiseworthy or harmful, other people would likely regard it the same way, and that, consequently, we could use our own knowledge of what we liked and disliked as a basis for how to treat others; and, moreover, that people were sufficiently capable of reflection and self-control to put the rule into practice.

Knowledge of our inner reasoning and how it works also informs our behavior in public life. Consider a politician who claims he sought the answer to a complex policy issue by looking for "the truth in his own heart." Some of the politician's search within is probably trustworthy, particularly when it comes to identifying his basic moral reactions. The psychologist Jonathan Haidt has argued, in fact, that our moral sense has evolved to guide our behavior in society. Haidt points out that our ancestors who felt moral reactions—including moral disgust and approval—were better able to cooperate with one another as a consequence and to enhance their likelihood of their survival. The politician who examined his heart for the truth is simply introspecting—from the standpoint of personal intelligence—drawing responses from his memories and emotional and other systems into awareness to assess how he felt. Yet our understanding of personality reminds us that introspection can tell us only so much. Haidt points out that people differ in their moral reactions in certain respects; some may prioritize "helping the poor," as a key goal whereas others may emphasize "security for the community"; this leaves room for discussion among ourselves and compromise.

We run into difficulties if we try to decide public policy on the basis of our inner moral sense alone, as William Reddy of Duke University pointed out with a historical example. Reddy argues that philosophers of the eighteenth and nineteenth centuries who championed sentimentalist philosophy ended up contributing—albeit unintentionally—to the violence of the French Revolution. In a nutshell, sentimentalism was the idea that a person could discern absolute truths by checking on their inner feelings and sincerely held attitudes toward a given issue. As a French intellectual of the time put it: "There was a kind of 'evidence of the heart' that was as irresistible as the 'evidence which the mind attaches to speculative truths.'"

French revolutionaries looked into their own hearts and equated what they felt with Truth—and used those truths to guide their revolution against the French monarchy. Believing that they knew the truth from looking within themselves, and that they therefore understood what was best for their country, they were unwilling to compromise with others who felt differently—even those within their own movement—whom they regarded as hypocrites. Because the truth was obviously in us all, they believed anyone who dissented from their "truth" was likely the enemy. As the revolutionaries fought among themselves as to the best way to govern France, the move-ment's leaders identified and executed more than sixteen thousand suspected "traitors to the revolution" by guillotine (and more by other means) during the bloodbath referred to as "the Terror." Many French revolutionaries discovered their innermost hearts weren't 100 percent with their new regime. The logic of personal intelli-gence tells us we can't be "sincere" under force or coercion. Reddy describes the dilemmas of the leaders:

A requirement to have certain "natural" feelings or else face the death penalty is likely to inspire furtive doubts in most people. Am I being sincere? It is always hard to say. Such doubts, under the Terror, only helped feed an escalating spiral of suspicion, because everyone felt like a hypocrite in the face of such laws.

The revolutionary bloodshed rose, and the sentimentalist project ultimately disintegrated. Looking into one's heart for moral wisdom may be helpful, but it's less wise to rely on introspection as to what feels right without the checks and balances of the rest of our intellect. That's the logic of personality.

Along related political lines, why not begin to scientifically evaluate politicians' personalities and share that information with the public, so as to encourage voters to choose the leaders with the most likelihood of success, and to avoid supporting anyone who is especially likely to pose a danger to the country's citizens? As a young man, Christopher Hitchens would have objected to that idea: he believed that it was impolite to discuss another's character: "At my old English boarding school we had a sporting saying that one should 'tackle the ball and not the man.'" Yet some philosophers now argue that considering the character of a person who expresses a political opinion is quite relevant to evaluating her beliefs and leadership. Moreover, a politician's personality clearly affects her public conduct. Over time, Hitchens revised his "tackle the ball" philosophy: "I carried on echoing this sort of unexamined nonsense for quite some time . . . when it hit me very forcibly that the 'personality' of one of the candidates was itself an 'issue.'"

Some clinical psychologists have developed methods for estimating how dangerous a leader is to his own nation and its neighbors. They've called upon governments to use formal personality assessments of world leaders "to predict, understand, and better control their behavior for common good." And particularly promising leaders could be singled out for praise as well.

The idea of whether to publicly discuss a politician's personality is a specific case of a more general issue: the degree to which we should speak frankly about one another's characters in the first place. Talking about personalities no doubt allows us to apply and to develop our personal intelligence using the real people around us. Yet as we know, many of us are easily offended by hearing comments about ourselves. Although many philosophers and religious figures have cautioned us to speak about others' personalities only with great care, we might also consider John Stuart Mill's position on free speech: that "the silencing of discussion is an assumption of infallibility." *Not* talking about people allows them to behave without being questioned. Only under conditions of free speech, Mill explained, can our opinions about a person be exposed as wrong—or be revealed as informative and helpful to understanding a fellow human being.

When we gossip, we can inadvertently spread misinformation about someone (or worse, do so maliciously), yet such conversations often carry with them valuable information. In "The Vindication of Gossip," the philosopher Aaron Ben-Ze'ev argues that gossiping is instructive and we should feel more comfortable talking about other people. On the meaning of gossip, he remarks, with a figurative wink:

> When people are involved in serious, practical, and purposive talk, they are not gossiping. Thus, when two psychiatrists analyze the love affair of my neighbor, their discussion is not gossip; however, when my wife and I consider the same information, gossip it is. The psychiatrists' discussion is not idle talk (or so they claim).

From the standpoint of personal intelligence, both types of conversations involve learning about personality. Roy Baumeister and his colleagues have argued that gossip and commentaries involve stories we tell one another to convey the practical aspects of people's life choices and the consequences of their decisions.*

How we talk about someone's personality obviously depends on many conditions, from whether we are praising or criticizing, to how our comments might be used. To take just one example, we

---

*My colleague Michelle Leichtman and I have considered the ethics of discussing the personalities of public figures in an article in *Psychology of Popular Media Culture,* and we have treated some of the points here in greater detail in that article.

sometimes bring up another person's faults to make ourselves feel better. Social psychologists label our comments a "downward social comparison" because we regard the person with whom we're comparing ourselves as beneath us on a specific quality. (We also compare ourselves upwardly with people who seem better than us, so as to follow their practices.) We are particularly prone to use downward comparisons when we feel unhappy, dissatisfied, or insecure—this is very human but less than ideal in terms of communicating about personality because of its negative focus. Additionally, some people comment on personality not to provide helpful information but to carry out a social agenda—for example, to control another person by undermining his confidence and thereby discouraging him from, say, applying for a job they don't want him to have. Or worse, we speak out so as to damage someone's reputation for revenge.

But if our intentions are good, personal intelligence can help us improve our appraisals of people. We can remember that a troublesome trait often has a positive side: disagreeable people can be independent thinkers; depressed and anxious individuals often see real flaws that other people miss; and careless, disorganized individuals can also be fun and creative. We remember that a person who behaves poorly in one context may set a positive example in another. And good personal intelligence helps us keep our own character flaws in mind, which allows us to view other people's weaknesses with greater kindness.

Just as it may be helpful to talk about other people, it can be helpful to talk about our own personalities. The psychologist Sidney Jourard referred to individuals who disclose a great deal about themselves as having a *transparent* personality. The value of this transparency for Jourard is that it leads to our greater ability to see ourselves and to be clearly seen by others. He argued: "The individual who . . . can express his thoughts, feelings, and opinions honestly is in a better position to learn his real self . . . because as he reveals himself to another, *he is also revealing himself to himself.* The act . . . permits one to 'get outside oneself' and see oneself . . ." Yet as healthy as this is between friends, if we speak of ourselves in too much detail, people can feel overwhelmed by the level of specificity in our storytelling.

My general point is that talking about personalities in a fair and constructive manner is a skill worth acquiring. And if people are judicious in what they say about us, then we might benefit from being more welcoming of their comments (though it can be challenging at times to hear what they may say).

Personality also intersects with the economics of the workforce. Our worth as employees depends in part on our matching our capacities and interests to what a job calls for. And when we're satisfied at work, we not only help ourselves but also the economy by doing our jobs with greater energy and skill. Economists refer to the knowledge, skills, and abilities we bring to the workplace as "human capital"—and they regard our work performance as a driving force for business, nonprofits, and government. In fact, economists suggest that the economic growth of the United States and similar countries over the twentieth century was due in part to the nation's human capital—developed through the extensive public education available to its citizens—and possibly also because of the freedom we have to match ourselves to jobs that energize us.

Frank Schmidt and John Hunter examined the individual differences among employees' work. More-productive workers in unskilled and low-skill positions outperform their average peers by 19 percent, they estimated. Better workers in more-skilled positions outperform the average of their peers by 48 percent. Schmidt and Hunter concluded that even a modest improvement in selection procedures could result in hiring a worker who contributed $18,000 more in value, on average, to the organization than another potential worker. Once that effect is multiplied by the number of employees in a firm, it could spell the difference between the organization's success and bankruptcy. Their implication is that organizations should carefully choose their employees—and, I might add, that if society promotes a person's good occupational choice it will contribute to the broader economy.

That said, Micki McGee, a sociologist at Fordham University, raised some crucial reservations about such visions of ever-increasing worker productivity. McGee is concerned that we're increasingly required to shape our personalities to fit our jobs, and points out that workers are facing mounting economic insecurities, which we experience as pressure to conform to whatever the organization wants of us. McGee argues that society today expects us to be altogether too positive, too motivated, too responsible, and too "appropriate" in our work behavior. In response, many of us are developing a "belabored self" for which we must regularly invent and reinvent ourselves to meet societal demands. Developing a healthy and socially acceptable self, she goes on, "is increasingly required as a new form of 'immaterial labor'—mental, social, and emotional tasks—required for participation in the labor market." In other words, we need to develop our personalities just to find or keep a decent job. McGee would like to remedy this situation by redirecting the energies of people away from self-reinvention and into progressive social movements that demand a more equitable distribution of wealth and resources.

My point here is that personal intelligence not only guides our own personalities, but that we are also in the business of taking personality into account when we create, evaluate, and enact social policy. Another example of this is Dr. Allen Frances's recent argument in *Saving Normal* that we need to defend the notion of a normal personality from the ever-expanding definitions of psychiatric disorders published in the *Diagnostic and Statistical Manual of Mental Disorders*. For Frances, normal personalities enable us to maintain our stable functioning much of the time, so that we can adequately manage our lives. He reminds us that it is also normal to be thrown off course from time to time by uncontrollable events, and to react emotionally or irrationally to obstacles and setbacks. According to Frances, it is poor psychiatry indeed to label any short-term detours from equilibrium that our personalities may take as either abnormal or diseased; rather, this is an expectable part of how personality functions. As I see it, Frances is drawing on his scientific expertise, his knowledge of the field, and his personal intelligence in advocating for a broader definition of what normal is.

Personal intelligence can help us understand and evaluate these important public discussions, whether the topic is realizing that introspection can be inappropriate for settling policy debates, or questioning how much cheerful behavior we need at work, or examining what's psychiatrically healthy.

I believe it also makes sense to teach people more about the basics of personality so they can better understand themselves and others, and apply their knowledge to evaluating social policy. Most of us already have enough personal intelligence to learn more about personality, yet we receive little instruction when it comes to the subject, and it would be easy enough to orchestrate the basics of such learning. Such education would surely enhance our reasoning and capability in the area. Beyond that, I'm agnostic about whether we can raise personal intelligence itself: psychologists mean something rather specific when they talk about raising an intelligence: raising a person's *potential* or *capacity* to think—and it's difficult to demonstrate changes in potential. But we can improve problem-solving independently of intelligence; for example, we teach math to help people solve basic algebra problems, and we succeed without reference to raising their IQ.

The reason educators don't teach much about personality today, I believe, is a consequence in part of when universal education was introduced, back in the eighteenth and nineteenth centuries. During that period, the leaders of the industrialized nations recognized the crucial importance of an educated populace to ensure their society's economic growth and to support an increasingly technological workplace. They created national education systems; and, within these, educators wrote textbooks for arithmetic and algebra, grammar, and how to read a poem. These books (and the curricula more generally) communicated key areas of knowledge that young people could readily be taught. My colleagues and I refer to the drawing together of this previously scattered difficult-to-access information as institutionalizing knowledge.

But information about psychology and the personality system weren't institutionalized at that time—there wasn't anything to institutionalize, as the psychological sciences didn't emerge until a century or more after the implementation of universal education in many nations. And one might argue that it took at least until the mid-twentieth century for psychologists to collect enough information about personality to be of general use. The institutionalization of information in the field is still a work in progress.

At the grade school level today, recently developed curricula in social and emotional learning fall short of providing an organized or uniform treatment of personality and its aspects. Character-education programs often focus on values and moral character, but without much perspective on how personality works. Even college courses still sometimes focus on "theories of personality"—an antiquated mix of theories by Freud, Jung, Rogers, Maslow, and more recent theorists, often with little contact with contemporary research.

Better college courses describe the central parts of personality, such as a person's traits and mental models, along with personality's major areas of functions—how we develop our individual energies, use knowledge to guide ourselves, and plan for the future. These courses further examine how we carry out actions by recruiting motives, emotions, and social skills from across our major psychological systems—and how we engage in self-control; and these better courses cover personality development and change. It's reasonable to expect that those of us who learn this material will be better able to contribute to the public debates that impact personality, and better guide our own personal development as well. The reason to invest in such learning is to unleash our personal energies in directions that work for us all.

The expression "It takes all kinds to make a world" entered the English language from a 1620 translation of Cervantes's *Don Quixote*. The fact that we all differ in many ways enables our contemporary society, which depends on ever more specialization, to function as smoothly as it does. Some people will prefer to become veterinarians, others accountants, and still others to make videos. It means that we can choose our friends from those who are shy and quiet, or those who are party animals who like to hang glide.

Some professionals benefit from knowing more about personality than the rest of us; these include psychologists and psychiatrists, social workers, human-resource professionals, teachers, police officers, parole officers, and others. Many professionals in these fields already know a lot about personality. Many of them acquire extensive on-the-job experience in dealing with people. The one ingredient experts often miss in their professional work, however, is the opportunity to receive good feedback as to how they're doing when it comes to assessing others. We develop expertise faster if we have good reports about how we're performing; in fact, such feedback is one of the three key elements of expertise identified by psychologists, along with ability and practice.

For example, none of us receives much information about whether our introspection is accurate in a given case. True, it's easy enough to ask someone what they're thinking about as it is going on. In the Descriptive Experience Sampling (DES) method, people carry around a beeper and record what they're experiencing when the alarm goes off; then they're asked to elaborate on whatever they wrote, in a follow-up interview. Because the research participants record their introspections at the time they occur, memory distortions are minimized. Yet neither a scientist using the DES nor anyone else has methods to check the participants' accuracy. And even monitoring people's inner states in the laboratory is little better. Researchers can check a person's claim to be sad, for example, against the biological and cognitive markers of sadness, but if the person claims she is sad and the markers don't indicate it, there could be something wrong with the markers in the specific individual's case.

Psychotherapists, who are supposed to cultivate a certain degree of equanimity and neutrality when listening to their patients, generally don't have anyone who can help them introspect by "traveling inside" their minds to see what they see. Perhaps the closest they may get is to use a training analyst—a highly trained supervisor of other therapists—who guides their self-discovery in therapy. In one study, more than 80 percent of therapists-in-training who made use of training analysts believed that the insight they gained helped them to understand their own reactions to their patients—and to keep their reactions from interfering with the treatment of those individuals. They may be right, but skeptics might argue that their positive evaluations are justifications after the fact for the effort they put into their extra training. And although findings show that psychotherapy heals distress, I don't know of any rigorous studies of whether clients who undergo such treatments are more insightful, although I believe such learning could occur under the right conditions.

It's much easier to evaluate the accuracy of how we perceive and predict other people. It's plausible to me, for example, that many of us become expert at understanding our family members and friends. We have ability in the area, we observe them for many hours, and we get frequent feedback as to whether our guesses are right. As children, we learn that if we ask our mother for permission to walk downtown, she will let us do it during the day but not at night. And we learn that among our relatives Uncle Herb is always kind and welcoming, even when our own parents are mad at us.

People in many careers, such as human resources and social work, spend their time learning about others. Yet psychotherapists (who may be the most studied), for one, rarely receive systematic feedback about their work outcomes. In one article examining the variation in therapist quality, the authors noted that

> psychotherapists . . . are not particularly adept at identifying treatment success and failure. Indeed . . . therapists do not recognize treatment deterioration. Exacerbating this problem is that therapists typically are not cognizant of the trajectory of change of patients seen by therapists in general. That is to say, they have no way of comparing their treatment outcomes with those obtained by other therapists.

The authors' conclusion was that therapists ought to have feedback as to treatment outcomes—but usually they do not; I suspect the same is true of many of the other occupations I have mentioned.

Psychotherapists already bring about considerable positive change among the clients they treat—the research evidence is clear on that point. My purpose here is simply to suggest that psychotherapists and many other professionals may have an opportunity to develop their expertise above what they can now do if their workplaces were slightly reengineered to make feedback a more regular part of their work experience.

In certain instances, professionals may be better off applying formulae based on psychological tests and other information to make decisions about people. By the 1950s, psychologists began to realize that a good formula often outperformed their own clinical judgment in assessment and prediction. For example, a clinician might administer a psychological test, and then use software that interprets the test profile to recommend a certain diagnosis or course of treatment. This is artificial expertise—a limited form of artificial intelligence—and it works well when formulae are available (often, they are not).

William Grove and his colleagues at the University of Minnesota looked over 136 studies that had pitted formulae against professionals' judgments across a variety of work settings. The nature of the professionals' judgments varied depending upon their occupations and included, for example, educational counselors' estimates of their students' academic performance in school, managers' predictions of advertising sales in a media company, and physicians' predictions of the likelihood of death following a heart attack. Across the studies, predictive formulae outperformed the professionals' opinions by about a 10 percent margin in forecasting outcomes. We commonly think that we want experts who make decisions about us to "take in" our personality and to care about us. But back in 1955, Paul Meehl of the University of Minnesota, who had already argued for the superiority of formulaic prediction, upended that idea, opining that everyone would be better off if clinicians used a formula and made sure in regard to a client "to avoid talking to him, and . . . to avoid thinking about him!" Put another way, a formula may "know us" in some manner better than an expert.

There is an important addendum to the research findings about using formulae: predictive formulae about people get better if they include observations of the target individuals by other people around them. Researchers have drawn together studies covering eighty-five years of research to explore the best predictors of occupational success, comparing such variables as general mental ability, job samples, handwriting analysis, and how the employee was perceived in job interviews and by coworkers. The single most effective measure of job performance, they found, was general mental ability as measured by IQ tests or their near-equivalents. Beyond that, however, the employee's personality—as evaluated either by their coworkers or by interviewers—was an important predictor of job success, adding to the forecasts that were possible using general mental ability by itself. By contrast, adding a measure of the person's interest added very little to the prediction, and adding in a person's age, or a handwriting analysis, added nothing. So *personality mattered*—in the form of observers predicting the employees' success.

One of the exciting things about the theory of personal intelligence is that it provides an explanation of why we pay attention to personality and why it matters, and explains the principles we use to reason about personality. Here, I've drawn together key scientific studies that, collectively, depict an essential set of rules, methods, and procedures we use to reason about ourselves and other people. To be sure, this is just a beginning. Psychologists will continue to seek out further examples of such problem-solving; they'll further develop and refine measures of personal intelligence; they will continue to explore how these abilities at reasoning fit together and relate to other intelligences, and will explore how our capacity to understand personality affects our lives. There's plenty more to learn in each of these areas. That said, I've built on the theory here by drawing together some of the key techniques we use to solve problems relating to ourselves and other people, and this integration allows for a new level of understanding of how we reason about personality, and of the adaptive purposes of such thought.

•

Personal intelligence begins with our curiosity about people; but of course we're interested in many subjects other than personality. In the late 1950s, for example, President Eisenhower established the National Aeronautics and Space Administration (NASA) at Cape Canaveral in Florida to explore space travel and outer space. This was at about the same time that Michael Murphy and Richard "Dick" Price, along with the journalist George Leonard, began investigating our psychological selves at a place called the Esalen Institute, in Big Sur on the California coast. Their institute became known as "a Cape Canaveral of inner space," and it would attract leading intellectuals from across the nation thanks to the young men's vision and timing—and people's interest in understanding their own personalities.

The Esalen Institute was founded on land owned by the Murphy family, on which there was an inn and natural hot springs. A few colorful characters were living on the grounds at the time. These included the renowned folksinger Joan Baez and a young author by the name of Hunter S. Thompson, whom Michael Murphy's mother had hired to maintain security. One night, Murphy and Price held a midnight session in which they brainstormed to find a phrase or slogan they could use to wake people up to the possibilities of their personal lives. At the time, Aldous Huxley, the author of *Brave New World* and *The Doors of Perception*, lived several hours to the south of them in Los Angeles and had been lecturing nearby about people's "human potentialities." Murphy and Leonard tweaked Huxley's phrase to describe a new "human potential movement."

The personality theorist Abraham Maslow visited Esalen and found the philosophy there sympathetic to his own views—that our inner personalities hold great potential within them. Esalen's spirit was unique in combining then-current psychological thought with hope of deep self-understanding, if only our inner secrets could be unlocked. Ideas from Esalen swirled and mixed with other conceptions of personality in strange and sometimes seductive ways. Although Walter Mischel never visited the institute so far as I know, his work emphasized how much people altered their behavior from one situation to the next to adapt to the tasks they were carrying out. If you believe personality isn't fixed and that our behavior is fluid and adapted to the moment—which many people took as Mischel's message—then you might also believe that any of us can become whomever we wish, without bounds. All it requires is some personal seeking, coupled with support from society.

Today, psychologists still regard our characters as changeable, but within limits. And various psychological movements continue to champion how we can better ourselves. For example, today's positive psychology is a related aspirational movement, albeit more empirically focused. Psychologists who participate in the positive-psychology program focus on how we can improve our minds through expressing gratitude, developing personal virtues, and making our everyday lives more fulfilling.

I have ever so briefly considered Esalen, the human-potential movement, and the more recent positive-psychology movement to acknowledge that there are many reasons we look inward—and they share in common a desire to improve our own lot and that of society. One of the wishes that animated Esalen's founders and its visitors was that somehow we could peer within ourselves and discern the truth: Are we just biological organisms? Do we have some kind of soul? The human potential movement asked how we could become better versions of ourselves. And psychologists in the positive-psychology movement of today ask how we can improve our well-being. Although these questions have emerged again and again throughout history, in the twentieth century they became inter-twined with the thinking of modern psychologists.

Personal intelligence speaks both to our human potential and to our capacity for well-being. But although it contributes to our growth as individuals and to our skills at engaging with society, it also speaks to the value of knowing our boundaries and limits. Per-sonal intelligence tells us how to look within and what to trust under what conditions—and what remains unknowable about us, at least for today. It invites us to look inward but reminds us that introspec-tion can be confining, and reminds us to direct our attention back to the outer world to navigate it well.

In one sense personal intelligence is very much a part of the human potential that many psychologists have sought to understand. The theory encourages us to expand our notions of human intelligence by describing a previously undervalued human skill that we now can measure and explore. We use our personal intelligence to better function with one another and to contribute to civilization and its progress. On any given day, we may encounter personality after personality, and as we do, we often appreciate the humor and the drama that other people bring to our lives. Sometimes we can predict what people will do, and at other times they take us by surprise; we ourselves may go off in a new direction that startles us. I find inspiration in the idea that looking inward, we discover the many attributes we share with other people, as well as our differences from others and a sense of our inner uniqueness. Part of the art of being a person is to recognize the great beauty in the personalities around us, in their commonalities and in their striking variations.

NOTES

INTRODUCTION: DOES PERSONALITY MATTER? . . .
AND OTHER PRELIMINARIES

4 *Wundt and his students asked research participants* . . . See pp. 1081 and 1086 of Blumenthal, A. L. (1975). A reappraisal of Wilhelm Wundt. *American Psychologist, 30,* 1081–1088. Wundt's laboratory work also is described in Farr, Robert M. (1983). Wilhelm Wundt (1832–1920) and the origins of psychology as an experimental and social science. *British Journal of Social Psychology, 22,* 289–301.

4 *"psychical personality"* . . . From p. 26 of Wundt, W. (1897). *Outlines of psychology* (C. H. Judd, Trans.). Leipzig, Germany: Wilhelm Englemann.

5 *Carl Jung drew on Western, Hindu, and Buddhist traditions* . . . An example of Jung's borrowing and adapting from one yogic tradition is covered in Coward, H. G. (1985). Jung and Kundalini. *The Journal of Analytical Psychology, 30,* 379–392. More about the grand theorists can be found in Hall, C. S., & Lindzey, G. (1957). *Theories of personality.* New York: John Wiley & Sons.

5 *In 1959, Professors Calvin Hall and Gardner Lindzey* . . . Their recommendations appeared in the section "Some reflections on current personality theory" beginning on p. 550 of Hall, C. S., & Lindzey, G. (1957). *Theories of personality.* John Wiley & Sons. The statement is further developed in the 1978 edition.

6 *Their conclusions upended at least a few* . . . See the controversies about repression in Bowers, K. S., & Farvolden, P. (1996). Revisiting a century-old Freudian slip—from suggestion disavowed to the truth repressed. *Psychological Bulletin, 119,* 355–380. And more generally for more about theorizing in the area, see de Jong, L. (2010). From theory construction to deconstruction: The many modalities of theorizing in psychology. *Theory & Psychology, 20,* 745–763.

7 *Thomas Hobbes argued that all men are equal* . . . See pp. 133–134 of Kidder, J. (1983). Acknowledgements of equals: Hobbes's Ninth Law of Nature. *The Philosophical Quarterly*, 33, 133–146. Hobbes's doubts about equality are from the same page.

7 *"I am, perhaps, like no one"* . . . This and his claim to be no better than others are both from Book 1, Paragraph 2 of Rousseau, J. J. (2006). The confessions of Jean-Jacques Rousseau. (Original work 1782). D. Widger (Prod.). Retrieved from www.gutenberg.org/files/3913/3913-h/3913-h.htm.

7 *"no matter what part of the world we come from"* and *"We all seek happiness"* . . . Both are from the third paragraph of the Dalai Lama's acceptance speech for the Nobel Peace Prize, awarded in 1989. Retrieved from www .dalailama.com/messages/acceptance-speeches/nobel-peace-prize.

8 *As a brief aside to illustrate this idea* . . . The several different types of yoga and yoga students are summarized on p. 28 of Smith, H. (1991). *The world's religions*. San Francisco: HarperCollins. A longer treatment can be found on pp. 29–50. Jnana teaching is described on p. 31; Bhakti is described on pp. 34–35. The atman as self is described on pp. 37–39 of Hopkins, T. J. (1971). *The Hindu religious tradition*. Encino, CA: Dickenson Publishing.

8 *"easy"; "difficult"*; and *"slow to warm up"* . . . As described in Thomas, A., Chess, S., & Birch, H. G. (1970). The origin of personality. *Scientific American*, 102–109.

9 *Protecting the sensitivities of others is* . . . Such comments have been handed down to us from philosophers of the ancient world. For a collection of some of their teachings, see Mayer, J. D., Lin, S. C., & Korogodsky, M. (2011). Exploring the universality of personality judgments: Evidence from the Great Transformation (1000 BCE–200 BCE). *Review of General Psychology*, 15, 65–76.

11 *"imitates in words a sequence"* and *"actions and thoughts vis-à-vis the human"* . . . Both from p. 621 of Crane, R. S. (1952). The concept of plot and the plot of *Tom Jones*. In R. S. Crane (Ed.). *Critics and criticism: Ancient and modern*. Chicago: University of Chicago Press.

11 *By 1983, Wendy Lehnert, Michael Dyer, and colleagues at Yale University* . . . Their work on emotions in narratives appeared in Lehnert, W. G., Dyer, M. G., Johnson, P. N., Yang, C. J., & Harley, S. (1983). BORIS—An experiment in in-depth understanding of narratives. *Artificial Intelligence, 20, 15–62*, and in Dyer, M. G. (1983). The role of affect in narratives. *Cognitive Science*, 7, 211–242.

11 *For example, when the researchers gave BORIS* . . . The example appears in "The role of affect" (see above), p. 220.

12 *The day before the 2004 draft, scouts* . . . The story of Pedroia's recruitment from Arizona State to the major leagues is told on pp. 77–78 in Pedroia, D., with Delaney, E. J. (2008). *Born to play: My life in the game*. New York: Simon Spotlight Entertainment.

13 *The Inquiry project was massive* . . . Some of the scope is described on pp. 183–184 of Cunningham, C. A. (2005). A certain and reasoned art: The rise and fall of character education in America. In Lapsley, D. K., & Power, F. C. (Eds.), *Character psychology and character education* (pp. 183–184). Notre Dame, IN: University of Notre Dame Press.

13 *Using approaches like this, the investigators* . . . As described on p. 36 of Kenyon, E. W. (1979). *The Character Education Inquiry, 1924–1928: A historical examination of its use in educational research.* (Unpublished doctoral dissertation). The University of Texas, Austin, TX.

14 *Given the zero-to-one scale for a positive relationship* . . . In speaking about unrealistic expectations concerning the correlation from tests to behavior, I am echoing W. Mischel's 1968 *Personality and Assessment* (see p. 20, for example). It seems to me equally likely that the correlation coefficient was so new that there were few expectations of any sort during that decade concerning the prediction from traits to behaviors, but that, knowing little or nothing about a zero-to-one scale, .30 simply seemed low.

14 *The researchers at the Character Education Inquiry* . . . The correlation of about .30 is discussed on p. 383 of Hartshorne, H., & May, M. A. (1928). *Studies in the nature of character. Vol. 1: Studies in deceit.* New York: Macmillan—as cited on p. 24 of Mischel, W. (1968). *Personality and assessment.* New York: John Wiley & Sons.

14 *"no evidence"* . . . The idea that the effects were negligible was expressed in Hartshorne, H. (1930). Sociological implications of the Character Education Inquiry. *American Journal of Sociology, 36,* 251–262. The authors of one of the reports wrote, regarding the project, "There is no evidence of any trait of goodness or character if what is meant by goodness or character is just what may be observed or measured by conduct"; as cited on p. 186 of Cunningham, C. A. (2005). A certain and reasoned art: The rise and fall of character education in America. In Lapsley, D. K., & Power, F. C. (Eds.), *Character Psychology and Character Education* (pp. 166–200). Notre Dame, IN: University of Notre Dame Press.

15 *Once we have pegged someone as* . . . For the idea that people perceive others according to prototypes, see Cantor, N., & Mischel, W. (1977). Traits as prototypes: Effects on recognition memory. *Journal of Personality and Social Psychology, 35,* 38–48.

15 *They concluded, after reviewing a number of studies* . . . These reviews estimated the influence of situations on people's behavior as at about same level as the influence of personality. The first article to make this comparison may have been Bowers, K. (1973). Situationism in psychology: An analysis and a critique. *Psychological Review, 80,* 307–336 (see Table 1). Other key contributions to the discussion included Funder, D. C., & Ozer, D. J. (1983). Behavior as a function of the situation. *Journal of Personality and Social Psychology, 44,* 107–112, and

Epstein, S., & O'Brien, E. J. (1985). The person-situation debate in historical and current perspective. *Psychological Bulletin, 98,* 513–537.

16 *"freaky and unpredictable events"* and *"good teams usually win"* . . . From p. 129 of Abelson, R. P. (1985). A variance explanation paradox: When a little is a lot. *Psychological Bulletin, 97,* 129–133.

17 *And it seems entirely possible that still more perceptive individuals might choose the more suitable member of the pair 65 percent of the time versus 35 percent . . .* To the best of my knowledge, there are no research findings that directly address how well people might perform in making the "better choice" of a person from a pair of people, so these figures represent an educated guess. The 65 versus 35 percent split I advanced in the text represents a conversion of the correlation of .30 between an observer's choice and a desired outcome, as I'll explain toward the end of this note.

I chose the .30 correlation because correlations between .30 and .40 represent a relationship often found between traits (as measured by tests) and behaviors. A correlation of about .30 (.33, specifically) also describes the approximate level at which interviewers, using their own preferred styles of questioning, are able to predict a job candidate's success. It seems plausible to me that the same approximately .30 correlation might describe the "making better choices" example I have laid out, for which a chooser must compare the differences between the two people and from those differences (which likely are multivariate normal) estimate which candidate is the better choice. My estimate is necessarily approximate, and I invite others who are interested in this problem to improve on this initial treatment.

The relevant references for the .30-to-.40 correlations between traits and behavior are reviewed in Chapter 4, see especially pp. 114–115 of Funder, D. R. (2013). *The personality puzzle (6th ed.).* W. W. Norton. The .33 correlation between unstructured interviews and job performance (one of several results) is reported in McDaniel, M. A., Whetzel, D. L., Schmidt, F. L., & Maurer, S. D. (1994). The validity of employment interviews: A comprehensive review and meta-analysis. *Journal of Applied Psychology, 79,* 599–616.

To convert a correlation of .30 to decision-making outcomes expressed as percents, I used a Binomial Effect Size Display (BESD). Based on the correlation of .30, I used calculations of .30/2 × 100 = 15, or 50 +/–15, that is, of 65 and 35, for the relevant cells of the table. The method is outlined in Rosenthal, R., & Rubin, D. B. (1982). A simple, general purpose display of magnitude of experimental effect. *Journal of Educational Psychology, 74,* 166–169. In essence, I formed a 2 (cue to pair member's personality indicates selecting) × 2 (choice of pair member actually leads to a better outcome) table as shown on the facing page and read across the "better outcome" column, ignoring the rest, to get the 65–35 percent success rate.

		Choice of pair member actually leads to . . .		
		Worse outcome	Better outcome	Total overall
Cue to pair member's personality indicates selecting the individual is a:	Better choice	35	65	100
	Worse choice	65	35	100
Total Overall		100	100	200

17 *By the time he was a young child* . . . According to family lore, friends of the Pedroia family remarked, "Wow, your son's really good," from p. 10 of Pedroia, D., with Delaney, E. J. (2008). *Born to play: My life in the game.* New York: Simon Spotlight Entertainment.

17–18 *"fire the ball off the bricks"* and *"Don't worry about the clock"* . . . Ibid., p. 24.

18 *"the only tool I saw he had was"* and *"I can't think the Red Sox are this smart"* . . . Ibid., pp. 4–5.

18 *Walter Mischel—who had pointed out people's inconsistencies* . . . Mischel noted that "correlations across situations tend to be highest for cognitive and intellectual functions . . . Considerable stability over time has been demonstrated for some domains, and again particularly for ability and cognitive measures," on p. 36 of Mischel, W. (1968). *Personality and assessment.* New York: John Wiley and Sons.

19 *The term itself had been used on an occasional basis* . . . Earlier uses of the term "personal intelligence" included magazine columns or features on prominent individuals. See, for example, Anonymous. (1851, February 27). General Jackson and the clerk. *New Hampshire Patriot & State Gazette*, p. 4, and Guernsey, A. H. (1857, July). Editor's table. *Harper's New Monthly Magazine.* The use of personal intelligence as a reflection of aspects of an individual's traditional IQ was used by Thorne, S. (1990). *The theory of intelligence: A sensory-rational view.* Springfield, IL: Charles C. Thomas.

19 *Howard Gardner had proposed an intrapersonal intelligence* . . . Gardner describes intrapersonal intelligence as a blend of emotional discernment and identity; he emphasizes emotion-related abilities on p. 239, and refers to identity multiple times throughout the chapter. His interpersonal intelligence was focused on recognizing individual differences on p. 239, and broadened into

understanding social and cultural laws on the top of p. 251, in Gardner, H. (1993). *Frames of mind: The theory of multiple intelligences* (10th anniversary ed.). New York: Basic Books.

19 *At least a few researchers shortened Gardner's term* . . . Park and Park refer to Gardner's work and, through it, introduce their own expansion of the idea in regard to its evolutionary theory and its potential applications to psychiatry: Park, L. C., & Park, T. J. (1997). Personal intelligence. In McCallum, M., & Piper, W. E. (Eds.), *Psychological mindedness: A contemporary understanding* (pp. 133–167). Mahwah, NJ: Lawrence Erlbaum Associates Publishers.

19 *And Imrich Ruisel, of the Institute of Experimental Psychological Sciences* . . . Ruisel used the term to describe work on "reflexics," a cognitive representation of the self, in Ruisel, I. (1994). From academic and personal intelligence to wisdom. *Studia Psychologica, 36,* 137–152, and then again as a lay theory of one kind of intelligence by Ruisel, I. (1996). Implicit theories of intelligence in adolescents. *Studia Psychologica, 38* (1–2), 23–34.

20 *In a 1948 report* . . . I have been unable to find out any information about J. Wedeck beyond this single published study: Wedeck, J. (1947). The relationship between personality and 'psychological ability'. *British Journal of Psychology, 37,* 133–151.

20 *I also discussed the idea with Peter Salovey* . . . Shortly after our conversation, Peter became provost of Yale and is now president of Yale University.

1. WHAT IS PERSONAL INTELLIGENCE?

27 *By contrast, our ability to remember nonsense words* . . . A more controversial candidate for an intelligence involves musical ability. Although problem-solving in music about notes and melodic structure, scales, and rhythms qualifies as a mental ability, many experts regard it as a talent rather than an intelligence, because it is narrower and apparently involves fewer different skills and (they believe) is less valued than the ability to understand words. Whether you consider musical ability to be a talent or an intelligence is a matter of taste to some degree; to my mind music might well qualify.

27 *Among the most successful investigations* . . . For a broader biographically oriented history of intelligence testing, see Fancher, R. E. (1987). *The intelligence men: Makers of the IQ controversy.* New York: W. W. Norton.

27 *Binet was appointed a member of the commission* . . . The French government's appointment of Binet as a commissioner is described ibid., p. 69. Fancher then goes on to describe Binet's 1905 intelligence test over the next pages.

28 *The 1905 version of Binet and Simon's test* . . . Binet, A. (1905). New methods for the diagnosis of the intellectual level of subnormals. *L'Année Psychologique, 12,* 191–244. Reprinted in Kite, S. (Trans.) (1916). *The development of intelligence in children.* Vineland, NJ: Publications of the Training School at Vineland. Retrieved from psychclassics.yorku.ca/Binet/binet1.htm.

29 *Although Spearman regarded intelligence* . . . My qualification that Spearman regarded intelligence as "mostly" general refers to the fact that Spearman supposed each person possessed skills in specific areas of problem-solving that varied from one another, and that were a part of their general level of intelligence.

29 *"The primary fact is that intelligence . . ."* From p. 287 of Thorndike, E. L. (1920). The reliability and significance of tests of intelligence. *Journal of Educational Psychology, 11*, 284–287.

29 *"the ability to understand and manage"* . . . In *Harper's*, Thorndike more completely divided the intellectual sphere into the verbal, mechanical, and social. The quote is from p. 228 of Thorndike, E. L. (1920). Intelligence and its use. *Harper's Magazine, 140*, 227–235.

29 *"shows itself abundantly . . . on the playground"* . . . Ibid., p. 231. Thorndike saw this intelligence in nonverbal communication between people.

29 *After briefly raising his idea* . . . Although treated only in brief, Thorndike's ideas were highly intriguing, and other psychologists' approaches and their attempts to measure social intelligence represented groundbreaking work at the time, from which I and others have greatly benefited.

29 *"ability to get along with others"* and *"social technique"* . . . The phrases are quoted from p. 359 of a review by Kihlstrom, J. F., & Cantor, N. (2000). Social intelligence. In Sternberg, R. J. (Ed.), *Handbook of intelligence* (2nd ed., pp. 359–379). Cambridge, UK: Cambridge University Press.

30 *David Wechsler finally coaxed psychologists* . . . Wechsler, in turn, drew on the works of many earlier psychologists, including Edward Thorndike (who introduced social intelligence). Wechsler's performance IQ, for example, found a precursor in Thorndike's earlier idea of a mechanical intelligence.

31 *Perceptual-organizational IQ, in other words* . . . When verbal-comprehension and perceptual-organizational intelligence were correlated among English speakers, their relation was about .75, reflecting a strong positive relationship, as reported on p. 80 of Kaufman, A. S., & Lichtenberger, E. O. (2005). *Assessing adolescent and adult intelligence*. New York: Wiley.

32 *From this perspective, any new IQ* . . . But there were nonetheless eloquent arguments for multiple intelligences in the field as well. Two particularly influential researchers were J. P. Guilford, who proposed 120 intelligences based on combinations of various mental functions, and Robert J. Sternberg of Yale University, who proposed three intelligences—academic, practical, and creative.

32 *"the Puluwat people of the Caroline Islands . . ."* The quote is from p. 202 of *Frames of Mind*, but Gardner leads off his book with reference to the Puluwat people on p. 4; both from Gardner, H. (1993). *Frames of mind: The theory of multiple intelligences* (10th anniversary ed.). New York: Basic Books.

33 *And he proposed intra- and interpersonal intelligences* . . . Gardner's intelligences could be characterized in many ways, as they are very rich descriptions and, as he acknowledges, they are not fully specified. My characterization of interpersonal intelligence pays particular attention to ibid., pp. 239 and 251.

33 *But Gardner rather inexplicably brushed off* . . . For example, in a 1999 book, Gardner wrote under the heading "Myth 1" that now that he had identified multiple intelligences, "researchers can—and perhaps should—create a variety of tests . . ." He continued that "having a battery of MI tests is not consistent with major tenets of the theory," on p. 80 of Gardner, H. (1999). *Intelligence reframed.* New York: Basic Books. He had expressed similar sentiments, though less explicitly, in *Frames of Mind*, arguing that intelligences cannot be fairly assessed through traditional forms of intelligence testing, and then expressing a mildly critical view of intelligence testing on p. 16. Gardner, H. (1993). *Frames of mind: The theory of multiple intelligences* (10th anniversary ed.). New York: Basic Books.

34 *Even advocates of multiple intelligences* . . . Robert Sternberg's concerns over the theory were expressed pointedly in the *Phi Delta Kappan*, where he wrote, "In fact, no experiments to test Gardner's theory exist yet, and Gardner's test of his intelligences do not exist yet either," from p. 700 of Sternberg, R. J. (1984). Fighting butter battles: A reply. *The Phi Delta Kappan, 65*, 700. Similarly, Earl Hunt opined, using MI as an abbreviation for multiple intelligences, that "Despite the popularity of the MI idea in some educational circles, there is virtually no evidence for the theory." From p. 119 of Hunt, E. (2010). *Intelligence.* New York: Cambridge University Press.

34 *When psychologists did attempt to test Gardner's theory* . . . See, for example, Visser, B. A., Ashton, M. C., & Vernon, P. A. (2006). Beyond *g*: Putting multiple intelligences theory to the test. *Intelligence, 34*, 487–502.

34 *To measure this, Wagner and Sternberg* . . . The example of the manager facing a decision comes from the appendix of Sternberg, R. J., Wagner, R. K., Williams, W. M., & Horvath, J. A. (1995). Testing common sense. *American Psychologist, 50*, 912–927. More recent evidence for this approach comes from Sternberg, R. J., Grigorenko, E. L., & Zhang, L. (2008). Styles of learning and thinking matter in instruction and assessment. *Perspectives on Psychological Science, 3*, 486–506.

34 *Although scientists at the time often bickered* . . . My more historically minded colleagues may object to my statement that psychologists were reaching a new détente vis-à-vis general versus specific intelligences, remarking that Spearman himself had recognized the existence of a hierarchy of intelligences at the turn of the twentieth century. They are right, in part. My basis for making this statement is that a richer understanding of factor analysis, and new developments in hierarchical factor analysis, made it easier to appreciate an empirically grounded hierarchy of intelligences.

34 *John Carroll, an emeritus professor* . . . In my report of Carroll's three-strata theory, I have made a few very small changes to his terminology to better connect his work with the earlier discussions of intelligences in this chapter. To see the original, refer to Carroll, J. B. (1993). *Human cognitive abilities.* New York: Cambridge University Press.

35 *And a person's profile of broad intelligences matters* . . . Jonathan Wai and his colleagues' study of spatial intelligence was reported in Wai, J., Lubinski, D., Ben-

bow, C. P., & Steiger, J. H. (2010). Accomplishment in science, technology, engineering, and mathematics (STEM) and its relation to STEM educational dose: A 25-year longitudinal study. *Journal of Educational Psychology, 102,* 860–871.

35 *This was the intellectual landscape in 1990 . . .* I have focused on the aspects of the intelligence field I regarded as most relevant to the beginnings of Peter's and my work. The depiction, I acknowledge, omits a great deal. Some issues not touched upon here included models of fluid versus crystallized intelligence, issues of test fairness, and emerging brain research in the area.

35 *And although they have not been shy about pointing out . . .* For example, we have been criticized for reporting test reliabilities (which can be thought of as the consistency of measurement) at a level somewhat above that found by researchers in other laboratories. We respond to a recent exchange on the topic in Mayer, J. D., Salovey, P., & Caruso, D. R. (2012). The validity of the MSCEIT: Additional analyses and evidence. *Emotion Review, 4,* 403–408. In addition, we have acknowledged that our tests of EI are valid, although at least one subscale may not work adequately (for details, see the same issue of *Emotion Review*).

36 *Those with emotional intelligence were better . . .* See, for example, Mayer, J. D., Salovey, P., & Caruso, D. R. (2008). Emotional intelligence: New ability or eclectic traits? *American Psychologist, 63,* 503–517, and Mayer, J. D., Roberts, R. D., & Barsade, S. G. (2008). Human abilities: Emotional intelligence. *Annual Review of Psychology, 59,* 507–536.

36 *Some journalists had . . . equated our theory of intelligence with a person's overall character . . .* For a review, see Hughes, J. (2005). Bringing emotion to work: Emotional intelligence, employee resistance and the reinvention of character. *Work Employment Society, 19,* 603–625. The problem with such an equation is that by stretching emotional intelligence to refer to character, the concept loses its precision. Hughes points out that the expansion of EI's meaning has led to a "gulf between the version of EI provided the 'serious scientists' . . ." and the quite different version employed by some consultants and journalists (note 6, p. 621).

36 *I began to look for common rules and principles . . .* I compiled these ideas into a framework called the Personality Systems Framework. It's presented in Mayer, J. D. (2005). A tale of two visions: Can a new view of personality help integrate psychology? *American Psychologist, 60,* 294–307, and in Mayer, J. D., & Korogodsky, M. (2011). A really big picture of personality. *Personality and Social Psychology Compass, 5,* 104–117.

37 *Through gossip, Dunbar argues . . .* See Dunbar, R.I.M. (1998). The social brain hypothesis. *Evolutionary Anthropology, 6,* 178–190. Dunbar had written earlier about some of the same ideas under the name of "Machiavellian Intelligence"—so he inferred an intelligence at work as well.

37 *Martie Haselton and David Funder added . . .* See Haselton, M. G., & Funder, D. C. (2006). The evolution of accuracy and bias in social judgment. In M. Schaller, J. A. Simpson, & D. T. Kenrick (Eds.), *Evolution and social psychology* (pp. 15–37). Madison, CT: Psychosocial Press.

37 *David Buss of the University of Texas at Austin* . . . A recent summary of some
    of his thinking about individual differences is in Buss, D. M. (2009). How can
    evolutionary psychology successfully explain personality and individual differ-
    ences? *Perspectives on Psychological Science, 4*, 359–366.

38 *Many of these writings* . . . The material on Buddhism, ancient Greece, China,
    and Theophrastus is reviewed in Mayer, J. D., Lin, S. C., & Korogodsky, M.
    (2011). Exploring the universality of personality judgments: Evidence from the
    Great Transformation (1000 BCE–200 BCE). *Review of General Psychology,*
    15, 65–76.

38 *Forer was teaching a class in introductory* . . . The study is described in Forer,
    B. R. (1948). A diagnostic interest blank. *Rorschach Research Exchange, 12*,
    119–129.

38 *"You have a great need"* . . . to *"Security is one of your major goals"* . . . From p.
    120 of Forer, B. R. (1949). The fallacy of personal validation: A classroom dem-
    onstration of gullibility. *The Journal of Abnormal and Social Psychology, 44*,
    118–123.

39 *They referred to Forer's finding* . . . A check of PsycINFO on March 18, 2013,
    indicated that Forer's research had been referred to as a "Barnum effect" in
    seventy-two journal articles since 1949.

39 *In fact, if test-takers receive* two *sets of feedback* . . . In one study, test-takers
    thought that feedback tailored specifically to them was 76 percent accurate ver-
    sus 70 percent accurate for feedback based on the sample in general. The study
    was conducted by Guastello, S. J., & Rieke, M. L. (1990). The Barnum effect and
    validity of computer-based test interpretations: The Human Resource Develop-
    ment Report. *Psychological Assessment: A Journal of Consulting and Clinical*
    Psychology, 2, 186–190. A carefully designed double-blind study replicates the
    findings: Wyman, A., & Vyse, S. (2008). Science versus the stars: A double-blind
    test of the validity of the NEO Five-Factor Inventory and computer-generated
    astrological natal charts. *The Journal of General Psychology, 135*, 287–300. For
    a related result, see Andersen, P., & Nordvik, H. (2002). Possible Barnum effect
    in the Five Factor model: Do respondents accept random NEO Personality
    Inventory-Revised scores as their actual trait profile? *Psychological Reports, 90*,
    539–549.

40 *"in cynical and cutting tones"* . . . From p. 48 of Ipp, H. (2001). The case of
    Gayle. In Goldberg, A. (Ed.), *The narcissistic patient revisited: Progress in self*
    psychology (pp. 47–56). Mahwah, NJ: Analytic Press.

41 *One of the examples I found that nicely illustrates* . . . Although I believe Gra-
    ham possessed personal intelligence, it wasn't to the exclusion of her remarkable
    verbal-comprehension intelligence. Graham describes how she read a lot in her
    Montessori school (p. 42). During just one summer before entering the fifth
    grade she read, by her account, one hundred books, including all of Dumas and
    Louisa May Alcott (p. 50). She then found success in an occupation requiring
    written communication, first joining the school magazine in high school and

then working as a journalist in the summer (p. 74). After graduating from the University of Chicago, Graham found work as a journalist at the *San Francisco News* and then moved to *The Washington Post* the next year, 1939, to work on the editorial page of the paper (p. 95). Graham, K. (1997). *Personal history.* New York: Alfred A. Knopf.

41 *"having stood by my father and husband"* . . . Ibid., p. 348.

41 *"an ignorant intruder"* . . . Ibid., p. 346.

42 *"Not only had I mythologized him"* . . . Ibid., p. 341.

43 *"I am a colored girl born in Mississippi"* . . . Quoted in LaGesse, D. (2005, October 31). Heeding her own voice. *U.S. News & World Report, 44.*

43 *"I relate to the core of everyone's pain"* . . . Kantrowitz, B., Peterson, H., & Wingert, P. (2005, October 24). How I got there. *Newsweek, 146,* 48–62.

44 *Philosophers sometimes call these categories "fuzzy"* . . . For a general overview of nonclassical logic, see Priest, G. (2001). *An introduction to non-classical logic.* Cambridge, UK: Cambridge University Press. For specifics about fuzzy categories, see Kosko, B. (1993). *Fuzzy thinking: The new science of fuzzy logic.* New York: Hyperion.

44 *We wrote more than a hundred such items* . . . In describing the TOPI, I mention that all items were multiple choice with one correct answer per question. We relaxed this criterion slightly, allowing for two correct answers, for about 10 items (out of about 140) for version 1.2 of the TOPI.

45 *According to the psychologist David Funder* . . . The list appears on p. 658 of Funder, D. C. (1995). On the accuracy of personality judgment: A realistic approach. *Psychological Review, 102,* 652–670.

45 *Funder finds that we are particularly good* . . . Funder, D. C., & Dobroth, K. M. (1987). Differences between traits: Properties associated with interjudge agreement. *Journal of Personality and Social Psychology, 52,* 409–418.

46 *A. A. Roback, who wrote a 1927 textbook* . . . The conventional wisdom assigns priority to Gordon Allport, but Roback's text preceded Allport's 1937 book by almost a decade, and Roback, in his introduction, plainly indicates his book reached its second printing because it was being used in new courses on personality psychology. The text is Roback, A. A. (1931). *The psychology of character with a survey of temperament.* New York: Harcourt, Brace and Company. (Original work 1927)

46 *For Roback, it was the* inner *personality* . . . This is the implication of the section on the "Double Phase of Personality," from ibid., p. 159 of Chapter IX, defining terms.

2. CLUES TO OURSELVES: CONCEALED AND REVEALED

51 *Each of us is like a detective* . . . The idea of searching for clues about mental life is found repeatedly through the scientific literature, but the best contemporary treatment might be in David Funder's textbook. Funder, D. (2010). *The personality puzzle.* New York: W. W. Norton.

51 *Panzarella used clues about the suspect* . . . The case is drawn from Michaels, P. A. (1994). *The detectives.* New York: St. Martin's.

51 *"You know, you're really breaking my balls"* and *"Officer, there's a jacket in the backseat"* . . . Ibid., p. 23.

53 *"a feel"* and *"Detectives have been taking people off"* . . . Both ibid., p. 25.

53–54 *"how exhausting it is"*; *"feeling sad—as if"*; and *"her baby is her top priority"* . . . The ideas about what new mothers think are from p. 1042 of Lewis, K. L., Hodges, S. D., Laurent, S. M., Srivastava, S., & Biancarosa, G. (2012). Reading between the minds: The use of stereotypes in empathic accuracy. *Psychological Science, 23,* 1040–1046.

55 *For example, Penton-Voak and his team took photographs* . . . Reported in Penton-Voak, I. S., Pound, N., Little, A. C., & Perrett, D. I. (2006). Personality judgments from natural and composite facial images: More evidence for a "kernel of truth" in social perception. *Social Cognition, 24,* 607–640.

55 *For every group of fifteen extreme scorers* . . . Duncan Rowland and David Perrett have developed several computer approaches to capturing and modifying the human face (including an iPhone app called "Face Transformer" by Abertec; see itunes.apple.com/gb/app/facetransformer-art-edition/id442729566?mt=8\). The more serious business of morphing faces is described in Rowland, D., & Perrett, D. I. (1995). Manipulating facial appearance through shape and color. *IEEE Computer Graphics and Applications, 15,* 70–76.

56 *The composite extraverted woman* . . . I am describing faces from Figures 1 (men) and 2 (women) from pp. 622 and 623 of Penton-Voak and his colleagues' study of composite faces in Penton-Voak, I. S., Pound, N., Little, A. C., & Perrett, D. I. (2006). Personality judgments from natural and composite facial images: More evidence for a "kernel of truth" in social perception. *Social Cognition, 24,* 607–640.

56 *Researchers also distinguish between individuals with "baby-faced"* . . . See Zebrowitz, L. A., & Collins, M. A. (1997). Accurate social perception at zero acquaintance: The affordances of a Gibsonian approach. *Personality and Social Psychology Review, 1,* 204–223.

56 *Between opponents, the candidate with the face* . . . Some votes were held before the study, and some after; there was no difference. Reported in Todorov, A., Mandisodza, A. N., Goren, A., & Hall, C. C. (2005). Inferences of competence from faces predict election outcomes. *Science, 308,* 1623–1626.

56 *For example, circulating testosterone may affect both* . . . Reported in Penton-Voak, I. S., & Chen, J. Y. (2004). High salivary testosterone is linked to masculine male facial appearance in humans. *Evolution and Human Behavior, 25,* 229–241.

56 *James M. Dabbs of Georgia State* . . . See Dabbs, J. M. (1992). Testosterone and occupational achievement. *Social Forces, 70,* 813–824.

57 *In other comparisons, actors and football players* . . . See Dabbs, J. M. (1990). Testosterone and occupational choice: Actors, ministers, and other men. *Journal of Personality and Social Psychology, 59,* 1261–1265; and Dabbs, J. M., Allford,

E. C., & Fielden, J. A. (1998). Trial lawyers and testosterone: Blue-collar talent in a white-collar world. *Journal of Applied Social Psychology, 28*, 84–94.

57 *Not surprisingly, high levels of estrogen* . . . See Law Smith, M. J., Deady, D. K., Moore, F. R., Jones, B. C., Cornwell, R. E., Stirrat, M., Lawson, J. F., Feinberg, D. R., & Perrett, D. I. (2012). Maternal tendencies in women are associated with estrogen levels and facial femininity. *Hormones and Behavior, 61*, 12–16.

58 *Samuel Gosling and his colleagues* . . . See Gosling, S. D., Ko, S. J., Mannarelli, T., & Morris, M. E. (2002). Room with a cue: Personality judgments based on offices and bedrooms. *Journal of Personality and Social Psychology, 82*, 379–398.

59 *The judges could have done better* . . . From p. 6 of Gosling, S. (2009). *Snoop*. New York: Basic Books.

59 *At the beginning of a lecture course in psychology* . . . Back, M. D., Schmukle, S. C., & Egloff, B. (2010). Why are narcissists so charming at first sight? Decoding the narcissism-popularity link at zero acquaintance. *Journal of Personality and Social Psychology, 98*, 132–145.

59 *"I insist on getting the respect that is due me"* . . . From p. 13 of Emmons, R. A. (1987). Narcissim: Theory and measurement. *Journal of Personality and Social Psychology, 52*, 11–17.

59 *This study and others like it make clear* . . . See, for example, Table 1 in particular of Zebrowitz, L. A., & Collins, M. A. (1997). Accurate social perception at zero acquaintance: The affordances of a Gibsonian approach. *Personality and Social Psychology Review, 1*, 204–223.

60 *The philosopher Theophrastus* . . . In Theophrastus. (372–287 B.C./1929). Demarcated characters. In Edmunds, J. M. (Ed.), *The characters of Theophrastus*. Cambridge, MA: Harvard University Press.

60 *Tera Letzring of Idaho State University* . . . As reported in Letzring, T. D. (2008). The good judge of personality: Characteristics, behaviors, and observer accuracy. *Journal of Research in Personality, 42*, 914–932.

61 *"a clear-cut internally consistent personality"* . . . The quote is from p. 924 (Table 1) of Letzring, T. D. (2008). The good judge of personality: Characteristics, behaviors, and observer accuracy. *Journal of Research in Personality, 42*, 914–932.

62 *For example, studies have found that people's membership* . . . See Schlenker, B. R., Chambers, J. R., & Le, B. M. (2012). Conservatives are happier than liberals, but why? Political ideology, personality, and life satisfaction. *Journal of Research in Personality, 46*, 127–146.

62 *Generally, liberals are more open to others' perspectives* . . . According to Carney, D. R., Jost, J. T., Gosling, S. D., & Potter, J. (2008). The secret lives of liberals and conservatives: Personality profiles, interaction styles, and the things they leave behind. *Political Psychology, 29*, 807–840.

62 *And according to Jacob Hirsch and his colleagues* . . . As reported in Hirsh, J. B., DeYoung, C. G., Xu, X., & Peterson, J. B. (2010). Compassionate liberals and

polite conservatives: Associations of agreeableness with political ideology and moral values. *Personality and Social Psychology Bulletin, 36,* 655–664.

62 *High-activity people prefer to be doing things* . . . In O'Sullivan, D. M., Zuckerman, M., & Kraft, M. (1998). Personality characteristics of male and female participants in team sports. *Personality and Individual Differences, 25,* 119–128.

62 *Club membership also provides clues* . . . As reported in Zambon, A., Morgan, A., Vereecken, C., Colombini, S., Boyce, W., Mazur, J., Lemma, P., & Cavallo, F. (2010). The contribution of club participation to adolescent health: Evidence from six countries. *Journal of Epidemiology and Community Health, 64,* 89–95.

63 *Marc Brackett, Kevin Carlsmith, Heather Chabot, and I* . . . As of this writing, Marc Brackett is at Yale University, Heather Chabot is at New England College, and Kevin Carlsmith, after a short, brilliant career, passed away at too young an age; he is missed by many of us from many places. The most recent study discussed is Brackett, M. A., & Mayer, J. D. (2006). The life space: A framework and method to describe the individual's external traits. *Imagination, Cognition and Personality, 26,* 3–41. The initial study was Mayer, J. D., Carlsmith, K. M., & Chabot, H. F. (1998). Describing the person's external environment: Conceptualizing and measuring the Life Space. *Journal of Research in Personality, 32,* 253–296.

64 *Bem illustrated the effect of watching ourselves* . . . The "truth" and "false" light study was Study 3 of Bem, D. J. (1965). An experimental analysis of self-persuasion. *Journal of Experimental Social Psychology, 1,* 199–218.

65 *When people are paid to perform a task, Deci showed* . . . Deci, E. L. (1971). The effects of externally mediated rewards on intrinsic motivation. *Journal of Personality and Social Psychology, 18,* 105–115.

66 *"run the asinine verses week after next"* . . . Quoted on page 45 of Parker, D. M. (2005). *Ogden Nash: The life and work of America's laureate of light verse.* Chicago: Ivan R. Dee. Nash's use of scrap paper and his tossing them on his coworkers' desks is on p. 27; the story about Nash's friend submitting his satirical poem to a newspaper appears on p. 46.

66 *"Candy is dandy"* and *"Why did the Lord give us"* . . . The poems are titled, respectively, "Reflections on Ice-Breaking" and "Common Sense," and appear on pp. 3 and 10 of Nash, O. (1975). *I wouldn't have missed it.* Boston: Little, Brown and Company. (Original works 1930).

66 *"I am not very adept at picking up subtle social clues"* . . . From p. 58 of Max, T. (2006). *I hope they serve beer in hell.* New York: Citadel Press.

66 *"I get excessively drunk at inappropriate times"* and *"I do contribute to humanity"* . . . The two quotes can both be found on the home page of TuckerMax.com. Retrieved November 8, 2011, from www.tuckermax.com/on.

67 *"out all night and I couldn't see anything"* and *"I took this as carte blanche to keep doing"* . . . From pp. 56 and 59, respectively, of Max, T. (2006). *I hope they serve beer in hell.* New York: Citadel Press.

67 *Perhaps Max was as he described himself* . . . Max reflects on the events in ibid., p. 67.

67 *Cameron Anderson and Aiwa Shirako of the University of California* . . . Reported in Anderson, C., & Shirako, A. (2008). Are individuals' reputations related to their history of behavior? *Journal of Personality and Social Psychology, 94,* 320–333.

68 *Most of us do keep track* . . . See, for example, Carlson, E. N., Vazire, S., & Furr, R. M. (2011). Meta-insight: Do people really know how others see them? *Journal of Personality and Social Psychology, 101,* 831–846.

68 *Even narcissistic people* . . . As reported in Carlson, E. N., Vazire, S., & Oltmanns, T. F. (2011). You probably think this paper's about you: Narcissists' perceptions of their personality and reputation. *Journal of Personality and Social Psychology, 101,* 185–201.

69 *"I am not thinking"* through *"take part in a new physical activity"* . . . Examples from pp. 591–592 in Lippke, S. Z., Jochen, P., & Schwarzer, R. (2005). Stage-specific adoption and maintenance of physical activity: Testing a three-stage model. *Psychology of Sport and Exercise, 6,* 585–603.

70 *A classic series of research studies* . . . See pp. 170–171 of Wilson, T. D. (2002). *Strangers to ourselves.* Cambridge, MA: Belknap Press of Harvard University Press.

71 *a "little something extra"* . . . See p. 334 of Wilson, T. D., Lisle, D. J., Schooler, J. W., Hodges, S. D., Klaaren, K. J., & LaFleur, S. J. (1995). Introspecting about reasons can reduce post-choice satisfaction. *Personality and Social Psychology Bulletin, 19,* 331–339.

71 *For example, students in the poster study* . . . The observation is from p. 172 of Wilson, T. D. (2002). *Strangers to ourselves.* Cambridge, MA: Belknap Press of Harvard University Press.

72 *It wasn't like they "met yesterday"* and *"Who had taught her the fine art"* . . . From p. 156 of Reik, T. (1983). *Listening with the third ear.* New York: Farrar, Straus and Giroux. (Original work, 1948).

3. THE PEOPLE OUT THERE

76 *"its power to parallel or model external events."* through *"the* Queen Mary . . . *with the aid of a model in a tank"* . . . Craik adds that such models are built on the ground of "cheapness, speed, and convenience." From Craik, K. (1967). *The nature of explanation.* New York: Cambridge University Press.

76 *One of the fundamental purposes of memory* . . . See, for example, Schacter, D. L. (2012). Adaptive constructive processes and the future of memory. *American Psychologist, 67,* 603–613.

76 *Two founders of this field, Susan T. Fiske and Shelley E. Taylor* . . . Their original work was dated 1984 and published by Longman Higher Education. The in-print version is Fiske, S. T., & Taylor, S. E. (1991). *Social cognition.* New York: McGraw-Hill.

77 *"Kennedy prepared meticulously"* and *"of a crude, opinionated peasant"* . . .

See p. 542 of O'Brien, M. (2005). *John F. Kennedy: A biography*. New York: Macmillan.

77 *In this way Kennedy hoped to exhibit his confidence* . . . As described in Beschloss, M. R. (1991). *The crisis years: Kennedy and Khrushchev, 1960–1963*. New York: Edward Burlingame Books.

78 *"roughest thing in my life"* through *"He just beat the hell out of me"* . . . The quote is from Thrall, N., & Wilkins, J. J. (2008). Kennedy talked, Khruschev triumphed. *New York Times* [op-ed]. Retrieved from www.nytimes.com/2008 /05/22/opinion/22thrall.html.

78 *But perhaps not all was lost* . . . From p. 551 of O'Brien, M. (2005). *John F. Kennedy: A biography*. New York: Macmillan.

79 *"significant other"* . . . Michael Kraus and Serena Chen's study is reported in Kraus, M. W., & Chen, S. (2011). Facial-feature resemblance elicits the transference effect. *Psychological Science, 21*, 518–521.

79 *"At times she is extraverted, affable"* . . . Ibid., p. 519.

80 *"She was horrified at [the suggestion]"* and *"many years earlier . . . that the man"* . . . From p. 348 of Freud, S. (1895/1966). The psychotherapy of hysteria. In Freud, S., & Breuer, J. (Eds.). *Studies on hysteria* (pp. 299–351). J. Strachey and A. Freud (Trans). (1895, Original edition in German). A note suggests that this is Freud's first use of the term in this sense.

80 *Freud concluded that the young woman had transferred* . . . From Salvard, A. (1992). Freud's narrow escape and the discovery of transference. *Psychoanalytic Psychology, 9*, 347–367; Makari, G. J. (1994). Toward an intellectual history of transference: 1888–1900. *Psychiatric Clinics of North America, 17*, 559–570.

80 *Professors and psychotherapists Merton Gill and Irwin Hoffman* . . . Merton Gill was a faculty member at the University of Illinois at Chicago, and both Gill and Hoffman served on the faculty of analytic institutes in the Chicago area. Their work was an unusual and bold entry in the realm of empirical research, to which they brought a uniquely subtle touch to the empirical study of clinical processes. Reported in Gill, M., & Hoffman, I. (1982). Analysis of transference: Studies of nine audio-recorded psychoanalytic sessions. *Psychological Issues, Monograph 54*, 1–229.

81 *"[He] was keeping me from reading and"* . . . Ibid., p. 152.

81 *"Well, now I'm getting that same feeling that, you know"* . . . Ibid., p. 154.

81 *Researchers in the area had found that an inner model* . . . The idea that a person's mental models also appear in dreams in the form of thematic preoccupations comes from Mikulincer, M., Shaver, P., & Avihou-Kanza, N. (2011). Individual differences in adult attachment are systematically related to dream narratives. *Attachment and Human Development, 13*, 105–123. See also Popp, C. A., Diguer, L., Luborsky, L., Faude, J., Johnson, S., Morris, M., Schaffer, N., Schaffler, P., & Schmidt, K. (1996). Repetitive relationship themes in waking narratives and dreams. *Journal of Consulting and Clinical Psychology, 64*, 1073–1078.

82 *After that, Tricia and I played again* . . . After the encounter, the school took up the issue of "Tricia's" treatment at home. The school at which I met Tricia was the Mental Development Center (MDC). Founded in 1959, it was the first university school for children with developmental disabilities in the United States. At the time I worked there, it was directed by Professor Jane Kessler, a child psychoanalyst who worked in (and later chaired) the Psychology Department of Case Western Reserve University. In 1994, the school became administered by the Murtis H. Taylor Multi-Service Center, and the university created a replacement program: The Schubert Center for Child Development. A shorter form of this story served as an introduction to an earlier article on transference, coauthored with Henry C. Rapp & Lizette Williams in 1993.

83 *"It sounds stupid, but it does scare me"* . . . From p. 60 of O'Connell, M. (2008). *The marriage benefit: The surprising rewards of staying together.* New York: Springboard Press.

83 *She was overlooking the decency and sincerity* . . . See ibid., in particular p. 53, for this part of the story of Noah and Devon.

84 *"If you are investigating / the character"* . . . From 33, p. 143, in Ptahhotep (c. 2450 BCE/2003). The maxims of Ptahhotep. V. A. Toben (Trans). In W. K. Simpson (Ed.), *The Literature of Ancient Egypt* (pp. 129–148). New Haven: Yale University Press. (Please note that there are "extreme difficulties" with translating the text, and translations vary.)

84 *"our children will be the better for it"* . . . From p. 3 of Theophrastus. (Trans. 1970). *Theophrastus characters.* W. Anderson (Ed. & Trans.). Kent, OH: Kent State University Press. This passage is often attributed to a student of Theophrastus', as it seems to have been added at some point after the original manuscript was compiled.

85 *"There was a time when I used to listen"* . . . From 5.10, p. 11 of Leys, S. (Ed. & Trans.) (1997). *The analects of Confucius.* New York: W. W. Norton (Original work c. 300 BCE).

85 *Professors Jerry Wiggins, of the University of British Columbia, and Krista Trobst* . . . During the time of this study, Wiggins had moved briefly to York University. The report of the study is in Wiggins, J. S. (2003). *Paradigms of personality assessment.* New York: Guilford Press.

85–86 *As part of the study, Madeline traveled by jet, first* . . . Madeline's itinerary for the assessment was described in ibid., p. 210.

86 *"was not what she had in mind at all!"* . . . Ibid., p. 229.

86 *"When she arrived for the testing session"* . . . See pp. 227–228 in Behrends, R. S., & Blatt, S. J. (2003). Psychodynamic assessment. In J. S. Wiggins (Ed.), *Paradigms of personality assessment* (pp. 226–245). New York: Guilford Press.

87 *"apt to making sexually suggestive remarks"* through *"with individuals who are made"* . . . From p. 313 of Trobst, K. K., & Wiggins, J. S. (2003). Constructive alternativism in personality assessment. In Wiggins, J. S. (Ed.), *Paradigms of personality assessment* (pp. 226–245). New York: Guilford Press.

87 *For example, Behrends noticed that Madeline* . . . From p. 230 of Behrends,
    R. S., & Blatt, S. J. (2003). Psychodynamic assessment. In Wiggins, J. S. (Ed.),
    Paradigms of personality assessment (pp. 226–245). New York: Guilford Press.

88 *The researchers conjectured* . . . Madeline's vision of the monster with fire and
    the person being burned, as well as other details of Madeline's content, is dis-
    cussed in ibid., pp. 239 and 240. I acknowledge that many of my colleagues have
    their well-argued doubts about the Rorschach, but although I see the measure's
    limits, I regard it as a useful measurement instrument.

88 *"Childhood," "Jail," and "The Present"* . . . See p. 215 of McAdams, D. P. (2003).
    Personological assessment: The life story of Madeline G. In Wiggins, J. S. (Ed.),
    Paradigms of personality assessment (pp. 213–225). New York: Guilford Press.

89 *She then worked defending Native American* . . . Madeline's low, high, and turn-
    ing points are described in ibid., pp. 216–217.

89 *She regarded her survival and eventual flourishing* . . . Ibid., p. 224.

89 *"for us or against us"* . . . The point is made in Malle, B. F. (2008). Fritz Heider's
    legacy: Celebrated insights, many of them misunderstood. *Social Psychology,*
    39, 163–173.

89 *"She experiences the nagging question"* . . . See p. 245 in Behrends, R. S., &
    Blatt, S. J. (2003). Psychodynamic assessment. In Wiggins, J. S. (Ed.), *Paradigms*
    of personality assessment (pp. 226–245). New York: Guilford Press.

90 *"IF a person is at a party"* . . . These examples are drawn from p. 1289 of
    Chen, S. (2003). Psychological-state theories about significant others: Implica-
    tions for the content and structure of significant-other representations. *Personal-*
    ity and Social Psychology Bulletin, 29, 1285–1302. See also Chen, S. (2001).
    The role of theories in mental representations and their use in social perception:
    A theory-based approach to significant-other representations and transference.
    In Moskowitz, G. B. (Ed.), *Cognitive social psychology: The Princeton Sympo-*
    sium on the legacy and future of social cognition (pp. 125–142). Mahwah, NJ:
    Lawrence Erlbaum Associates.

90 *Glenn Reeder of Illinois State University has illustrated people's logic* . . . In
    Reeder, G. D. (2009). Mindreading: Judgments about intentionality and motives
    in dispositional inference. *Psychological Inquiry, 20,* 1–18.

91 *Paul Costa and Ralph Piedmont of the National Institute on Aging* . . . Paul Costa
    is a coauthor with Robert McCrae of the "NEO-PI-R," a benchmark test of the Big
    Five. Their report on Madeline is in Costa, P. T., & Piedmont, R. L. (2003). Multi-
    variate assessment: NEO PI-R profiles of Madeline G. In Wiggins, J. S. (Ed.), *Para-*
    digms of personality assessment (pp. 226–245). New York: Guilford Press.

91 *In fact, the Big Five approach had its start in 1936* . . . The 17,953 words and
    4,504 traits were reported in Allport, G. W., & Odbert, H. S. (1936). Trait names:
    A psych-lexical study. *Psychological Monographs, 47,* 1–171.

91 *Similar lists have been developed in German, Italian, and Chinese* . . .
    McCrae, R. R., & Alik, J. (Eds.), *The Five-Factor model of personality across*
    cultures. New York: Kluwer Academic Publishers.

92 *"I generally prefer to go along with others"* through *"This person generally prefers"* . . . From the NEO-PI-R, the Neuroticism-Extraversion-Openness Personality Inventory, Revised (to measure Agreeableness and Conscientiousness as well), developed by Paul Costa and Robert "Jeff" McCrae. Her assessment is described in Costa, P. T., & Piedmont, R. L. (2003). Multivariate assessment: NEO PI-R profiles of Madeline G. In Wiggins, J. S. (Ed.), *Paradigms of personality assessment* (pp. 226–245). New York: Guilford Press.

92 *Based on averaging her own and her partner's responses* . . . Madeline was well above average on extraversion; see ibid., p. 266.

92 *"She is active and energetic"* . . . Ibid., p. 268.

93 *"is characteristically suspicious of other people"* . . . Ibid., p. 267.

93 *"Coworkers who tend to express skepticism and cynicism"* . . . From p. 148 of Christiansen, N. D., Wolcott-Burnam, S., Janovics, J. E., Burns, G. N., & Quirk, S. W. (2005). The good judge revisited: Individual differences in the accuracy of personality judgments. *Human Performance, 18,* 123–149.

93 *"an athlete you know who was largely"* . . . Ibid., p. 148.

94 *"Madeline and her partner are likely to butt heads"* . . . The quote is from Aaron Pincus of the Pennsylvania State University and Michael Gurtman of the the University of Wisconsin, Parkside, from p. 261 of Pincus, A. L., & Gurtman, M. B. (2003). Interpersonal assessment. In Wiggins, J. S. (Ed.), *Paradigms of personality assessment* (pp. 246–261). New York: Guilford Press.

94 *"to be controlled"* and *"helps with self-control"* . . . The discussion arose on p. 280 of Costa, P. T., & Piedmont, R. L. (2003). Multivariate assessment: NEO PI-R profiles of Madeline G. In Wiggins, J. S. (Ed.), *Paradigms of personality assessment* (pp. 226–245). New York: Guilford Press.

95 *"the protagonist in this narrative"* . . . From p. 225 of McAdams, D. P. (2003). Personological assessment: The life story of Madeline G. In Wiggins, J. S. (Ed.), *Paradigms of personality assessment* (pp. 213–225). New York: Guilford Press.

95 *A latent variable is a psychological attribute* . . . It's something we infer from observations. This idea is my informal translation of Bollen's "sample realization" definition of latent variables. Bollen, K. A. (2002). Latent variables in psychology and the social sciences. *Annual Review of Psychology, 53,* 605–634.

95 *In 2012, we reported a successful attempt* . . . See Mayer, J. D., Panter, A. T., & Caruso, D. R. (2012). Does personal intelligence exist? Evidence from a new ability-based measure. *Journal of Personality Assessment, 94,* 124–140.

96 *So skill at using one tool correlated positively with skill at using another* . . . New data we are analyzing as I write continue to indicate that overall personal intelligence is a unitary ability. Our most recent analyses suggest the overall ability may subdivide into two or three related problem-solving abilities. One ability area is primarily focused on associating parts of personality with one another, such as traits with other traits, or traits with behaviors. The other ability area is focused on logical reasoning about personality, such as integrating feedback and inferring motivations. Nonverbal perceptions of personality appear to

form a third area of reasoning; their relationship with the other areas is less strong. Findings like these, once better understood, will likely influence specifics of the future models of personal intelligence we develop.

96 *"on a roll"* . . . See p. 224 of McAdams, D. P. (2003). Personological assessment: The life story of Madeline G. In Wiggins, J. S. (Ed.), *Paradigms of personality assessment* (pp. 213–225). New York: Guilford Press.

97 *The two organizers had hoped* through *Madeline had participated* . . . Discussed on pp. 322–333 of Wiggins, J. S. (Ed.). (2003). *Paradigms of personality assessment*. New York: Guilford Press.

97 *"Madeline tolerates a great deal in herself"* . . . On p. 238 in Behrends, R. S., & Blatt, S. J. (2003). Psychodynamic assessment. In Wiggins J. S. (Ed.), *Paradigms of personality assessment* (pp. 226–245). New York: Guilford Press.

98 *"Wow! Did everyone get me like that?"* On p. 323 of Wiggins, J. S. (2003). *Paradigms of Personality Assessment*. New York: Guilford Press.

98 *"I love that. I love the idea of this"* . . . Ibid.

4. FEELING INFORMATION

100 *"I don't know what to do"* . . . From "Who am I?" p. 7 of Wooten, H. R. (1994). Cutting losses for student-athletes in transition: An integrative transition model. *Journal of Employment Counseling, 31,* 2–9. Further evidence that college students who are less sure of who they are find it harder to choose a career is indicated in the structural equation model based on a study of measurements of 285 students by Downing, H. M., & Nauta, M. M. (2010). Separation-individuation, exploration, and identity diffusion as mediators of the relationship between attachment and career indecision. *Journal of Career Development, 36,* 207–227.

100 *the cognitive scientist Ulric Neisser* . . . Neisser outlined five kinds of selves in his article. Neisser, U. (1988). Five kinds of self-knowledge. *Philosophical Psychology, 1,* 35–59.

100 *"everything that happened before October 5, 1957"* . . . From p. 16 of Hickam, H. H. (1998). *Rocket boys.* New York: Delacorte Press.

100 *As the child of a coal mine supervisor* . . . Hickam's skill at fighting was recounted in ibid., p. 21. His paper route and bicycle are described on p. 2.

101 *His lower-grade teachers, "The Great Six"* . . . The teachers acquired that nickname because they taught grades 1 through 6. From ibid., p. 10.

101. *Hickam's own list of his qualities as a boy* . . . I gleaned the list of "happy," "hopeful," "imaginative," "industrious," and "tough" from Hickam's self-descriptions in the chapters on Coalwood and *Sputnik.* Ibid.

101 *After a deafening explosion* . . . Hickam's story of his first rocket launch occurs in ibid., pp. 54–57.

101 *"Sonny, do you think"* . . . Ibid., p. 42.

102 *"I-am-counting-on-you"* and *"Show him you can do something!"* . . . From ibid., p. 46.

102 *As a result of his brain injury* . . . K.C.'s personality change is described on p. 993 of Rosenbaum, R. S., Kohler, S., Schacter, D. L., Moscovitch, M., Westmacott, R., Black, S. E., Fuqiang, G., & Tulving, E. (2005). The case of K.C.: Contributions of a memory-impaired person to memory theory. *Neuropsychologia, 43,* 989–1021.

103 *Not only could K.C. describe his personality* . . . I am relying on a summary of the case described on p. 926 of Klein, S. B., & Lax, M. L. (2010). The unanticipated resilience of trait self-knowledge in the face of neural damage. *Memory, 18,* 918–948.

103 *W.J. was asked to indicate qualities of her personality* . . . The most detailed report is in Klein S. B., Loftus J., & Kihlstrom, J. F. (1996). Self-knowledge of an amnesic patient: Toward a neuropsychology of personality and social psychology. *Journal of Experimental Psychology, General, 125,* 250–260.

103 *W.J. had somehow noticed changes* . . . As described on pp. 926–927 of Klein, S. B., & Lax, M. L. (2010). The unanticipated resilience of trait self-knowledge in the face of neural damage. *Memory, 18,* 918–948.

103 *Cases such as K.C.'s and W.J.'s are rare* . . . Described in ibid., p. 933.

103 *We may think of our episodic memories* . . . The idea that we use our memory to simulate the future is developed in Schacter, D. L. (2012). Adaptive constructive processes and the future of memory. *American Psychologist, 67,* 603–613.

104 *Regarding our sense of self* . . . Hazel Markus developed the idea of possible selves at the University of Michigan, as reported in Markus, H., & Nurius, P. (1986). Possible selves. *American Psychologist, 41,* 954–959.

104 *"Maybe one day we'll have a trophy"* . . . From p. 79 of Hickam, H. H. (1998). *Rocket boys.* New York: Delacorte Press.

104 *"My thought belongs with my other thoughts"* . . . From p. 153 in the chapter on "the Stream of Consciousness" in James, W. (1892). *Psychology: Briefer course.* New York: Henry Holt and Company.

105 *"each one of them mentally reaches"* . . . Ibid., p. 158.

105 *Within our working memory* . . . For an overview of working memory, see Baddeley, A. (2012). Working memory: Theories, models, and controversies. *Annual Review of Psychology, 63,* 1–29.

106 *It was dusk, he said* . . . I set the stage for my description of Hickam's conscious experience of his mother's talk to him by drawing on pp. 43–45 of Hickam, H. H. (1998). *Rocket boys.* New York: Delacorte Press.

106 *The philosopher Daniel Dennett believed* . . . Dennett's analogy between the brain and computers can be found in Chapter 9: Toward a cognitive theory of consciousness. In Dennett, D. C. (1981). *Brainstorms: Philosophical essays on mind and psychology.* Cambridge, MA: MIT Press. I note that Dennett has further developed his views on consciousness since writing this essay, but his earlier thoughts remain useful.

106 *We then access the responses* . . . The idea that if we introspect, our minds respond with a set of results is from p. 156 (Section III) of "Toward a cognitive theory of consciousness." In ibid.

107 *In fact, we recruit different sets* . . . One set of findings that thinking about ourselves involves overlapping but different brain regions from thinking about others is reported in Saxe, R., Moran, J. M., Scholz, J., & Gabrieli, J. (2006).
Overlapping and non-overlapping brain regions for theory of mind and self-
reflection in individual subjects. *Social Cognitive and Affective Neuroscience, 1,*
229–234. See also the more recent Whitfield-Gabrieli, S., Moran, J. M., Nieto-
Castañón, A., Triantafyllou, C., Saxe, R., & Gabrieli, J.D.E. (2011). Associations
and dissociations between default and self-reference networks in the human
brain. *NeuroImage, 55,* 225–232.

108 *"an overall intelligence within expectations, given their sociocultural back-*
ground" and *"They never construct an appropriate theory about their*
persons" . . . Both quotes are from p. 58 of Damásio, A. (2005). *Descartes's*
error: Emotion, reason, and the human brain. New York: Penguin Books.

108 *"And after all this, I still wouldn't know what to do!"* . . . Ibid., p. 49.

108 *The participants' pain responses* . . . Reported in Kross, E., Berman, M. G.,
Mischel, W., Smith, E. E., & Wager, T. D. (2011). Social rejection shares somato-
sensory representations with physical pain. *PNAS, 108,* 6270–6275.

109 *It turns out, in fact, that acetaminophen* . . . Reported in DeWall, C. N., Mac-
Donald, G., Webster, G. D., Masten, C. L., Baumeister, R. F., Powell, C., Combs,
D., Schurtz, D. R., Stillman, T. F., Tice, D. M., & Eisenberger, N. I. (2010).
Acetaminophen reduces social pain: Behavioral and neural evidence. *Psychologi-*
cal Science, 21, 931–937.

109 *Beyond brain studies, the tragedy of* . . . The statistics indicating that suicide is
the third leading cause of death among adolescents in the United States, and the
second leading cause in Canada, are from Steele, M. M., & Doey, T. (2007).
Suicidal behaviour in children and adolescents. Part 1: Etiology and risk factors.
Canadian Journal of Psychiatry, 52, 21S–33S. Supplement 1.

109 *The "better-than-average" effect* . . . A description of the concept and the findings I report are from Guenther, C. L., & Alicke, M. D. (2010). Deconstructing
the better-than-average effect. *Journal of Personality and Social Psychology, 99,*
755–770.

109 *We take responsibility for positive events* . . . This effect, sometimes referred to
as "beneffectance," was introduced in Greenwald, A. G. (1980). The totalitarian
ego: Fabrication and revision of personal history. *American Psychologist, 35,*
603–618. The study of taking credit in groups is by Johnston, W. A. (1967). Individual performance and self-evaluation in a simulated team. *Organizational*
Behavior and Human Performance, 2, 309–328.

110 *Freud described the painful ideas* . . . A nice contemporary viewpoint of ego
threat is offered in Leary, M. R., Terry, M. L., Allen, A. B., & Tate, E. B. (2009).
The concept of ego threat in social and personality psychology: Is ego threat
a viable scientific construct? *Personality and Social Psychology Review, 13,*
151–164.

110 *Consider the following: More than 91 percent* . . . The percentages are drawn

from pp. 7 and 8 of Buss, D. M. (2005). *The murderer next door: Why the mind is designed to kill*. New York: Penguin.

110 *Conservative estimates are that 22 percent* . . . The statistics are drawn from Wiederman, M. W. (1997). Extramarital sex: Prevalence and correlates in a national survey. *The Journal of Sex Research, 34*, 167–174. I also looked at Parker-Pope, T. (2008, October 27). Love, sex, and the changing landscape of infidelity. *New York Times*: Health. Retrieved from www.nytimes.com/2008/10/28/health/28well.html. This article reported on a study by David C. Atkins of the University of Washington.

110 *As a consequence, few of us recognize the prevalence* . . . The reference to Forer is to his study reported in Forer, B. R. (1949). The fallacy of personal validation: A classroom demonstration of gullibility. *The Journal of Abnormal and Social Psychology, 44*, 118–123. See also the coverage of Forer in Chapter 1.

110 *Freud cataloged a number of practices* . . . See, for example, p. 975 of Loewenberg, P. (2005). Wild analysis: A new Freud translation. *Journal of the American Psychoanalytic Association, 53*, 973–979.

111 *"a blessing in disguise"* . . . The example is quoted from p. 33 of Banja, J. D. (2004). *Medical errors and medical narcissism*. Sudbury, MA: Jones and Bartlett.

111 *We can arrange these, from the more immature* . . . For a contemporary ordering of mechanisms of coping and defense, see Vaillant, G. E., Bond, M., & Vaillant, C. O. (1986). An empirically validated hierarchy of defense mechanisms. *Archives of General Psychiatry, 43*, 786–794. See also Vaillant, G. E. (2000). Adaptive mental mechanisms: Their role in a positive psychology. *American Psychologist, 55*, 89–98.

112 *there is some agreement between the two assessment techniques* . . . The various methods of measuring defense—through self-judgments, thematic storytelling, and interviews—show some convergence when they are correlated with one another (the correlation is $r = .35$), as reported on p. 792 of Vaillant, G. E., Bond, M., & Vaillant, C. O. (1986). An empirically validated hierarchy of defense mechanisms. *Archives of General Psychiatry, 43*, 786–794. See also Vaillant, G. E. (2000). Adaptive mental mechanisms: Their role in a positive psychology. *American Psychologist, 55*, 89–98. Although this is not as high as one might wish, it is a familiar pattern for different sources of information about a given personality characteristic. (There may be many reasons different information sources disagree: a test of a given type often picks up information that is different but complementary to a test of another type.) In this instance, one finding in common to all the measures is that defense styles predict quality-of-life outcomes in diverse groups.

112 *"Carli, who had just entered college, kept agreeing"* . . . This story was a composite of several similar stories told by participants in Allen's study. Details are forthcoming in Allen, J., & Mayer, J. D. (2013). *What do people learn about personality?* Manuscript in preparation.

113 *"seemed to want to please everyone she knew"* and *"People only do favors be-cause"* . . . These and the relationship to the TOPI in ibid.

113–14 *"The two children are playing together and having fun"* through *"The child playing with blocks isn't sharing very nicely and the other boy is mad"* . . . The card I described is fictional (so as to avoid revealing the actual content of the TAT). I have applied Cramer's scoring system, drawn from her Defense Mecha-nism Manual, to it, as described in Cramer, P. (2006). *Protecting the self: Defense mechanisms in action.* New York: Guilford. Also see Cramer, P. (2008). Identification and the development of competence: A 44-year longitudinal study from late adolescence to late middle age. *Psychology and Aging, 23,* 410–421.

114 *Cramer finds that adolescents* . . . Cramer, P. (2009). An increase in early adoles-cent undercontrol is associated with the use of denial. *Journal of Personality Assessment, 91,* 331–339; and Cramer, P. (2002). Defense mechanisms, behavior, and affect in young adulthood. *Journal of Personality, 70,* 103–128.

115 *"they are all the same—cousins, aunts, and everybody"* . . . From p. 789 of Vail-lant, G. E., Bond, M., & Vaillant, C. O. (1986). An empirically validated hierarchy of defense mechanisms. *Archives of General Psychiatry, 43,* 786–794.

115 *"take things in stride"* through *"I want to make sure I know what I am hollering about before I start hollering"* . . . Ibid., pp. 790–791.

115 *Vaillant's work shows that accurate self-perception* . . . See p. 96 of Vaillant, G. E. (2000). Adaptive mental mechanisms: Their role in a positive psychology. *American Psychologist, 55,* 89–98.

116 *Thomas Oltmanns and Eric Turkheimer studied* . . . Reported in Oltmanns, T. F., & Turkheimer, E. (2006). Perceptions of self and others regarding pathological personality traits. In Kruger, R. F., & Tackett, J. L. (Eds.), *Personality and psy-chopathology* (pp. 71–111). New York: Guilford.

116 *A. T. Panter, David Caruso, and I* . . . From Table 6 of Mayer, J. D., Panter, A. T., & Caruso, D. R. (2012). Does personal intelligence exist? *Journal of Personality Assessment, 94,* 124–140.

117 *Toward the end of the decade, he was arrested and jailed* . . . See, for example, the story on p. 82 of Carr, D. (2008). *The night of the gun.* New York: Simon & Schuster.

119 *"a complicated asset as a friend"* . . . Ibid., p. 39.

119 *"a fat thug who"* and *"I was a recovered addict"* . . . Ibid., p. 24.

119 *"I often feel I have very little"* and *"until he turns into this guy"* . . . Ibid., p. 186.

200 *By contrast, people with unrealistically high self-esteem* . . . From Baumeister, R. F., Campbell, J. D., Krueger, J. I., & Vohs, K. D. (2003). Does high self-esteem cause better performance, interpersonal success, happiness, or healthier lifestyles? *Psychological Science in the Public Interest, 4,* 1–44. A 2007 study by Christopher Barry and his colleagues complicates this depiction slightly. Their work indicated that a lack of self-questioning, coupled with narcissistic, self-involved attitudes, is associated with criminal behavior—but so is low self-esteem; in other words, narcissism and low self-esteem can go together sometimes. Barry,

C. T., Grafeman, S. J., Adler, K. K., & Pickard, J. D. (2007). The relations among narcissism, self-esteem, and delinquency in a sample of at-risk adolescents. *Journal of Adolescence, 30,* 933–942.

120 *the Greek philosopher Plato anticipated this finding* . . . Plato (fourth century BCE). *Philebus,* sections 49a, 49b, 49c. Retrieved September 21, 2013, from the Perseus Project of Tufts University, data.perseus.tufts.edu/hopper/text?doc=Per seus%3Atext%3A1999.01.0174%3Atext%3DPhileb.%3Asection%3D49c.

5. A GUIDE TO MAKING CHOICES

121 *Experts in decision-making often* . . . An example of a book like this is Russo, J. E., & Schoemaker, P. J. (2001). *Winning decisions: Getting it right the first time.* New York: Crown Business.

122 *"shall forevermore become impossible"* . . . From "Five chief kinds of decisions" on p. 433 in the chapter on Will by James, W. (1920). *Psychology: Briefer course.* (Original work 1892).

123 *"too far for anyone to jump"* through *"I quickly forced from"* . . . From pp. 34 and 39 of Greenlaw, L. (1999). *The hungry ocean.* New York: Hyperion.

123 *She reflected on her desires* . . . Ibid., p. 50.

123 *Rebecca Schlegel and her colleagues* . . . Reported in Schlegel, R. J., Hicks, J. A., Arndt, J., & King, L. A. (2009). Thine own self: True self-concept accessibility and meaning in life. *Journal of Personality and Social Psychology, 96,* 473–490.

124 *Schlegel also examined how knowledge of one's true self* . . . Schlegel's studies of the true self and decision-making are reported in Studies 4 and 3 (in the order discussed in the text) of Schlegel, R. J., Hicks, J. A., Davis, W. E., Hirsch, K. A., & Smith, C. M. (2013). The dynamic interplay between perceived true self-knowledge and decision satisfaction. *Journal of Personality and Social Psychology, 104,* 542–558.

124 *Solomon Asch of the University of Pennsylvania* . . . The classic study described here was originally reported in Asch, S. E. (1955). Opinions and social pressure. *Scientific American, 193,* 31–35.

125 *Edward Deci and Richard Ryan of the University of Rochester* . . . An overview of their work can be found in Deci, E. L., & Ryan, R. M. (1985). *Intrinsic motivation and self-determination in human behavior.* New York: Plenum.

125 *"You can't fight fires with books"* . . . From Rector, K. (2012, December 2). City firefighters face new education requirements for promotion. *Baltimore Sun.* Retrieved December 17, 2012, from articles.baltimoresun.com/2012-12-02 /news/bs-md-ci-fire-education-requirements-20121202_1_fire-department -local-fire-chief-james-s-clack.

126 *"Because I'll get in trouble"* through *because "I want people to like me"* . . . From Table 2, p. 752, of Ryan, R. M., & Connell, J. P. (1989). Perceived locus of causality and internalization: Examining reasons for acting in two domains. *Journal of Personality and Social Psychology, 57,* 749–761.

126 *Press shot baskets behind the house* . . . From pp. 3, 34, and 35 of Berger, P. (1999). *Forever showtime: The checkered life of Pistol Pete Maravich*. Dallas, TX: Taylor Publishing Company.

126 *"knew any son would want"* . . . From pp. 56–57 of Maravich, P., & Campbell, D. (1987). *Heir to a dream*. Nashville, TN: Thomas Nelson. I was directed to this quote by Kriegel, who reproduced it on p. 50 of Kriegel, M. (2007). *Pistol: The life of Pete Maravich*. New York: Free Press.

127 *because "I want to understand the subject"* . . . From Table 2, p. 752, of Ryan, R. M., & Connell, J. P. (1989). Perceived locus of causality and internalization: Examining reasons for acting in two domains. *Journal of Personality and Social Psychology, 57,* 749–761.

127 *"I saw him do things"* through *"He's going to be the first"* . . . From p. 61 of Kriegel, M. (2007). *Pistol: The life of Pete Maravich*. New York: Free Press.

127 *Wooden recalled warning Press* . . . Ibid., p. 80.

127 *"hard, very hard, to contain"* Ibid., p. 253.

127 *"hit by a baseball once"* and *"That's why I stuck with basketball"* . . . From p. 30 of Federman, W., Terrill, M., & Maravich, J. (2006). *Pete Maravich: The authorized biography of Pistol Pete*. Carol Stream, IL: Tyndale House.

128 *"Don't worry about that"* . . . Ibid., p. 25.

128 *By high school, other players* . . . From p. 78 of Kriegel, M. (2007). *Pistol: The life of Pete Maravich*. New York: Free Press.

128 *"And I wasn't going to give him anything"* . . . From p. 32 of Federman, W., Terrill, M., & Maravich, J. (2006). *Pete Maravich: The authorized biography of Pistol Pete*. Carol Stream, IL: Tyndale House.

128 *"don't ever come home again"* . . . Ibid., p. 60.

128 *"basketball android"* . . . Ibid., p. 35.

128 *To be sure, Pete faced challenges as a player* . . . From p. 303 of Kriegel, M. (2007). *Pistol: The life of Pete Maravich*. New York: Free Press.

129 *"All I could think of were the expectations"* . . . Quoted from p. 169 of Maravich, P., & Campbell, D. (1987). *Heir to a dream*. Nashville, TN: Thomas Nelson. The quote appears also on p. 253 of Kriegel, M. (2007). *Pistol: The life of Pete Maravich*. New York: Free Press.

129 *Deci and Ryan believe that those who act* . . . Here I am paraphrasing some of the argument on p. 69 of Ryan, R. M., & Deci, E. L. (2000). Self-determination theory and the facilitation of intrinsic motivation, social development, and well-being. *American Psychologist, 55,* 68–78.

129 *He brought his own sons* . . . Described on pp. 285–286 of Kriegel, M. (2007). *Pistol: The life of Pete Maravich*. New York: Free Press.

129 *Michael Jordan's father* . . . Described on p. 17 of Halberstam, D. (2000). *Playing for keeps: Michael Jordan and the world he made*. New York: Three Rivers Press/Broadway Books.

129–30 *"There was no way I could live with that"* and *"do what I always had done"* . . . From p. 5 of Jordan, M. (1998). *For the love of the game: My story.* New York: Crown Publishers.

130 *The rest is basketball history* . . . See, for example, Anonymous (n.d.). "Michael Jeffrey Jordan." NBA encyclopedia (playoff edition). Retrieved September 24, 2012, from www.nba.com/history/players/jordan_bio.html. The article's first sentence is "By acclamation, Michael Jordan is the greatest basketball player of all time."

130 *"Family members should stick together"* through *"It is important that I do my job better than others"* . . . From Table 2 of Triandis, H. C., & Gelfand, M. J. (1998). Converging measurement of horizontal and vertical individualism and collectivism. *Journal of Personality and Social Psychology, 74,* 118–128. Items of this type were used in the Chirkov and Ryan study, as summarized on p. 103 of Chirkov, V., Ryan, R. M., Kim, Y., & Kaplan, U. (2003). Differentiating autonomy from individualism and independence: A self-determination theory perspective on internalization of cultural orientations and well-being. *Journal of Personality and Social Psychology, 84,* 97–109.

130 *"to depend on oneself"* through *"to maintain harmony"* . . . From items representing cultural practices on p. 110 (the appendix) of Chirkov, V., Ryan, R. M., Kim, Y., & Kaplan, U. (2003). Differentiating autonomy from individualism and independence: A self-determination theory perspective on internalization of cultural orientations and well-being. *Journal of Personality and Social Psychology, 84,* 97–109.

130 *"feel free in choosing it"* and *"because someone else insists"* . . . From ibid., p. 102.

131 *"involves competition"* through *"includes sensuous stimuli"* and *"talking is permitted"* . . . Items drawn from Table 1, p. 337, of Sherman, R. A., Nave, C. S., & Funder, D. C. (2010). Situational similarity and personality predict behavioral consistency. *Journal of Personality and Social Psychology, 99,* 330–343.

131 *Ryne Sherman of Florida Atlantic* . . . Reported in Sherman, R. A., Nave, C. S., & Funder, D. C. (2012). Properties of persons and situations related to overall and distinctive personality-behavior congruence. *Journal of Research in Personality, 46,* 87–101.

131 *We also make decisions by picking alternatives* . . . Studied by Niedenthal, P. M., Cantor, N., & Kihlstrom, J. F. (1985). Prototype matching: A strategy for social decision making. *Journal of Personality and Social Psychology, 48,* 575–584.

132 *"unconventional, friendly"* and *"practical, responsible"* . . . From Studies 1 and 2 of Setterlund, M. B., & Niedenthal, P. M. (1993). "Who am I? Why am I here?" Self-esteem, self-clarity, and prototype matching. *Journal of Personality and Social Psychology, 65,* 769–780.

132 *Similar research indicates that teenagers* . . . The smokers were studied in Chassin, L., Presson, C. C., Sherman, S. J., Corty, E., & Olshavsky, R. W. (1981). Self-images and cigarette smoking in adolescence. *Personality and Social Psychology Bulletin, 7,* 670–676. The college students were studied in Burke, P. J., &

Reitzes, D. C. (1981). The link between identity and role performance. *Social Psychology Quarterly, 44*, 83–92.

132 *Geher found that his sample of students* . . . Reported in Geher, G. (2000). Perceived and actual characteristics of parents and partners: A test of a Freudian model of mate selection. *Current Psychology, 19*, 194–214.

133 *This preference for similar others* . . . I relied on two articles in particular: McCrae, R. R., Martin, T. A., Hrebíčková, M., Urbánek, T., Willemsen, G., & Costa, P. T., Jr. (2008). Personality trait similarity between spouses in four cultures. *Journal of Personality, 76*, 1137–1163; and Chen, H., Luo, S., Yue, G., Xu, D., & Zhaoyang, R. (2009). Do birds of a feather flock together in China? *Personal Relationships, 16*, 167–186.

133 *That said, studies indicate that among couples* . . . See, for two examples, Gonzaga, G. C., Carter, S., & Buckwalter, J. G. (2010). Assortative mating, convergence, and satisfaction in married couples. *Personal Relationships, 17*, 634–644; and Luo, S., & Klohnen, E. C. (2005). Assortative mating and marital quality in newlyweds: A couple-centered approach. *Journal of Personality and Social Psychology, 88*, 304–326.

133 *Adult children of alcoholics* . . . Reported in Kearns-Bodkin, J. N., & Leonard, K. E. (2008). Relationship functioning among adult children of alcoholics. *Journal of Studies on Alcohol and Drugs, 69*, 941–950.

133 *As expected, given the love between parent and child* . . . The risk factors are covered in Hasin, D. S., Stinson, F. S., Ogburn, E., & Grant, B. F. (2007). Prevalence, correlates, disability, and comorbidity of DSM-IV alcohol abuse and dependence in the United States: Results from the national epidemiologic survey on alcohol and related conditions. *Archives of General Psychiatry, 64*, 830–842. See also Olmsted, M. E., Crowell, J. A., & Waters, E. (2003). Assortative mating among adult children of alcoholics and alcoholics. *Family Relations, 52*, 64–71.

134 *(The longevity of a marriage is also related to* . . .) . . . Larson, J. H., & Holman, T. B. (1994). Premarital predictors of marital quality and stability. *Family Relations, 43*, 226–237.

135 *For example, when a young adult considers* . . . The perplexities of getting engaged are drawn from Table 2 of Carroll, J. S., Badger, S., Willoughby, B. J., Nelson, L. J., Madsen, S. D., & McNamara, B. C. (2009). Criteria for marriage readiness among emerging adults. *Journal of Adolescent Research, 24*, 349–375.

135 *When we encounter two people who* . . . The idea that (dis)similarity among partners is relatively consistent across couples is found in Caspi, A., & Herbener, E. S. (1990). Continuity and change: Assortative marriage and the consistency of personality in adulthood. *Journal of Personality and Social Psychology, 58*, 250–258. Examples of positive coping such as negotiation and optimistic comparisons can be found in Menaghan, E. (1982). Measuring coping effectiveness: A panel analysis of marital problems and coping efforts. *Journal of Health & Social Behavior, 23*, 220–234. See also Bowman, M. L. (1990). Coping efforts and marital satisfac-

tion: Measuring marital coping and its correlates. *Journal of Marriage & Family*, 52, 463–474.

135 *an international matchmaker* . . . Reverend Moon's mass marriages took place in New York and Washington, D.C., for example. See Talbot, M. (1997, December 22). Married in a mob. *New Republic, 217* (25), 14–15; and Associated Press (1997, November 30). 28,000 couples gather for Rev. Moon rites. *New York Times*, p. 30.

136 *As it turned out, the married participants* . . . As reported in Galanter, M. (1984). Engaged members of the Unification Church. Impact of a charismatic large group on adaptation and behavior. *Archives of General Psychiatry, 40*, 1197–1202.

136 *The* Washington Post *reporter Michelle Boorstein; "when you're in the kitchen duking it out"*; and *"old-fashioned patience"* . . . From Boorstein, M. (2012, September 15). Though united in a crowd by Rev. Sun Myung Moon, couples say marriages succeeded or failed on their own. *Washington Post Local*. Retrieved from www.washingtonpost.com/local/though-united-in-a-crowd-by-rev-sun-my ung-moon-couples-say-marriages-succeeded-or-failed-on-their-own/2012/09/15 /b0bfa176-fe77-11e1-8adc-499661afe377_print.html.

137 *A study of female staff nurses* . . . Reported in Williams, G., Dean, P., & Williams, E. (2009). Do nurses really care? Confirming the stereotype with a case control study. *British Journal of Nursing, 18*, 163–165.

137 *Holland arranged his careers* . . . Reviewed in Armstrong, P. I., Day, S. X., McVay, J. P., & Rounds, J. (2008). Holland's RIASEC model as an integrative framework for individual differences. *Journal of Counseling Psychology, 55*, 1–18. See also Armstrong, P. I., & Rounds, J. (2010). Integrating individual differences in career assessment: The Atlas Model of Individual Differences and the Strong Ring. *The Career Development Quarterly, 59*, 143–153.

138 *Lynette Sutherland and her colleagues* . . . Reported in Sutherland, L. F., Fogarty, G. J., & Pithers, R. T. (1995). Congruence as a predictor of occupational stress. *Journal of Vocational Behavior, 46*, 292–309.

138 *reviewed forty-one such studies* . . . Reported in Assouline, M., & Meir, E. I. (1987). Meta-analysis of the relationship between congruence and well-being measures. *Journal of Vocational Behavior, 31*, 319–332.

138 *David Oleski and Linda Subich of the University of Akron* . . . Reported in Oleski, D., & Subich, L. M. (1996). Congruence and career change in employed adults. *Journal of Vocational Behavior, 49*, 221–229.

139 *"malevolent, stubborn, misanthropic"* . . . From p. 118 of Lockwood, L. (2003). *Beethoven: The music and the life.* New York: W. W. Norton.

139 *"It seemed to me impossible to leave"* . . . Ibid., p. 119.

139 *"Oh, Friends, not these tones!"* . . . Ibid., p. 434.

139 *"You millions, I embrace you"* . . . Ibid., p. 436.

140 *After the final notes of the performance* . . . The story of Beethoven conducting the premiere of his Ninth Symphony is told in Lockwood, pp. 352–353.

140 *"They are created . . . by individuals"* . . . Ibid., p. 19.

6. GROWING UP WITH PERSONAL INTELLIGENCE

143 *"Five-month-olds already recognize"* . . . See Woodward, A. L. (2009). Infants'
grasp of others' intentions. *Current Directions in Psychological Science, 18*,
53–57.

143 *By ten months old, most infants* . . . See Thomsen, L., Frankenhuis, W. E.,
Ingold-Smith, M., & Carey, S. (2011, January 28). Big and mighty: Preverbal infants mentally represent social dominance. *Science, 331*, 477–480. To see the
video of larger and smaller cartoon figures, go to news.sciencemag.org/science-
now/2011/01/babies-size-up-the-social-scene.html.

144 *For each correct answer, a person receives one point.* This description applies
solely to the 104 all-verbal items of the scale on the TOPI 1.2Rf; each of these is
scored "0" or "1." Another set of thirty mostly visual items are scored somewhat
differently and are not included in the analyses I report here.

144 *So someone with no insight . . . who guesses on every question would select . . .
25 percent correct on the test* . . . My colleagues and I screen out anyone we detect is intentionally responding in a haphazard way; we believe nearly everyone
else in the sample has put some effort into answering the questions.

144 *That bell-like distribution of scores points to* . . . More technically, the bell curve
approximates a binomial distribution. A binomial distribution arises when one or
more binary events (the "bi" of the binomial), each one random, collectively take
place and add together. You can produce a simple binomial distribution by tossing two coins into the air and adding up the number of heads after they land.
There could be 0, 1, or 2 heads from your single toss. If you then repeat this
twenty times, you are likely to see a pattern: that the probability of 0 heads is
roughly 25 percent, of one head is 50 percent, and of two heads is 25 percent. As
you add more events (tossing, say, twenty coins in the air three hundred times),
the result smooths into a curve that resembles the bell curve. The fact that the
distribution of TOPI scores looks like a bell curve tells us that many events are
summing together to cause a person's score.

There was, however, a noticeable deviation from the bell-like shape: more
people scored at the high-performing end than expected, and this meant that
we need more difficult items in our test if it is possible to write them. We may
not have had enough hard items either because we underestimated people's
abilities, or because the fuzzy logic of personal intelligence rules out difficult
items in this domain of reasoning. That is, because the answers are fuzzy, plausible items may need to be obvious to select compared with incorrect items,
thereby making the test as a whole appear "too easy." We will try to decide
which alternative is correct by writing harder items (and other test-makers may
try as well). If we cannot succeed in writing a large group of hard items, it would
argue for the fuzzy-logic limit on difficulty.

145 *This is called the equal-environment assumption* . . . Scientists using the classical model of twin genetics make a further assumption that the family environment is similar for identical twins, fraternal twins, and for other siblings, insofar

as those influences might affect a particular trait. The original Equal Environmental Assumption assumed the environment for identical twins and nonidentical twins was equal overall; that version is known to be incorrect, and the revised version of the assumption I describe assumes an equal environment only insofar as it pertains to influences on a specific trait. The classical twin model and the equal-environment assumption and its updated version, the trait-specific equal-environment assumption, are discussed in Charney, E. (2012). Behavior genetics and postgenomics. *Behavioral and Brain Sciences, 35*, 331–410. See also Plomin, R. (2004). *Nature and nurture: An introduction to human behavioral genetics.* Stamford, CT: Wadsworth.

145 *So, if a person had an IQ* . . . Scientists have estimated that genetic influences on general intelligence account for roughly 60 percent of a person's intellectual difference from average. The range of estimates is mostly from 40 to 80 percent. I have taken the midpoint. Nisbett, R. E., Aronson, J., Blair, C., Dickens, W., Flynn, J., Halpern, D. F., & Turkheimer, E. (2012). Intelligence: New findings and theoretical developments. *American Psychologist, 67*, 130–159.

145 *In the 1980s, for example . . . macaque monkeys* . . . See Perrett, D. I., Smith, P. A., Mistlin, A. J., Chitty, A. J., Head, A. S., & Potter, D. D. (1985). Visual analysis of body movements by neurons in the temporal cortex of the macaque monkey: A preliminary report. *Behavioral and Brain Research, 16*, 153–170.

145 *"specific, meaningful hand movements"* . . . From p. 176 of di Pellegrino, G., Fadiga, L., Fogassi, L., Gallese, V., & Rizzolatti, G. (1992). Understanding motor events: A neurophysiological study. *Experimental Brain Research, 91*, 176–180.

146 *They called the cell a mirror neuron* . . . See Casile, A., Caggiano, V., & Ferrari, P. F. (2011). The mirror neuron system: A fresh view. *Neuroscientist, 17*, 524–538.

146 *To do so, Heberlein asked* . . . See Heberlein, A. S., Adolphs, R., Tranel, D., & Damasio, H. (2004). Cortical regions for judgments of emotions and personality traits from point-light walkers. *Journal of Cognitive Neuroscience, 16*, 1143–1158.

146 *In a second study, the scientists* . . . See Heberlein, A. S., & Saxe, R. R. (2005). Dissociation between emotion and personality judgments: Convergent evidence from functional neuroimaging. *NeuroImage, 28*, 770–777.

147 *Pillemer and his colleagues* . . . See Pillemer, D. B., Picariello, M. L., & Pruett, J. C. (1994). Very long-term memories of a salient preschool event. *Applied Cognitive Psychology, 8*, 95–106.

148 *Jenkins, Turrell, and their colleagues* . . . See Jenkins, J. M., Terrell, S. L., Kogushi, Y., Lollis, S., & Ross, H. S. (2003). A longitudinal investigation of the dynamics of mental state talk in families. *Child Development, 74*, 905–920.

148 *terms such as* want, hope, wish, *and* care *(as in "I don't care")*; sad, hurt, angry, *and* happy; *and* think, know, believe, remember, *and* guess . . . The terms I report here are from ibid., pp. 908–909.

148 *"Emily puts her M&M's"* . . . My story here closely follows the story that appears

in Perner, J., Leekam, S. R., & Wimmer, H. (1987). Three-year-olds' difficulty with false belief: The case for a conceptual deficit. *British Journal of Developmental Psychology, 5,* 125–137.

148 *Older children understand . . .* See ibid.

148 *Children who spoke . . .* The relation between false belief and mental-state talk is described in Jenkins, J. M., Terrell, S. L., Kogushi, Y., Lollis, S., & Ross, H. S. (2003). A longitudinal investigation of the dynamics of mental state talk in families. *Child Development, 74,* 905–920. The control for the children's verbal abilities was done by holding constant (statistically) their "mean length of utterance," a measure of verbal fluency. The results suggested that mental-state talk is a special area of skill.

149 *Evidence for the discrete brain . . .* See Leslie, A. M. (1992). Pretense, autism, and the theory-of-mind module. *Current Directions in Psychological Science, 1,* 18–21.

149 *For example, deaf children . . .* See Peterson, C. C., & Siegal, M. (2000). Insights into theory of mind from deafness and autism. *Mind and Language, 15,* 123–145.

149 *And when psychologists studied the Junín Quechua . . .* See Vinden, P. G. (1996). Junín Quechua children's understanding of mind. *Child Development, 67,* 1707–1716.

150 *With this insight, Binet . . .* For a discussion of Binet's insight into age and intelligence see, in particular, p. 71 of Fancher, R. E. (1985). *The intelligence men: Makers of the IQ controversy.* New York: W. W. Norton. Also, the "quotient" part of the term "intelligence quotient," abbreviated as IQ, reflects that comparison between age and mental ability.

150 *"Tell me how you usually have been"; "I have been good"; and "Tell me what you did in school today" . . .* From p. 1220 of Eder, R. A. (1989). The emergent personologist: The structure and content of 3½-, 5½-, and 7½-year-olds' concepts of themselves and other persons. *Child Development, 60,* 1218–1228.

150 *"writing a story about kids your age" . . .* From p. 852 of Eder, R. A. (1990). Uncovering young children's psychological selves: Individual and developmental differences. *Child Development, 61,* 849–863. The children varied in age from three and a half to seven years old.

150 *"I don't climb things that are high" . . . "I climb really high things" . . .* From Table 1, p. 853, of Eder, R. A. (1990). Uncovering young children's psychological selves: Individual and developmental differences. *Child Development, 61,* 849–863.

150 *"Puppet 1: My friends tell me what to do" . . .* The conversation is from ibid., p. 861.

151 *"these children possessed an elaborate self-concept" . . .* Ibid.

151 *Children could perform better than chance . . .* Reported in Yuill, N., & Pearson, A. (1998). The development of bases for trait attribution: Children's understanding of traits as causal mechanisms. *Developmental Psychology, 34,* 574–586.

151 *"Who knows best what you are thinking?"* and *"Who knows best what you want for your birthday?"* . . . From p. 427 of Burton, S., & Mitchell, P. (2003). Judging who knows best about yourself: Developmental change in citing the self across middle childhood. *Child Development, 74*, 426–443.

152 *Researchers at Leiden University* . . . Their article was Rieffe, C., Villanueva, L., & Terwogt, M. (2005). Use of trait information in the attribution of intentions by popular, average and rejected children. *Infant and Child Development, 14*, 1–10.

152 *"patient and nice"* and *"often bossy"* . . . Ibid., p. 5.

153 *"might be in danger"* . . . From p. 6 of Canada, G. (1995). *Fist stick knife gun: A personal history of violence*. Boston: Beacon Press.

153 *Letting the children find* . . . The study was conducted by Ed Deci and Yasmin Haddad of the University of Rochester, and is reported on p. 148 in Deci, E., & Flaste, R. (1995). *Why we do what we do: Understanding self-motivation*. New York: Penguin.

153 *Psychologists distinguish between childhood environments* . . . Harsh versus secure environments—my terminology combines what some argue to be two separate dimensions of harshness-warmth and riskiness-security; for the purposes of this overview, this general description will suffice. For more on the distinction, see Belsky, J., Schlomer, G. L., & Ellis, B. J. (2011). Beyond cumulative risk: Distinguishing harshness and unpredictability as determinants of parenting and early life history strategy. *Developmental Psychology 48*, 662–673.

154 *Jay Belsky of the University of California* . . . In Belsky, J., Schlomer, G. L., & Ellis, B. J. (2011). Beyond cumulative risk: Distinguishing harshness and unpredictability as determinants of parenting and early life history strategy. *Developmental Psychology, 48*, 662–673. NICHD in this instance is the United States National Institute of Child Health and Development.

154 *As predicted, girls who faced* . . . Ibid.

155 *"dysfunctional"*; *"over-the-top;"* *"grotesque"*; and *bitten by one of her children* . . . "Grotesque" is from Rutten, T. (2009, February 11). The excesses of Nadya Suleman. *Los Angeles Times*. Retrieved from articles.latimes.com /print/2009/feb/11/opinion/oe-rutten11. The "over-the-top" and "dysfunctional" descriptions appear on p. 2, paragraph 2, and the description of being bitten by one of the children appeared on p. 4, paragraph 2, both from Bowe, J. (2009, November 15). The Octomom and her babies prepare for prime time. *New York Times Magazine*. Retrieved from www.nytimes.com/2009/11/15/magazine /15octomom-t.html?pagewanted=prin.

155 *Yet some evolutionary psychologists* . . . See Belsky, J. (2012). The development of human reproductive strategies: Progress and prospects. *Current Directions in Psychological Science, 21*, 310–316.

155 *"Tiger Mother"*; *"get in the trenches"*; and *"if a Chinese child"* . . . All from Chua, A. (2011, January 8). Why Chinese mothers are superior. Can a regimen of no playdates, no TV, no computer games and hours of music practice create happy kids? And what happens when they fight back? *Wall Street Journal*: The Saturday

Essay. Retrieved from online.wsj.com/article/SB10001424052748704111504576 059713528698754.html.

156 *"we're hardworking and successful"* . . . From the last paragraph of Loh, S. T. (2011, April). Sympathy for the tiger moms. *Atlantic Monthly*: Books. Retrieved from www.theatlantic.com/magazine/archive/2011/04/sympathy-for-the-tiger -moms/308399/?single_page=true.

156 *Aurelio Figueredo and his colleagues* . . . The MIDUS study included 2,141 questions in its original survey; the team identified about 8 percent of the total items as especially relevant to life-history theory, and divided them into three broad content areas. As reported in Figueredo, A. J., Vásquez, G., Brumbach, B. H., & Schneider, S.M.R. (2007). The K-Factor, covitality, and personality: A psychometric test of life history theory. *Human Nature, 18*, 47–73.

156 *"I find it helpful to"* and *"How much love and affection"* . . . The quotes are from pp. 65–68 of the appendix, ibid.

158 *"I may know why she is the way she is"* . . . From p. 14 of Summer, L. (2005). *Learning joy from dogs without collars*. New York: Simon and Schuster.

158 *Among many details, her mother told Lauralee* . . . Ibid., p. 25.

158 *After many difficult years* . . . Ibid., p. 158.

158 *On a whim, she joined the men's wrestling team* . . . Ibid., p. 161.

159 *"where she emerged laden down"* . . . Ibid., p. 242.

159 *"conventionally dressed"* and *"robotlike"* . . . From the story of the "robotlike" young man on p. 114 of Deci, E., & Flaste, R. (1996). *Why we do what we do: Understanding self-motivation*. New York: Penguin.

160 *Seana Moran of Stanford University* . . . Reported in Moran, S. (2009). Purpose: Giftedness in intrapersonal intelligence. *High Ability Studies, 2*, 143–159.

160 *"planful competence"; "satisfied with self"; "calm, relaxed in manner"; and "rebellious"* . . . From pp. 74, 77–78 of Clausen, J. A., & Jones, C. J. (1998). Predicting personality stability across the life span: The role of competence and work and family commitments. *Journal of Adult Development, 5*, 73–83.

161 *Joseph Durlak, Roger Weissberg, and their colleagues* . . . As reported in Durlak, J. A., Weissberg, R. P., Dymnicki, A. B., Taylor, R. D., & Schellinger, D. B. (2011). The impact of enhancing students' social and emotional learning: A meta-analysis of school-based universal interventions. *Child Development, 82*, 405–432.

161 *"self-awareness, self-management, social awareness"* . . . Ibid., p. 406.

161 *Regarding the adolescents* . . . The Perkins study is described in Mayer, J. D., Perkins, D. M., Caruso, D. R., & Salovey, P. (2001). Emotional intelligence and giftedness. *Roeper Review: A Journal on Gifted Education, 23* (3), 131–137. Perkins assessed the participants' reasoning using the Multifactor Emotional Intelligence Scale—Adolescent version (MEIS-A). Although the MEIS-A is nonoverlapping with the TOPI in its content, it's likely that the MEIS-A and TOPI, like other measures of hot intelligence, correlate at moderate levels with each other.

162 *"Violence makes me uncomfortable"* and *"I fought so that"* . . . From Participant 5 in ibid., p. 135.

162 *"It began as joking around"* . . . From Participant 7 in ibid., p. 136.

7. PERSONAL INTELLIGENCE IN ADULTHOOD

165 *I once asked participants in a study* . . . Mayer, J. D. (2007). The big questions of personality psychology: Defining common pursuits of the discipline. *Imagination, Cognition and Personality, 27,* 3–26.

165 *"what was best for the children of men"* . . . Hebrew Bible, Kohelet 2:3.

165 *"What is my future?"* . . . See p. 17 of Mayer, J. D. (2007). The big questions of personality psychology: Defining common pursuits of the discipline. *Imagination, Cognition and Personality, 27,* 3–26.

165 *Zimbardo and Boyd have studied* . . . In Zimbardo, P. G., & Boyd, J. N. (1999). Putting time in perspective: A valid, reliable individual-differences metric. *Journal of Personality and Social Psychology, 77,* 1271–1288.

165 *People who live in the present* . . . Reported in Keough, K. A., Zimbardo, P. G., & Boyd, J. N. (1999). Who's smoking, drinking, and using drugs? Time perspective as a predictor of substance use. *Basic and Applied Social Psychology, 21,* 149–164.

166 *Hal Ersner-Hershfield and his colleagues at Stanford University* . . . In Ersner-Hershfield, H., Garton, M. T., Ballard, K., Samanez-Larkin, G. R., & Knutson, B. (2009). Don't stop thinking about tomorrow: Individual differences in future self-continuity account for saving. *Judgment and Decision Making, 4,* 280–286.

167 *E. Tory Higgins, a professor at Columbia University* . . . Higgins, E. T. (1987). Self-discrepancy: A theory relating self and affect. *Psychological Review, 94,* 319–340.

167 *New parents who are focused* . . . See Alexander, M. J., & Higgins, E. T. (1993). Emotional trade-offs of becoming a parent: How social roles influence self-discrepancy effects. *Journal of Personality and Social Psychology, 65,* 1259–1269.

168 *"This Dream is usually articulated"* . . . From p. 23 of Levinson, D. J., Darrow, C. M., Klein, E. B., Levinson, M. H., & McKee, B. (1976). Periods in the adult development of men: Ages 18 to 45. *The Counseling Psychologist, 6,* 21–25.

168 *"Major shifts in life direction"* . . . Ibid.

168 *After the 2008 economic downturn* . . . The request by the class of 2010 for Christensen to address them in this way is described in the editors' introduction to Christensen's remarks. These can be found in the Editor's Note on p. 46, immediately preceding Christensen, C. M. (2010). How will you measure your life? *Harvard Business Review, 88,* 46–51.

169 *"When I was a Rhodes scholar"* . . . Ibid.

169–70 *"being creative is important"* to *"He tries always to be responsive"* . . . From pp. 687–688 of Schwartz, S. H., Cieciuch, J., Vecchione, M., Davidov, E.,

Fischer, R., Beierlein, C., Ramos, A., Verkasalo, M., Lönnqvist, J.-E., Demirutku, K., Dirilen-Gumus, O., & Konty, M. (2012) Refining the theory of basic individual values. *Journal of Personality and Social Psychology, 103*, 663–688.

170 *Ravenna Helson and Sanjay Srivasta studied* . . . The researchers examined a sample of women who were followed by the Institute of Personality and Social Research at UC Berkeley using Carolyn Ryff's measure of well-being to categorize the values of their groups, based on its two predominant dimensions of environmental mastery and personal growth, as illustrated in Table 3, p. 1074, of Ryff, C. D. (1989). Happiness is everything, or is it? Explorations on the meaning of psychological well-being. *Journal of Personality and Social Psychology, 57*, 1069–1081. Helson and Srivastava's article is Helson, R., & Srivastava, S. (2001). Three paths of adult development: Conservers, seekers, and achievers. *Journal of Personality and Social Psychology, 80*, 995–1010.

171 *"A 24-year-old can't sit down"* . . . From Brooks, D. (2010, August 3). The summoned self [op-ed]. *New York Times*, A23.

172 *Shmuel Shulman of Bar Ilan University* . . . The emerging adults interviewed by Shulman, Feldman, and their colleagues ranged in age from twenty-two to twenty-seven. Thirty-five lived independently (including with romantic partners) and thirty-five lived at home. The study is reported in Shulman, S., Feldman, B., Blatt, S. J., Cohen, O., & Mahler, A. (2005). Emerging adulthood: Age-related tasks and underlying self processes. *Journal of Adolescent Research, 20*, 577–603.

172 *"Confusion. I do many things"* . . . Ibid., p. 590.

172 *"My parents, though they are"* . . . Ibid., p. 591.

172 *"It is possible that some matters"* . . . Ibid., pp. 590–591.

173 *"It is not a matter of how many rewards"* . . . From p. 24 of Levinson, D. J., Darrow, C. M., Klein, E. B., Levinson, M. H., & McKee, B. (1976). Periods in the adult development of men: Ages 18 to 45. *The Counseling Psychologist, 6*, 21–25.

173 *The psychologists Robert Emmons and Laura King* . . . Emmons, R. A., & King, L. A. (1988). Conflict among personal strivings: Immediate and long-term implications for psychological and physical well-being. *Journal of Personality and Social Psychology, 54*, 1040–1048.

173 *"to appear more intelligent than I am"* and *"to dominate, control, and manipulate people and situations"* . . . From Emmons, R. A., & King, L. A. (1988). Conflict among personal strivings: Immediate and long-term implications for psychological and physical well-being. *Journal of Personality and Social Psychology, 54*, 1040–1048. A similar example, "getting straight A's" and to be "partying all the time" is in Sheldon, K. M., & Kasser, T. (1995). Coherence and congruence: Two aspects of personality integration. *Journal of Personality and Social Psychology, 54*, 1040–1048.

173–74 *Participants also had greater well-being* . . . Ibid.

174 *"Which goal would be problematic to meet"* . . . See Mayer, J. D., Panter, A. T., & Caruso, D. R. (2012). Does personal intelligence exist? Evidence from a new ability-based measure. *Journal of Personality Assessment, 94*, 124–140.

174 *"must be perfectly competent, adequate, talented, and intelligent"* . . . From p. 25 of Ellis, A. (1958). Neurotic interaction between marital partners. *Journal of Counseling Psychology, 5,* 24–28. For a further development, see Ellis, A. (1987). The impossibility of achieving consistently good mental health. *American Psychologist, 42,* 364–375.

174 *A team led by Daphna Oyserman* . . . Reported in Osyerman, D., Bybee, D., & Terry, K. (2006). Possible selves and academic outcomes: How and when possible selves impel action. *Journal of Personality and Social Psychology, 91,* 188–204.

176 *"If Margaret wants to become better"* . . . The items are slightly modified in some instances to protect the exact content of the TOPI itself; for more details see Mayer, J. D., Panter, A. T., & Caruso, D. R. (2012). Does personal intelligence exist? Evidence from a new ability-based measure. *Journal of Personality Assessment, 94,* 124–140.

176 *"I haven't really got any future plans"* . . . From p. 1136 of Devadason, R. (2008). To plan or not to plan? Young adult future orientations in two European cities. *Sociology, 42,* 1127–1145.

176 *"I'd like to get a more interesting and fulfilling job"* . . . Ibid., p. 1138.

178 *Lindblom would argue that the coach's recommendations* . . . For example, a book that describes approaches similar to those of the life coach is Simon, S. B., Howe, L. W., & Kirschenbaum, H. (1995). *Values clarification: A practical action-directed workbook.* New York: Grand Central Publishing. Lindblom is making the point that experts often follow alternative practices in real-world contexts.

178 *But no one really makes* . . . The description of recommendations for expert decision-making as unrealistic is in the introduction to Lindblom, C. E. (1959). The science of "muddling through." *Public Administration Review, 19,* 79–88.

178 *No one can state* . . . The description of the hypothetical decision-making is on p. 82 of the introduction to Lindblom, C. E. (1959). The science of "muddling through." *Public Administration Review, 19,* 79–88.

179 *"In creating an integrated life structure"* . . . From pp. 23–24 of Levinson, D. J., Darrow, C. M., Klein, E. B., Levinson, M. H., & McKee, B. (1976). Periods in the adult development of men: Ages 18 to 45. *The Counseling Psychologist, 6,* 21–25.

179 *"social clock"* . . . From p. 711 of Neugarten, B. L., Moore, J. W., & Lowe, J. C. (1965). Age norms, age constraints, and adult socialization. *American Journal of Sociology, 70,* 710–717.

179 *"Men and women compare themselves"* . . . From p. 887 of Neugarten, B. L. (1979). Time, age, and the life cycle. *American Journal of Psychiatry, 136,* 887–894.

180 *The end of the 1950s* . . . Helson, R., Mitchell, V., & Moane, G. (1984). Personality patterns of adherence and nonadherence to the social clock. *Journal of Personality and Social Psychology, 46,* 1079–1096.

181 *They were lower on self-acceptance* . . . As reported in ibid., pp. 1084, 1088, and 1089.

181 *Those in the No Social Clock* . . . As described in ibid., p. 1090.

181 *"Still another variant is"* . . . From p. 22 of Levinson, D. J., Darrow, C. M.,

Klein, E. B., Levinson, M. H., & McKee, B. (1976). Periods in the adult development of men: Ages 18 to 45. *The Counseling Psychologist, 6*, 21–25.

182 *"In some cases, the man"* . . . Ibid.

182 *Surveys from the 1990s* . . . Arnett, J. J. (2000). Emerging adulthood: A theory of development from the late teens through the twenties. *American Psychologist, 55*, 469–480.

183 *"You ship a product"* . . . From p. 49 of Christensen, C. M. (2010). How will you measure your life? *Harvard Business Review, 88*, 46–51.

183 *"unhappy, divorced, and alienated from their children"* . . . Ibid., p. 48.

184 *Angela Duckworth and her colleagues* . . . Duckworth, A. L., Peterson, C., Matthews, M. D., & Kelly, D. R. (2007). Grit: Perseverance and passion for long-term goals. *Journal of Personality and Social Psychology, 92*, 1087–1101.

184 *Rather, they expect to overcome* . . . Duckworth, A. L., & Quinn, P. D. (2009). Development and validation of the Short Grit Scale (Grit-S). *Journal of Personality Assessment, 91*, 166–174. www.sas.upenn.edu/~duckwort/images/Duck worth%20and%20Quinn.pdf.

184 *Gritty commitment is also found* . . . The statistical tests indicate that grit overlaps closely with the students' self-report of the hours they practiced. In this instance, one variable can be used in place of another; that is, grit does not add prediction of the competitive outcome over and above that of hours practiced; see ibid., p. 172.

184 *In general, we become increasingly influential* . . . Roberts, B. W., & Mroczek, D. (2008). Personality trait change in adulthood. *Psychological Science, 17*, 31–35.

185 *"How can I improve in this job"* . . . In Ashford, S. J., & Tsui, A. S. (1991). Self-regulation for managerial effectiveness: The role of active feedback seeking. *Academy of Management Journal, 34*, 251–280. See also Tuckey, M., Brewer, N., & Williamson, P. (2002). The influence of motives and goal orientation on feedback seeking. *Journal of Occupational and Organizational Psychology, 75*, 195–216.

185 *"My name is something"* through *"I am four years old"* . . . From the "World's Best Self Introduction" portion of the "Able Leader" newsletter, March 2007 (www.stevekaye.com/ezine-index.html), on the website "One great meeting." Retrieved February 24, 2013 from www.stevekaye.com/ez/ez_0703.html.

185 *As charming as the four-year-old's* . . . Bluck, S., & Habermas, T. (2001). Extending the study of autobiographical memory: Thinking back about life across the life span. *Review of General Psychology, 5*, 135–147.

186 *"When I started learning to read and write"* through *"I learned to walk"* From p. 330 of Fivush, R., Habermas, T., Waters, T., & Zaman, W. (2011). The making of autobiographical memory: Intersections of culture, narratives and identity. *International Journal of Psychology, 46*, 321–345.

187 *"how many good people there are in the world"* . . . From p. 97 of McAdams, D. P. (2006). *The redemptive self: Stories Americans live by.* New York: Oxford University Press.

187 *"I guess for me if you had to distill it into a nutshell, it would be redemption"* . . . Ibid., p. 96.

187 *Many of McAdams's more fortunate* . . . McAdams, D. P. (2008). American identity: The redemptive self. *The General Psychologist, 43*, 20–27.

187 *A woman described how* . . . This is a characterization of the findings from a dissertation by Martha Lewis, as described on pp. 216–217 of McAdams, D. P. (2006). *The redemptive self: Stories Americans live by.* New York: Oxford University Press. The original dissertation is abstracted as Lewis, M. S. (2000, January). The life stories of less generative adults: Identifying narrative and psychological features. *Dissertation Abstracts International: Section B: The Sciences and Engineering, 61 (6-B)*, 3315.

188 *"It was embarrassing"* . . . Quoted from the *Boston Globe* on p. 41 of Pillemer, D. B. (1998). *Momentous events, vivid memories.* Cambridge, MA: Harvard University Press.

188 *"when I want to learn"* through *"when . . . I think about"* . . . From p. 98 of Bluck, S., Alea, N., Habermas, T., & Rubin, D. C. (2005). A tale of three functions: The self-reported uses of autobiographical memory. *Social Cognition, 23*, 91–117.

188 *He became an educator* . . . In Moton, R. R. (c. 1920). *Finding a way out: An autobiography.* Garden City, NY: Doubleday, Page & Company. Retrieved from http://docsouth.unc.edu/fpn/moton/moton.html.

189 *"In all the years of my experience"* . . . Ibid., p. 287.

189 *Perhaps the most sophisticated* . . . The most sophisticated level of our storytelling involves spotting the themes across our lives and the causes of what we have done. From Bluck, S., & Habermas, T. (2001). Extending the study of autobiographical memory: Thinking back about life across the life span. *Review of General Psychology, 5*, 135–147.

189 *Researchers have asked people* . . . The conception of wisdom as involving empathy and self-assertion was proposed in Glück, J., Bluck, S., Baron, J., & McAdams, D. P. (2005). The wisdom of experience: Autobiographical narratives across adulthood. *International Journal of Behavioral Development, 29*, 197–208.

191 *"participates with vivid imagination"* . . . From p. 437 of Grafly, D. (1931). Robert Henri: Robert Henri memorial exhibition at the Metropolitan Museum. *American Magazine of Art, 22*, 435–446.

191 *"Henri would catch, in the life of an eyelid"* . . . Ibid., p. 441.

191 *"was the most influential teacher I had."* . . . In Perlman, B. B. (2007). Revolution in the classroom. *Art & Antiques, 30* (4), 77–83.

191 *"The object of painting"* . . . From Robert Henri, quoted on p. 401 of Goldwater, R., & Trever, M. (Eds.) (1945). *Artists on art.* Cited on p. 21 of Deci, E. L., & Flaste, R. (1995). *Why we do what we do: Understanding self-motivation.* New York: Penguin.

8. THE POWER OF PERSONALITY

193 *In his work* Leviathan, *the philosopher Thomas Hobbes* . . . The social contract was first described in Hobbes, T. (1991). *Leviathan* (R. Tuck, Ed.). New York: Cambridge University Press. (Original work published 1651.)

195 *"There was a kind of 'evidence of the heart'"* . . . The French intellectual was D'Alembert, who helped edit the groundbreaking French Encyclopedia. Cited on p. 123 of Reddy, W. M. (2000). Sentimentalism and its erasure: The role of emotions in the era of the French revolution. *The Journal of Modern History, 72,* 109–152.

195 *As the revolutionaries fought among themselves* . . . The name of "the Terror" itself reflected the highly emotional language of the times, as remarked upon on p. 210 of Reddy, W. M. (2001). *The navigation of feeling: A framework for the history of emotions.* New York: Cambridge University Press.

195 *"A requirement to have certain 'natural' feelings"* . . . From p. 143 of Reddy, W. M. (2000). Sentimentalism and its erasure: The role of emotions in the era of the French revolution. *The Journal of Modern History, 72,* 109–152.

196 *Yet some philosophers now argue that considering the character* . . . See van Eemeren, F., Meuffels, B., & Verburg, M. (2000). The (un)reasonableness of ad hominem fallacies. *Journal of Language and Social Psychology, 19,* 416–435.

196 *Moreover, a politician's personality* . . . See Elms, A. C. (1994). *Uncovering lives: The uneasy alliance of biography and psychology.* New York: Oxford University Press. Also Winter, D. G. (2010). Why achievement motivation predicts success in business but failure in politics: The importance of personal control. *Journal of Personality, 78,* 1637–1667. Also, for example, Simonton, D. K. (2009). The "other IQ": Historiometric assessments of intelligence and related constructs. *Review of General Psychology, 13,* 315–326.

196 *"I carried on echoing this sort of unexamined nonsense"* . . . in Hitchens, C. (2008). Vote for Obama. *Slate.* Retrieved from www.slate.com/id2202163/.

196 *Some clinical psychologists have developed methods* . . . Post, J. M. (2003). *The psychological assessment of political leaders: With profiles of Saddam Hussein and Bill Clinton.* Ann Arbor: University of Michigan Press.

196 *"to predict, understand, and better control"* . . . From p. 290 of Coolidge, F. L., & Segal, D. L. (2007). Was Saddam Hussein like Adolf Hitler? A personality disorder investigation. *Military Psychology, 19,* 289–299.

197 *"the silencing of discussion is an assumption of infallibility"* . . . From p. 60 in Chapter 2 of Mill, J. S. (1999). On liberty. In Alexander, S. (Ed.), *On liberty.* Peterborough, ON: Broadview Press.

197 *"When people are involved in serious"* . . . From p. 13 of Ben-Ze'ev, A. (1994). The vindication of gossip. In A. Ben-Ze'ev (Ed.), *Good gossip.* Lawrence: University Press of Kansas.

197 *Roy Baumeister and his colleagues have argued* . . . In Baumeister, R. F., Zhang, L., & Vohs, K. D. (2004). Gossip as cultural learning. *Review of General Psychology, 8,* 111–121.

198 *"The individual who . . . can express his thoughts, feelings"* . . . On pp. 168–169 of Jourard, S. M. (1974). *Healthy personality: An approach from the viewpoint of humanistic psychology.* New York: Macmillan.

199 *Economists refer to the knowledge, skills* . . . See p. 444 of Crook, T. R., Combs,

J. G., Todd, S. Y., Woehr, D. J., & Ketchen, D. J. (2011). Does human capital matter? A meta-analysis of the relationship between human capital and firm performance. *Journal of Applied Psychology, 96*, 443–456.

199 *In fact, economists suggest that the economic growth* . . . Acemoglu, D., & Autor, D. What does human capital do? A review of Goldin and Katz's *The race between education and technology. Journal of Economic Literature, 50*, 426–463.

199 *Frank Schmidt and John Hunter examined* . . . $18,000 per person—denominated in 1988 dollars—from p. 263 of Schmidt, F. L., & Hunter, J. E., (1998). The validity and utility of selection methods in personnel psychology: Practical and theoretical implications of 85 years of research findings. *Psychological Bulletin, 124*, 262–274.

200 *McGee argues that society today* . . . See p. 16 of McGee, M. (2005). *Self-Help, Inc.: Makeover culture in American life.* New York: Oxford University Press.

200 *"is increasingly required as a new form of 'immaterial labor'"* . . . Ibid., p. 24.

200 *McGee would like to remedy this situation* . . . Ibid., in particular, pp. 180–183.

201 *My colleagues and I refer to the drawing together* . . . See Mayer, J. D., Salovey, P., Caruso, D. L., & Sitarenios, G. (2001). Emotional intelligence as a standard intelligence. *Emotion, 1*, 232–242.

202 *At the grade school level today, recently developed curricula* . . . See p. 406 of the following article for a description of the coverage of the programs—but the evaluation that they don't fully cover personality is my own. Durlak, J. A., Weissberg, R. P., Dymnicki, A. B., Taylor, R. D., & Schellinger, D. B. (2011). The impact of enhancing students' social and emotional learning: A meta-analysis of school-based universal interventions. *Child Development, 82* (1), 405–432.

202 *Better college courses* . . . I have argued in a number of journal articles that better courses employ what I refer to as a "Personality Systems Approach." See, for example, Mayer, J. D. (1998). A systems framework for the field of personality psychology. *Psychological Inquiry, 9*, 118–144.

202 *The phrase "It takes all kinds"* . . . A near equivalent to the idea appeared in Shelton's 1620 translation of Cervantes's *Don Quixote*, II, xi. The exact phrase appeared in D. W. Jerrold's *Story of Feather*, xxviii. See Simpson, J., & Speake, J. (Eds.) (2009). *A Dictionary of Proverbs* (5th ed.). New York: Oxford University Press.

203 *We develop expertise faster if we have good reports about how we're performing* . . . Ericsson, K. A., & Ward, P. (2007). Capturing the naturally occurring superior performance of experts in the laboratory. *Current Directions in Psychological Science, 16*, 346–350.

203 *In the Descriptive Experience Sampling (DES) method* . . . Heavey, C. L., & Hurlburt, R. T. (2008). The phenomena of inner experience. *Consciousness and Cognition: An International Journal, 17*, 798–810.

203 *In one study, more than 80 percent of therapists-in-training* . . . Bosworth, H., Aizaga, K., & Cabaniss, D. L. (2009). The training analyst: Analyst, teacher, mentor. *Journal of the American Psychoanalytic Association, 57*, 663–675.

204 *"psychotherapists . . . are not particularly adept at identifying treatment success and failure"* . . . From pp. 921–922 of Wampold, B. E., & Brown, G. S.

(2005). Estimating variability in outcomes attributable to therapists: A naturalistic study of outcomes in managed care. *Journal of Consulting and Clinical Psychology, 73*, 914–923.

205 *William Grove and his colleagues at the University of Minnesota* . . . See, for example, Table 1 of Grove, W. M., Zald, D. H., Lebow, B. S., Snitz, B. E., & Nelson, C. (2000). Clinical versus mechanical prediction: A meta-analysis. *Psychological Assessment, 12*, 19–30.

205 *"to avoid talking to him, and . . . to avoid thinking about him!"* . . . From p. 263 of Meehl, P. E. (1955). Wanted—A good cookbook. *American Psychologist, 11*, 263–272.

205 *There is an important addendum to the research findings about using formulae* . . . For example, the idea that clinical observation is key to diagnosis, especially provided the observation becomes a part of the procedure or formula, was made by Drew Westen of Emory University and Joel Weinberger of Adelphi University in Westen, D., & Weinberger, J. (2004). When clinical description becomes statistical prediction. *American Psychologist, 59*, 595–613.

206 *Researchers have drawn together studies covering eighty-five years of research* . . . See Schmidt, F. L., & Hunter, J. E. (1998). The validity and utility of selection methods in personnel psychology: Practical and theoretical implications of 85 years of research findings. *Psychological Bulletin, 124*, 262–274.

206 *By contrast, adding a measure of the person's interest added very little* . . . All this is from ibid., Table 1.

207 *"a Cape Canaveral of inner space"* . . . Quoted from the obituary of George Leonard. Martin, D. (2010, January 18). George Leonard, voice of the '60s counterculture, dies at 86. *New York Times*, A22. Retrieved from www.nytimes.com /2010/01/18/us/18leonard1.html?_r=0.

207 *"human potential movement"* . . . The discussion of Murphy and Leonard's tweak of "human potentialities" in a midnight brainstorming session is from pp. 86–87 of Kripal, J. J. (2007). *Esalen: America and the religion of no religion.* Chicago: University of Chicago Press.

208 *today's positive psychology is a related aspirational movement* . . . See, for example, Seligman, M.E.P., & Csikszentmihalyi, M. (2000). Positive psychology: An introduction. *American Psychologist, 55*, 5–14.

209 *I find inspiration in the idea that looking inward* . . . The remainder of this sentence echoes an idea by Clyde Kluckhohn and Henry Murray, that we are like all others, some others, and no others. The original formulation is on p. 53 of Kluckhohn, C., & Murray, H. A. (1956). Personality formation: The determinants. In Kluckhohn, C., Murray, H. A., & Schneider, D. M. (Eds.), *Personality in nature, society and culture* (2nd ed.) New York: Alfred A. Knopf.

ACKNOWLEDGMENTS

Many people helped me with the development and writing of *Personal Intelligence*. The book has been greatly enriched by my collaboration with David R. Caruso, which extends back to our graduate school days at Case Western Reserve University. He and A. T. Panter, who has joined us more recently, have been actively involved from the beginning in conducting empirical research about personal intelligence—thereby giving me something to write about.

At the same time that David and Abigail developed the scientific side of the concept, David Miller and Lisa Adams of the Garamond Agency were instrumental in guiding me toward a book proposal on the topic. They patiently helped me shape the exposition of the material I was thinking about until it took on a form quite similar to the shape of the final book.

Peter Salovey, with whom I shared the excitement and pleasure of developing the concept of emotional intelligence, has a presence in this work as well: I drew on several of the strategies we had employed in analyzing the mental abilities of emotional intelligence, and updated them in the presentation of personal intelligence.

I was extremely fortunate to have Amanda Moon of Scientific American/Farrar, Straus and Giroux as my editor. She calmly and patiently guided me from the initial versions of the chapters I drafted for this book to the version you see here. Along the way, she expertly helped me to develop my voice as a writer so that I could better communicate with educated readers of diverse backgrounds, while also encouraging me to convey as much of the science behind the work as possible. She was relentless in drawing out my best efforts through every stage of the book, for which I am especially grateful.

I am particularly thankful to my wife, Deborah, who fully supported my taking on this project, understanding the sacrifices it would involve. She worked with me throughout the process, serving as an astute sounding board, and together we kept our household running as smoothly as possible during the demands of research, writing, and the life events that arise over the course of developing a book. Our daughter provided her own thoughtful remarks, which have influenced some of the contents of this work. I am grateful to both of them for tolerating the long hours I put in on the venture.

Many more people contributed to this work in meaningful though perhaps less obvious ways: the long line of teachers from whom I have learned; my students, colleagues, friends, and other family members. I have thought of them and their contributions many times as I worked on this book. A very partial list includes Gordon H. Bower, Robert Clancy, John Conroy, Douglas K. Detterman, Joel Fajans and Karen Zukor, Stephen F. Groth, Richard J. Israel, Elena Levine, Arthur C. Mayer, Edna Mayer, William C. Mayer, Charlie Murphy, Amy C. D. O'Connor, Sandra W. Russ, Thomas L. Schwarz and Sarah Luria, Eric Summergrad, Thomas Young, Michael Wein, and Irving B. Weiner. A few of those listed passed away before I had finished the book; I miss them greatly.

I am thankful, in addition, for the contributions of the many professionals at Scientific American/Farrar, Straus and Giroux and at the University of New Hampshire who helped with the book. Christopher Richards and Dan Gerstle assisted Amanda Moon and me during the development of the text. Louise Buckley, Deanna Wood, and Debbie Watson in the Reference Department of the UNH libraries repeatedly helped me with the project (and thanks also to Interlibrary Loan and Document Delivery). Susan Goldfarb at FSG oversaw the book's production; Jonathan Lippincott worked on the layout and design; John McGhee copyedited the work. At

UNH, Brendan C. Lortie helped ensure that the references followed APA style.

A key part of developing a book involves getting the word out about it, and many members of the marketing and publicity departments at FSG helped with that, including Nick Courage, Kathy Daneman, Sarita Varma, and Jeff Seroy. At UNH, Lori G. Wright assisted with publicity. I am also grateful to Devon Mazzone, Amber Hoover, and Amanda Schoonmaker in the subsidiary rights department of FSG for their efforts.

Finally, I am indebted just about every day to my colleagues in the Department of Psychology here at UNH and to the support we receive more generally from the university.

My many thanks to all of the above. Needless to say, any faults or errors associated with the contents of this book are my own.

INDEX

Tsui, Ann, 184–85
Tulving, Endel, 102–103
Turkey, 130
Turkheimer, Eric, 116, 117
Turrell, S. L., 148
Twin Cities Reader, 118
Tylenol, 109

U

Unger, Caroline, 140
Unification Church, 135–36, 239*n*
Upanishads, 37

V

Vaillant, George, 114–15
values, 88, 107, 169–71, 177–78, 182,
    189, 246*n*; in adolescence, 157, 175;
    in character education programs, 202;
    core, 186; individualistic versus
    collectivist, 130; internalization of,
    127; in sameness narrative, 7
Vanderbilt University, 35
van Gogh, Vincent, 70
verbal comprehension, 27–29, 32–34,
    217*n*, 220*n*
Veterans Administration, 38
Vietnam War, 180
"Vindication of Gossip, The" (Ben-Ze'ev),
    197
Virginia, University of, 70

W

Wagner, Richard K., 34
Washington University in St. Louis, 68
Washington City Paper, 118
Washington Nationals baseball team,
    53, 54

Washington Post, 41, 136, 220*n*
Wechsler, David, 30, 217*n*
Wechsler Adult Intelligence Scale
    (WAIS), 86, 87
Wedeck, J., 20
Wei, Jonathan, 35
Weinberger, Joel, 252*n*
Weissberg, Roger, 161
Welch, Jack, 43
West Berlin, 78
Westen, Drew, 252*n*
West Point, U.S. Military Academy at,
    184
West Virginia, University of, 128
Wiggins, Jerry, 85–86, 96–97,
    227*n*
Williams College, 113
Wilson, Quentin, 104
Wilson, Timothy, 70–71
Winfrey, Oprah, 43
Wooden, John, 127
Wooten, H. Ray, 99–100
working memory, 104–107
World War II, 14, 78
Wundt, Wilhelm, 4, 5

Y

Yale University, 11, 13, 16, 34, 35,
    86–87, 89, 94, 97–98, 168, 177, 224*n*
yoga, 8
York University, 85, 227*n*
Yuill, Nicola, 151
Yuroks, 157

Z

Ziegelmann, J. P., 68
Zimbardo, Philip, 165
Zuckerman-Kuhlman personality
    scale, 62